LEVERAGING WIKIPEDIA

ALA Editions purchases fund advocacy, awareness, and accreditation programs for library professionals worldwide.

LEVERAGING
WIKIPEDIA

Connecting Communities *of* Knowledge

EDITED BY **MERRILEE PROFFITT**

ALA
Editions

CHICAGO | 2018

MERRILEE PROFFITT is a senior program officer at OCLC Research. She provides project management skills and expert support to institutions represented within the OCLC Research Library Partnership. Among her many projects is looking at developing better relationships between Wikipedia and cultural heritage institutions. Proffitt started exploring this connection in 2011, and in 2012 she created OCLC's Wikipedian in Residence program. Along the way, Proffitt became a more confident member of the Wikipedia community, and she has contributed to dozens of Wikipedia articles and helped to run several edit-a-thons. She is a member of the GLAM US Advisory Group. She is a founding member of the Wikimedia and Libraries User Group.

© 2018 by the American Library Association

Extensive effort has gone into ensuring the reliability of the information in this book; however, the publisher makes no warranty, express or implied, with respect to the material contained herein.

ISBNs
978-0-8389-1632-2 (paper)
978-0-8389-1733-6 (PDF)
978-0-8389-1732-9 (ePub)
978-0-8389-1734-3 (Kindle)

Library of Congress Cataloging in Publication Control Number: 2018003536

Book design by Alejandra Diaz in the Minion Pro and Benton Sans typefaces.

♾ This paper meets the requirements of ANSI/NISO Z39.48–1992 (Permanence of Paper)

Printed in the United States of America
22 21 20 19 18   5 4 3 2 1

CONTENTS

Introduction
Why Wikipedia and Libraries?

MERRILEE PROFFITT

believe that Wikipedia is important for the future of libraries. I also believe that libraries are equally important to Wikipedia. This volume reveals the many ways in which the library and Wikipedia communities are beginning to work with one another for mutual benefit, but it is worth backtracking and stating why I believe Wikipedia and libraries are natural allies.

It's about scale . . . Wikipedia is immensely popular. It's the sixth most visited website in the United States, it is fifth globally, and according to Alexa it gets 21 percent of Internet traffic every day in the United states. English Wikipedia—that is, the English-language version of Wikipedia—receives an average of 200 million page views a day. This is popularity on a scale that cannot be ignored. Your library patrons are using Wikipedia weekly, if not daily—and if they are not going there directly, they are following a highly ranked search engine link which leads them to Wikipedia.

It's about vision . . . Wikipedia was launched in January 2001. From the beginning, the project envisioned a resource that provides every person with free access to knowledge in his or her own language. Over time, hundreds of thousands of people from around the world have worked to build and maintain the encyclopedia's content, which includes more than 40 million articles in about 290 languages. While most of the content in this volume pertains to activity and engagement with English Wikipedia (which tips the scales at over 5.4 million articles), there is also content built by a relatively tiny but dedicated number of volunteers who are working to make knowledge accessible for everyone in their own languages. Wikipedia is the tip of the Wikimedia iceberg, and there are a host of other related open knowledge projects such as Wikimedia Commons (a repository of freely usable media files to which anyone can contribute), Wikisource (a repository for texts), and Wikidata, a metadata repository that will be explored in depth in this volume. These projects act to support one another. For example, a Wikipedia article may draw metadata from Wikidata and show images from Wikimedia Commons. But beyond infrastructure, the Wikimedia universe represents what participants call a "movement" which represents not only the projects with their concrete outputs, but also a set of values that support freedom of information and the open sharing of knowledge.

It's about people. . . . All work that is done on Wikipedia is carried out by passionate volunteers. These people, Wikipedians, not only do the editing but also establish and maintain protocols and processes that support growing the knowledge base, and help keep the information credible (in addition to free and open). Although there are over 31 million registered user accounts on English Wikipedia, there are only 117,000 "active" registered users (that is, users who have made an edit in the last thirty days). The Wikimedia Foundation exists to support the activities of all the Wikimedia projects, and employs 280 people. It relies on grants and public donations to help keep servers up and running and to support projects that are of global interest. There are also dozens of Wikimedia chapters, which all have their own infrastructure to help support more local activities. The Wikimedia universe is so complicated that it is a wonder it runs at all, and yet it does, fueled by the passion of those who contribute their time and energy to it.

It is not without flaws . . . Wikipedia, as gigantic as it is, has some obvious flaws. There is a narrow demographic representation among Wikipedia contributors; for example, English Wikipedia contributors are overwhelmingly male. There are significant gaps on Wikipedia—for example, only 17 percent of the articles that are about people are about women. What has been typically characterized as a gender gap on Wikipedia extends well beyond topics having to do with women. As an example of a "gap" area in Wikipedia, look at articles that relate to librarianship—those articles have been neglected or have yet to be written. In addition to gaps, Wikipedia also has challenges posed by substandard articles; while the sheer quantity of articles has soared, their quality has not kept up. Wikipedians have their own process for peer review, and only a relative handful of articles have made it through the rigorous process to become a "featured" or even a "good" article. The rest are works in progress. Wikipedia articles rest on the notion of verifiability, and by its own measure, the project has some ways to go—there are currently over 351,000 "citation needed" tags in articles. Each one of these tags indicates the need for a quality source to back up an assertion in an article.

I see enormous opportunities for partnerships between Wikipedia and libraries based on this array of strengths and deficits in the encyclopedia. Wikipedia has the visibility on the open web that libraries lack. The communities of Wikipedians and librarians have a shared set of values. Wikipedians and librarians concur on what constitutes a quality source. It is because Wikipedians often seem unable to access quality sources that articles lack appropriate citations. What better place for Wikipedians to find and get access to those sources than at their library? Libraries, whether public or academic, hold collections that can bring depth to Wikipedia articles and can provide high-quality support materials in order to help build better articles. We librarians also serve diverse audiences, and there are many opportunities to develop programs and programming that will help lead our communities to connect with the new form of knowledge synthesis and creation that is Wikipedia.

Wikipedians are keenly interested in engaging with librarians. On the Wikipedia side, there is an established network of GLAM (Galleries, Libraries, Archives, and Museums) volunteers—in this book, Andrew Lih writes about GLAM and its origins, and Alex Stinson and Jason Evans outline how libraries can engage with an existing network of volunteers, chapters, and other resources. The Wikimedia movement has a deep history of engaging with higher education, and LiAnna Davis's chapter on Wikipedia and education outlines the outstanding successes the Wiki Education Foundation has had using Wikipedia as a pedagogical tool to improve information literacy. And Jake Orlowitz outlines his vision for supporting Wikipedians and librarians with an array of tools and initiatives to help improve the overall quality of articles, as well as build people-to-people connections that make a difference.

Even without formal networks to help them make connections, librarians have been finding innovative and effective ways of connecting both collections and communities to Wikipedia. Teri Embrey and Bob Kosovsky share their experiences connecting specialist collections to the encyclopedia. Lily Todorinova and Yu-Hung Lin shed some light on how students understand citations, in addition to hosting a Wikipedia Visiting Scholar. Monika Sengul-Jones shares rich and varied stories of engagement from public libraries, while Kelly Doyle explores addressing systemic bias and the gender gap in Wikipedia's content and coverage. Sara Snyder gives tips for holding the perfect edit-a-thon, and gives a peek at what lies "beyond" this tried-and-true format. Mairelys Lemus-Rojas and Timothy A. Thompson explain RAMP, a tool that helps "remix" archival collection descriptions into Wikipedia articles. Lemus-Rojas and Lydia Pintscher give a deep dive into Wikidata, while Kenning Arlitsch and Justin Shanks talk about the importance of Wikipedia and Wikidata for getting found on the Web. Many of the librarians who are represented here have had their own road to becoming Wikipedians (or a hybrid that I'll call Wikibrarians). We've felt our way in a new and unfamiliar landscape which is quite different from traditional librarianship. In this book's last chapter, I will share my own journey of going from being a curious outsider to becoming a Wikibrarian.

This is an exciting time for librarians and Wikipedians—we have many shared challenges and opportunities together. I hope this volume helps to illuminate some of the possibilities and inspires you to follow some of the existing models we've outlined here. Better yet, you may choose to adopt the Wikipedia motto, and "be bold" in exploring your own path.

I'd like to thank those who have contributed to this volume in large and small ways. First and foremost, thanks to the authors who were all willing to leap into this project with enthusiasm. OCLC has allowed me many years of time and space to develop my ideas around Wikipedia and libraries—I can't think of another organization that would have allowed the kind of time that this sort of deep exploration has required. Thanks to Lorcan Dempsey, Jim Michalko, and Rachel Frick for being my champions. A special thanks to Phoebe Ayers, Jake Orlowitz, Alex Stinson, and Andrew Lih for being wonderful Wikimedia connectors. And thanks to Cindy Aden for being a partner in crime for many years.

And where would we be without the libraries? Thanks to the Garden Grove Public Library (Chapman Branch) for letting me spend my teenage summers with you as a "volunteer." And thanks to the UC Berkeley libraries for letting me sprout my library wings as both a student employee and a staff member. Finally, thanks to the Oakland Public Library—I spent many hours at the Main and Montclair branches when I needed a different space where I could focus my mind while working on this project. I'm grateful for the library: a third place that gives me power, Wi-Fi, and doesn't want to sell me anything except the opportunity to access information.

What Are Galleries, Libraries, Archives, and Museums (GLAM) to the Wikimedia Community?

ANDREW LIH

n 2001, Wikipedia came into existence quietly and without much fanfare. It was an unusual project that was designed to allow anyone, even anonymous users, to edit any page of a nascent online encyclopedia. What most people don't know is that Wikipedia was an ad hoc experiment to help Nupedia, a struggling encyclopedia that depended on online volunteer contributors. However, Nupedia employed a strict publishing model with layers of oversight that required participants to prove they held a college degree. In hindsight, it is perhaps no surprise that Nupedia and its stringent rules failed to produce more than a dozen articles during its first year of existence. Wikipedia was launched alongside Nupedia to help spur article creation by allowing anyone to edit any page on its website. The hope was that articles created there might be moved to Nupedia, where more rigorous standards could be applied to create finished works.

What happened next was unexpected—not only were volunteers creating new articles on Wikipedia, but they were finishing and updating them while establishing new community norms and publishing guidelines that produced better and better content. The community, with the ability to self-organize and adapt to immediate needs, quickly wrote dozens of articles each day. By the next year, Wikipedia had generated nearly 20,000 entries. Nupedia was suddenly irrelevant and shut down. Wikipedia had become not just a greenhouse for starting articles, but a successful encyclopedia in its own right—edited, governed, and developed by a community of volunteer contributors. More than fifteen years later, Wikipedia has become one of the most visited websites in the world and is available in almost 300 languages while showing little sign of abating. It continues to operate as a volunteer-edited website, with no salaried editing staff, and it has expanded to become a greater Wikimedia movement encompassing new multimedia and structured data initiatives.

FIRST COLLABORATIONS

It is in this context that Wikipedia's relationship with traditional notions of knowledge at heritage institutions is so interesting. Just as Nupedia's assumptions about quality and authority have yielded to Wikipedia's crowd of self-organizing volunteers, so has the thinking of many memory institutions and the galleries, libraries, archives, and museums (GLAM) that have witnessed the rise of Wikipedia as the world's most notable and popular reference work.

Wikipedia's relationship with GLAM had an auspicious start in 2008, when Wikimania, the annual conference of Wikipedia contributors, was held at the Biblioteca Alexandrina in Egypt. The modern library funded by UNESCO was a revival of the original, ancient Library of Alexandria dating back to the third century BC. The conference of more than 600 volunteer contributors to Wikipedia and other Wikimedia projects was hosted by the Biblioteca, and included efforts to foster more Arabic-language content online and in Wikipedia. It was after this conference that Australian Wikipedia editor Liam Wyatt was inspired to propose an ongoing engagement between the Wikipedia community and cultural institutions. While serving as the multimedia coordinator at the Dictionary of Sydney project, he organized the first-ever conference of Wikipedia and GLAM organizations in Canberra, Australia in August 2009. The conference, called "Galleries, Libraries, Archives, Museums & Wikimedia: Finding the Common Ground," introduced the "GLAM-WIKI" terminology to the Wikimedia community and opened up more formal dialogues between the two sides.[1] That same month, English Wikipedia topped 3 million articles and was regularly ranked at the top of Google search results. Wikipedia was also receiving more than 300 million unique visitors a month in all languages, outpacing all but a few of the most popular sites on the Internet.

The magnitude of these numbers piqued the interest of Matthew Cock, website manager of the prestigious British Museum in London. "I looked at how many Rosetta Stone page views there were at Wikipedia . . . That is perhaps our iconic object, and five times as many people go to the Wikipedia article [on it] as to ours."[2] This realization inspired him to propose a novel idea to British Museum administrators—invite a Wikipedia contributor into the institution as the first ever "Wikipedian in Residence" to serve as a liaison within the museum. Despite his fears about proposing collaboration with unknown and uncredentialed Wikipedia volunteers, Cock did not get the internal pushback he expected. "Everyone assumed everyone else hated it and that I shouldn't recommend it," he recounted. Instead, he met with enthusiastic interest from numerous departments at the museum. With an invitation extended to him, Wyatt traveled to London in June 2010 and spent five weeks working with museum staff and Wikipedia volunteers to improve Wikipedia's content using the British Museum's resources. In addition to the Rosetta Stone article, one major initiative was to rally around a particular article to improve it to the highest rating in Wikipedia—featured article status. From the museum's collection, they chose to focus on the Hoxne Hoard, the largest cache of late Roman silver and gold ever discovered in Britain, and part of the British Museum's collection. The "Hoxne challenge" to improve the article was created, bringing the entry to top-quality featured status with volunteer efforts. During his five weeks in London, Wyatt helped establish new practices that have been employed by cultural heritage institution staff alongside Wikimedia volunteers at other institutions. Wyatt helped to pioneer "edit-a-thons," or meet-ups, with GLAM institutions to improve content, now a common engagement event. Another innovation was the "backstage pass," which has become another regular feature of GLAM collaboration, where Wikipedia editors are given special tours to nonpublic areas of an institution or receive access to work in progress there.

While these collaborations were relatively new to GLAM institutions and Wikipedia editors, the idea of cultural institutions interacting with volunteer Wikipedia editors should not be surprising. Volunteers, in the form of docents and guides, have had a long history in the life of museums and libraries. Noting this, Wyatt has proposed that GLAM institutions consider Wikipedia editors as "e-volunteers" who serve as an extension of the institutions' own established volunteer communities.

One of the biggest obstacles for the British Museum and GLAM institutions is knowing who they are working with. If editors to Wikipedia can be anonymous and don't need to register an account, what exactly do we know about Wikipedia's e-volunteers or Wikipedians? A survey in 2011 that randomly sampled editors of Wikipedia found that two-thirds of its contributors had at least a bachelor's degree, and one-third of all contributors had a master's degree or higher. With these numbers, GLAM entities have realized that while Wikipedia is the encyclopedia that anyone can edit, not just anyone does. A self-selecting class of elite contributors write the majority of Wikipedia. Unfortunately, self-selection has its downsides, since the same survey found that 90 percent of Wikipedia editors were male. Follow-up studies have also shown contributors to be predominantly Western-educated, which contributes a significant systemic bias to content in the encyclopedia. Trying to bridge such a wide gender gap has been a major initiative within the Wikipedia community ever since that eye-opening 2011 survey. By engaging GLAM institutions, in addition to library science programs, information science schools, and museum studies programs, there may be some possibilities to rebalance the profile of Wikipedia's contributors. A number of efforts, such as the Art+Feminism edit-a-thons run in conjunction with museums around the world, have helped recruit dozens of new editors. In 2015 Art+Feminism staged 70 events in 17 countries and engaged more than 1,300 volunteer editors.[3]

THE GREATER WIKIMEDIA MOVEMENT

While Wikipedia is the most prominent "wiki" project known to the public, it is important to note that there exists an array of projects inspired by Wikipedia within what is referred to as the greater Wikimedia movement. One of the earliest offshoots was Wikimedia Commons, a multimedia repository to share media assets across all Wikipedia language editions so that free-use images, audio, and video can be centralized in one place. Commons has developed its own norms, community, and administrators, many of whom never edit any Wikipedia text content and focus solely on multimedia content. This has led to robust activity around images and photography, including a number of popular annual contests such as the Pictures of the Year competition. Wiki Loves Monuments, an international contest designed to encourage the photography of heritage sites around the world, was declared the world's largest photo competition by the *Guinness Book of World Records* in 2011.[4]

When GLAM organizations donate images and other non-textual items from their holdings to Wikipedia, it is Wikimedia Commons that is often the point of contact, and the point of contention. Cultural institutions wishing to contribute large image collections need to navigate complex copyright, metadata, and bulk uploading concerns, which can be daunting given that all content on Commons must either be in the public domain or be released under a free content license. A common best practice has been to utilize third-party platforms, such as the photo-sharing site Flickr, to host image collections and use those sites to publicly declare the copyright details, such as a compliant Creative Commons license that allows commercial use. After such an upload, Commons has scripts and tools to import these Flickr-hosted collections in bulk. The Smithsonian Institution, the British Library, the U.S. National Archives, and many others have utilized this method of content donation to Commons with positive results. However, having the future of GLAM collaboration hinge on the longevity of a commercial service such as Flickr is somewhat precarious.

Another project, Wikisource, is a library of scanned textual sources that hosts transcription into multiple languages. While not as popular as Wikipedia, it has roughly 1,000 active contributors and transcribers per month across a dozen active languages. The Bibliothèque et Archives Nationales du Québec (BANQ) in Canada has been working with volunteers to help transcribe French-language content from its collections. In 2015, the Wikisource community worked with BANQ to help transcribe and resurrect a 1906 Quebec novel that had previously appeared only in serialized newspaper form. The work by Wenceslas-Eugène Dick, *Pirates of the Gulf of St. Lawrence,* is now available in a number of digital formats, such as PDF, ePub, and MOBI, for free download.[5]

Perhaps the most compelling development for GLAM institutions has been the launch of Wikidata in 2012. Wikidata is a collaboratively edited knowledge base that provides structured metadata for use on Wikipedia and for any number of other purposes and projects. This development of a Semantic Web version of Wikipedia content that is machine-readable and queryable is the culmination of many years of work.

Many GLAM organizations have already been working on linked open data initiatives of their own, or with peers. The promise of identifiers and authority control records that are familiar to librarians and memory institutions, such as VIAF (Virtual International Authority File), GND (German Integrated Authority File, Gemeinsame Normdatei), ULAN (the Getty Museum's Union List of Artist Names), or LCAuth (Library of Congress ID for authority control), being used by Wikidata is exciting. Having well-known authority control records accessible in a central hub at Wikidata allows for better access among federated databases across the world. By using industry standards like RDF and SPARQL, Wikidata is even more accessible and integrates into the efforts that cultural institutions are making to have information about collections be more visible on the open web. Wikidata's approach has become so successful in such a short amount of time that even Google has taken notice. In 2016 Google discontinued its own public-facing structured data project, Freebase, in favor of backing Wikidata. Efforts such as Linked Open Data in Libraries, Archives & Museums (LODLAM) and the American Art Collaborative Linked Open Data Initiative show great interest in the development of Semantic Web standards in the direction of Wikidata.

WIKIPEDIAN IN RESIDENCE PROGRAM

Since the 2010 experiment with the British Museum, the Wikipedian in Residence model has taken root, even leading to full-time positions for Wikipedia content experts on the staff of cultural institutions.

Inspired by Wyatt's work, one of the first contributors in the United States to follow the Wikipedian in Residence model was Lori Byrd-McDevitt, who took that position at the Children's Museum of Indianapolis while pursuing her master's degree in museum studies. While working with the world's largest children's museum, her experience in coordinating content donations and updating the collection's representation in Wikipedia formed part of her final thesis, "The Temple and the Bazaar: Wikipedia as a Platform for Open Authority in Museums."[6] In the paper, she challenges the traditional role of cultural institutions as authoritative experts, describing the emergence of Wikipedia as "a platform for facilitating new perspectives in collaborative knowledge-sharing between museums and communities." With GLAM institutions and Wikipedia contributors working together, she sees open authority as the "mixing of institutional expertise with the discussions, experiences, and insights of broad audiences." This two-way, participatory interpretation is something that is only possible with the advent of wiki software systems that allow easy online collaborative sharing and fulfill the original vision of the read-write web.

The museum curator Nina Simon describes the various levels of engagement between a GLAM institution and the public in her book *The Participatory Museum*[7] by defining contributory, collaborative, and ultimately, co-creative endeavors. Simon describes traditional ways in which cultural institutions solicit visitor contributions, like memory board reflections for exhibit-goers, and collaborative projects, such as harnessing community votes on content and uploading images. Engagement that goes beyond projects primarily shaped by the cultural institution enters the realm of the co-creative. New advances in interactive storytelling and visualization provide some exciting prospects. With Wikimedia projects becoming more multimedia-capable through new technological developments in 3D models and video, what is now primarily text-based co-creation will become richer and more interactive going forward. Because of the Wikimedia movement's commitment to using open standards and software, further work in this space has seen some delays. For example, the Smithsonian Institution has numerous detailed models at its X 3D project, which creates three-dimensional models of collection objects and items of scientific interest. However, Wikimedia Commons still lacks the technical capability to handle the upload of 3D objects and shape data, and the culture of Commons is resistant to the use of proprietary file formats.

As a United States federal employee, Dominic Byrd-McDevitt is the rare Wikimedia contributor who has a full-time staff designation. Since September 2013, he has been the digital content specialist and Wikipedian in Residence at the U.S. National Archives and Records Administration (NARA), where he has facilitated multimedia contributions and data sharing with the Wikimedia community. Byrd-McDevitt's extensive experience, which also includes a five-month stint as the Smithsonian Institution's Wikipedian in Residence before joining NARA, led to the creation of a comprehensive conflict-of-interest disclosure that is now used as a best practices template for other contributors who are serving as paid staff at cultural institutions. While trying to comply with Wikipedia's conflict-of-interest guidelines, Wikimedia community members who have a paid or formal role need to find a delicate balance between contributing on behalf of their institution while also steering clear of advocacy that violates Wikipedia's neutral point of view (NPOV) content policy. In many cases, Wikipedians in Residence pledge not to edit or are prohibited from editing articles in their institution's domain of expertise directly and work to provide volunteers with research aids and source material instead.

Much of NARA's leadership in Wikimedia engagement comes from the enthusiastic support of the archivist of the United States, David Ferriero, who stated that "the Archives is involved with Wikipedia because that's where the people are." The archivist has been an avid supporter of Wikimedia activities, with NARA hosting multiple GLAM and Wikipedia conferences at the National Archives facility in Washington, DC. Wikipedia is the largest driver of traffic to the National Archives site, going beyond even the Archives's commercial partner Ancestry.com. According to NARA's chief innovation officer, Pamela S. Wright, the roughly 100,000 digital objects it has uploaded to Wikimedia projects have been accessed more than 7.7 billion times over five years, far outpacing the traffic the National Archives gets for its digital files on its own website.

At any given moment, there are more than a dozen Wikipedians in Residence at institutions around the world, some as Wikipedia-focused staff members and others as temporary fellowships. Europeana, the digital platform for cultural heritage in the European Union, has a full-time Wikipedia coordinator in Wyatt who has helped develop an award-winning tool, the GLAM-Wiki toolset, which assists GLAM institutions in bulk uploading their image collections to Wikimedia Commons. Numerous libraries around the world have hosted a Wikipedian in Residence, including the National Library of Wales, the Biblioteca Nacional de Chile, the Metropolitan New York Library Council, and the University of Oxford—Bodleian Libraries.

CONNECTING PLACES OF KNOWLEDGE

The world's cultural institutions and the Wikimedia movement have found themselves constantly adapting to new communication technologies. How do we imagine them working together to gather the sum of all human knowledge? Libraries and museums have typically positioned themselves as a "third place" outside of home and work time, in which they serve as public spaces where citizens engage in cultural and civic life.

GLAM institutions now face a challenge that the third place is no longer necessarily an in-person experience. Increasingly, third place engagement is not a distinct slice of people's lives, consisting of a contiguous block of time or happening in a single locale. Work and leisure time encroach upon each other, substantially overlapping while our brains context-switch multiple times each hour. Our mobile phones that we constantly peek at are a permanent virtual third place where news alerts, social media snippets, and search engine results now make up a primary way we interact with knowledge. Public discourse becomes an ever-present virtual space, experienced dozens of times throughout the day via chats and micro-engagements. The user experience is controlled by the user more than ever, and knowledge institutions must adjust to this reality. When the Metropolitan Museum of Art's chief digital officer, Sree Sreenivasan, was asked what the Met museum's biggest competition is, it wasn't other museums. "Our competition is Netflix," he says. In this type of engagement economy, the scarcest commodity is human attention. How have GLAM institutions and Wikipedia adapted to this new reality?

We can turn to the origins of both the encyclopedia and our cultural institutions for guidance. The eighteenth-century Enlightenment produced three of the most important parts of our knowledge system—libraries, archives, and museums; encyclopedias; and periodicals. Outside of the formal schooling system, these provide the cornerstone of lifelong learning and education for the citizenry. The digital age has drastically altered all of these, yet they remain the bedrock of our information ecosystem.

If the news is considered the first rough draft of history, Wikipedia is the continuously edited working draft of history. Libraries, archives, and museums serve as our memory institutions and support long-term issues of preservation, access, curation, and interpretation. The news media, Wikipedia, and GLAM institutions all have complementary missions, with Wikipedia sitting at the nexus between immediate information and long-term knowledge. It is both current and historical. This is why Wikipedia's associations with GLAM institutions are vital: to bridge the current to the persistent. Through the collaborative capability provided by the Internet, Wikimedia projects achieve the impossible trinity of capturing the speed, depth, and breadth of all human knowledge.

The power of Wikimedia projects as this central hub of human knowledge is perhaps best described by this observation from Günter Waibel and Ricky Erway of OCLC in 2009:[8]

> Libraries, archives and museums (or LAMs) have each created an orderly world within their respective domains through the power of shared practices and standards. For the purposes of assembling a single body of LAM knowledge, however, those very practices and standards isolate cultural heritage institutions from one another. While the collections LAMs manage remain necessarily fragmented in the real world, potential users of these collections increasingly expect to experience the world of information as accessible from a single online search.

Wikipedia and its fellow Wikimedia projects are at the heart of this "single online search," with Google and other search sites using Wikimedia content extensively for their results. The best way GLAM institutions can stay current and relevant in the knowledge zeitgeist is by collaborating with Wikimedia projects now and into the future.

NOTES

1. Wikimedia Australia, proceedings from Galleries, Libraries, Archives, Museums & Wikimedia: Finding the common ground, https://wikimedia.org.au/wiki/GLAM-WIKI.

2. Noam Cohen, "Venerable British Museum Enlists in the Wikipedia Revolution," *New York Times*, June 4, 2010, www.nytimes.com/2010/06/05/arts/design/05wiki.html.

3. Hannah Ghorashi, "Art+Feminism's 2015 Wikipedia Edit-a-thon Adds 334 Articles on Female Artists," ARTnews, March 10, 2015, www.artnews.com/2015/03/10/artfeminisms -2015-wikipedia-edit-a-thon-adds-334-articles-on-female-artists/.

4. Wikimedia Blog, Wiki Loves Monuments breaks Guinness World Record for largest photo competition, October 9, 2017, https://blog.wikimedia.org/2012/10/09/wiki-loves -monuments-breaks-guinness-world-record-for-largest-photo-competition/.

5. This work, Wenceslas-Eugène Dick, *Pirates of the Gulf of St. Lawrence*, is available on the French language version of Wikisource: https://fr.wikisource.org/wiki/Les_pirates_du _golfe_St-Laurent.

6. Lori Byrd Phillips, "The Temple and the Bazaar: Wikipedia as a Platform for Open Authority in Museums," *Curator: The Museum Journal*, 56, no. 2 (2013), doi: 10.1111/ cura.12021.

7. Nina Simon, *The Participatory Museum* (Santa Cruz: Museum 2.0, 2010).

8. Günter Waibel and Ricky Erway, "Think Global, Act Local - Library, Archive and Museum Collaboration," *Museum Management and Curatorship*, 24, no. 4 (2009), www.oclc.org/content/dam/research/publications/library/2009/waibel-erway-mmc.pdf.

Connecting Citizens and the Military

The Experiences of the
Pritzker Military Museum & Library

THERESA A. R. EMBREY

The Pritzker Military Museum & Library, a nonprofit library in Chicago,
was founded in 2003 by Colonel Jennifer N. Pritzker, IL ARNG (Ret.).
The institution's mission "is to acquire and maintain an accessible collection of
materials and to develop appropriate programs focusing on the Citizen Soldier
in the preservation of democracy."[1] Participating as a GLAM institution
in Wikipedia was a natural alliance for the museum based on the shared mission
of information and knowledge provision.

BELIEF IN ACCESSIBILITY

Colonel Jennifer Pritzker and Ken Clarke, president and CEO of the Pritzker Military Museum & Library (PMML), strongly believe in the accessibility of information and in PMML's role as a "non-partisan research organization that attempts to increase the public understanding of military history and the sacrifices made by the men and women who have served."[2] By providing books and other materials on the history, current condition, and possible futures of the military, the Museum & Library facilitates an open, public forum for discussion and research.

This belief in accessibility is extremely important in today's world. Most Americans do not have firsthand knowledge of the military. Only one percent of Americans currently serve in the military.[3] Reliable information on military history and affairs is not necessarily easy to find. The amount of material available via the Internet can be overwhelming, out of date, or heavily biased. While there are military libraries across the United States, they are not easily accessible to the general public due to their locations on secure military bases. In recent years, some of the federally funded military libraries and military museums in the United States have scaled back their operations or closed due to budget cuts. Another round of military base closures is possible, since in 2017 the Pentagon reported that it has an excess of 22 percent in physical infrastructure.[4] Thus, by acting as a conduit for reliable information through the provision of an accessible collection both on-site and online, the Pritzker Military Museum & Library advances the understanding of citizen soldiers and their role in preserving democracy.

Originally, the Museum & Library's website was a gated collection that was truly open only to those who paid an annual membership subscription. In 2012, Ken Clarke forcefully led the Museum & Library staff in advocating for open access to the website and thus to the collections entrusted to the organization. Other structural changes at the institution occurred in 2013 that would later contribute to the ongoing success of the Museum & Library's participation in Wikipedia as a GLAM (Galleries, Libraries, Archives, and Museums) project.

In 2013, the Museum & Library migrated to a new library automation system offered by a vendor that provided the application programming interface to our web developer at no additional cost to the institution. As a result, the new library system brought scheduling and other workflow improvements, allowing the librarians to move from cataloging to curating. The time savings were allocated to the institution's GLAM initiative and to the expansion of the Veterans Information Center.

Museum & Library staff had edited Wikipedia prior to 2013, but the move from a cataloging to curating model marked the institution's participation in Wikipedia as an official GLAM project.[5]

JOINING WIKIPEDIA

When PMML first joined Wikipedia as a GLAM project partner, it did not have an official project page. PMML started by creating the "Wikipedia and Linked Data Project Internship" with the idea that this intern would edit Wikipedia, Citizendium, and other online wikis. The first intern to hold this position was a graduate student who had a military and technology background. She quickly helped set the bar for future PMML interns, who now contribute primarily to Wikipedia.

Wikipedia is organized behind the scenes via the talk pages into WikiProjects.[6] PMML staff received assistance from two Chicago-area Wikipedia administrators. These administrators set up the project table on PMML's project page (WP:GLAM/PMML) and were available for questions and assistance during the project's first year.

Edit-a-thons were an early way for the staff to engage with Wikipedia. For many libraries, hosting an edit-a-thon has become a regular reference/instructional service activity, which is reflected in the professional literature with essays like "Wikipedia Is Now a Reference Librarian's Job."[7]

The Museum & Library's first edit-a-thon was held on October 16, 2013, in cooperation with the existing WikiProject Chicago as part of Wikipedia's Wiki Loves Libraries 2013 outreach campaign. The experienced Wikipedians from WikiProject Chicago provided expertise in editing Wikipedia. The Museum & Library provided the location and boxed lunches from a local eatery for participants. Participants were encouraged to sign up on the WikiProject Chicago meet-up page in advance of the event.

For PMML, this first edit-a-thon was a success: ten individuals participated, with three new Wikipedia articles being created during the event. It allowed the institution to introduce local Wikipedians to PMML resources and introduced the PMML staff to Wikipedia's organizational culture. The Museum & Library hosted edit-a-thons in 2014 and 2015 with similar success.

WHAT REALLY WORKED

Edit-a-thons were useful in acclimating staff to Wikipedia and getting PMML's WikiProject started. But what has really worked is a more nuanced and integrated approach that heavily involves the use of interns and volunteers.

Due to this integrated approach, it is important to set aside time to manage the initiative and institutional contributions. As project lead, I regularly check my Wikipedia watch list for changes to articles identified with PMML's WikiProject. I roll back any vandalism edits and take note of which articles have been updated by other editors not associated with PMML's WikiProject. For editors who make substantial contributions to an article, I thank them using Wikipedia's thanks tools. Interns are encouraged to use these thank-you tools as well.

The project page lists articles to be created, and anyone can add requests for new articles to this list. PMML interns and volunteers have used this list as a jumping-off point for those times when they are unsure of what to work on next.

PMML librarians check the contributions of interns and volunteers. The time spent can range from twenty minutes at the end of an intern's shift to almost an hour, depending on how long they have been editing Wikipedia, their writing skill level, their previous research experiences, and other factors.

Interns range from junior and senior undergraduates to graduate students, and their ability levels for research and writing vary widely. As a result, grammar and other writing style issues are the most frequent corrections.

At the beginning of an internship or when onboarding a new volunteer, customized "cheat sheets" for the most frequently used Wikipedia template codes are given out. Coding errors can still occur and need to be checked for at the end of an intern's or volunteer's shift.

Copyright is another ongoing issue. Most Wikipedia contributors know not to copy text verbatim from other websites or printed sources, and Wikipedians have created tools to identify copyright violations. These tools have cut down on the number of close paraphrasing incidents in the work of PMML's interns and volunteers.

KNOWING PMML'S COLLECTION

Knowing our collection has significantly contributed to PMML's success as a GLAM project. The first step we took was defining the contributions PMML could make that would improve Wikipedia's coverage of military history and affairs. Since Wikipedia tends to skew a bit toward pop culture and current affairs, it quickly became evident that the majority of PMML's contributions would be historical sketches of people, places, and events. PMML librarians have also identified artists whose work is represented in our collections. A running list of artists the project has identified as notable is kept on PMML's project page.

Biographies of notable individuals have been one of PMML's ongoing initiatives. Wikipedia has another WikiProject that specializes in biographies called the WikiProject Biography. Interns and volunteers are careful to tag new articles with both project tags on the Wikipedia talk page that accompanies the article because this allows other Wikipedia editors to know which projects are interested in a Wikipedia article. Biographies contributed include artists, authors, historians, military personnel, musicians, and politicians.

Adding biographies of authors has been one of the areas in which PMML's project has excelled. Every author who visits PMML and tapes a television episode to air on local PBS channels is identified as needing a Wikipedia article, if they don't already have one. When ordering new books for the collection, we update the authors' Wikipedia pages as part of the acquisition process and include the ISBN and OCLC numbers for their new works. When Wikipedia readers click on the ISBNs and OCLC numbers, they are taken to a list of institutions that hold those titles. Some readers then ask their local libraries to borrow these items for them via interlibrary loan. Historians are another group of individuals for whom biographies are created. Particular attention is paid to situating their work into the historiography of the period they study, as opposed to simply listing their institutional affiliations and awards received.

The Museum & Library also contributes biographies of military personnel. WikiProject Military History is one of the more active and larger projects on Wikipedia and has special talk page tags for their project. PMML interns add these tags as well as the PMML tags and Biography project tags when they edit or create articles about current or former military personnel.

When the librarians evaluated what contributions our project could make to Wikipedia, we quickly realized that the materials in PMML's collection could fill a number of coverage gaps. One of the most notable gaps was American general officers from World War I. Since all general staff officers are considered notable under Wikipedia's guidelines for soldiers,[8] interns began to use Henry Blaine Davis, Jr.'s book *Generals in Khaki* to identify articles that needed to be created or expanded.[9] Since the Museum & Library is a founding sponsor of the United States World War One Centennial Commission[10] and the sponsor for the Illinois World War I Centennial Committee,[11] updating these articles in 2017 and 2018 is a high priority and a public service to those interested in America's involvement in World War I.

Wikipedia has a deficit of articles on notable women. Numerous academic studies document this deficit and give potential reasons for its occurrence. The Wikipedia project Women in Red has been actively trying to close this gender gap. One effort has been to create bot-generated lists of women for whom there are no articles, but for whom pictures or other data have been submitted to related Wiki initiatives, like WikiData (www.wikidata.org). PMML interns and volunteers use the Women in Red bot-generated list for the military as an index for articles that need to be created for females associated with the military. Because of the way this list is generated, it does not include some military women, like American Civil War nurses or women aviators. Biographical dictionaries, like Reina Pennington's *Amazons to Fighter Pilots: A Biographical Dictionary of Military Women*,[12] are used by PMML interns as an index tool in the creation of articles on military women.

Other WikiProjects have generated lists similar to the Women in Red. For example, interns are encouraged to select names from the early aviators list and use resources from the Museum & Library's Dr. Charles E. Metz Collection on World War II Aircraft and the Robin D. S. Higham Collection.

The Museum & Library, since its founding, has been known for the quality programs that it has produced in-house for broadcast on local PBS stations. The programs include author talks, interviews with military personnel, and panel discussions on military, history, and political science topics. Authors who have appeared at the Museum & Library include Sir Hew Strachan, Doris Kearns Goodwin, Mark Bowden, Richard Rubin, Rick Atkinson, Max Hastings, Gerhard Weinberg, A. J. Tata, and Elliot Ackerman. To date, the External Affairs team of the Museum & Library has produced more than 500 television episodes that have aired on the local stations WYCC (Channel 20), WTTW (Channel 11), and WTTW-Prime (Channel 11.2) as *Pritzker Military Presents* and *Citizen Soldier*. Data for the content, cast, and crew of each television episode are contributed to the IMDB (Internet Movie Database) by the Books and Library Services team as part of a larger linked data initiative. Some of this linked data is added to Wikidata and Wikipedia articles as appropriate and in keeping with Wikipedia guidelines.

PMML has hundreds of World War I and World War II sheet music scores in its holdings. Staff have identified the musicians represented therein. Many of these Tin Pan Alley artists did not have Wikipedia articles. So, as part of a larger World War I music project, a World War I curatorial intern added articles to Wikipedia for the songs, composers, and performers. Since the Museum & Library continues to receive donations of sheet music scores, these articles are edited and updated regularly. Articles that need to be created are added to the running list on PMML's GLAM project page.

PMML staff, interns, and volunteers have worked on a variety of Wikipedia articles, including articles on military units (both active and inactive), battle reports, notable books, notable works of art, military medicine, military aviation, war films and documentaries, television shows with military content, military vehicles, and technology as related to the military.

TAGGING AND ENGAGING WITH RELATED WIKIPEDIA PROJECTS

Often, an article is adopted by more than one Wikipedia project. Wikipedia has tools that allow editors to see how Wikipedia projects relate to one another. It is important to add related Wikipedia projects to talk pages because this informs other editors that articles have been created and may need updating or other improvements.

The WikiProject Military History with which PMML's GLAM project shares numerous articles highlights related projects on its project pages, including PMML's projects. WikiProject Military History runs monthly contests for article improvement and occasional special contests. PMML interns have participated in these friendly competitions.

Other Wikipedia projects with which PMML's GLAM project overlaps include WikiProject Songs, WikiProject Books, WikiProject Biography, WikiProject Aviation, WikiProject Television, WikiProject Piracy, WikiProject Nursing, and WikiProject Women.

INTERNS AND VOLUNTEERS

PMML's GLAM project has benefited from a formal internship program in which interns and volunteers help the staff fulfill their duties. The internship program allows the institution to give back to the community through mentoring and networking opportunities for its participants. In the fall and spring academic semesters, there are usually two or three interns and volunteers working on editing and creating Wikipedia articles. During the summer months, this number rises to between three and five interns and volunteers.

Every semester the Museum & Library's director of administration and operations suggests potential applicants for consideration as Wikipedia and linked data interns. Successful interns are considered for future internships with the institution based on their skill sets and interests.

Due to Wikipedia's policies on paid editing, interns who are solely editing Wikipedia are unpaid. Others, like the World War I curatorial intern, were paid, but they had job duties beyond Wikipedia. Some undergraduate interns receive academic credit for their participation. Because PMML actively seeks students from a variety of academic disciplines and provides a mentoring environment, participation in the project has been diverse. These interns have come from different fields of study including history, English, political science, and gender studies. Since 2013, PMML has had thirty-six interns with a near split demo-graphically by gender.

Wikipedians created a fun, space-themed tutorial called the Wikipedia Adventure.[13] New interns and volunteers are encouraged to move through the tutorial before they begin editing articles because this helps to introduce them to Wikipedia and its culture. Interns and volunteers are also encouraged to use Wikipedia's Teahouse, which is a social space on Wikipedia where editors can get help with coding, copyright questions, and related issues.[14] Informing the interns and volunteers of the many Wikipedia-supplied resources available helped them to become effective contributors since many of them did not have prior experience editing Wikipedia.

Interns are encouraged to document their internship experience. Interns who are getting academic credit may be required to do so by their university. For example, Stephen Hart, who interned with PMML in spring 2017, kept a blog for his internship in order to earn credit for his history major.[15]

INFLUENCE ON LIBRARIANS' PHILOSOPHY

Participating in Wikipedia as a GLAM project has had an influence on PMML staff. Librarians help patrons when they start in their quest for information. For many patrons, they start their search on Wikipedia. By working to improve Wikipedia articles related to their institution's holdings, PMML's librarians can confidently recommend Wikipedia articles as part of a more robust reference answer. Additionally, the librarians have the satisfaction of knowing that they are improving the English Wikipedia as a resource and providing reference outreach to patrons regardless of where they live or what time of day it might be.

The librarians realize that every "citation needed" tag in Wikipedia is an unanswered reference question. When time allows, staff update these tags by supplying an appropriate source from books and other resources in PMML's collection.

SHARING PMML'S EXPERIENCE

The Wikipedia Project Chart has been a very useful tool for communicating PMML's contributions to Wikipedia. Each Wikipedia Project Chart measures the quality class of the article as defined by standards spelled out by Wikipedia, and the importance of the article to a given Wikipedia project. Examples of some high-priority articles for the Museum & Library due to the strength of our holdings on these topics include the main article on World War I, the article on the Battle of Hamel (World War I), the article on the Battle of Iwo Jima (World War II), the article on the Guadalcanal Campaign (World War II), and the article on the Medal of Honor, the United States' highest award for valor.

Each month as part of the Museum & Library's internal reporting process, Wikipedia contributions to the PMML are documented. The Books and Library Services team includes such items as the Wikipedia Project Chart, views of approximately three to six specific Wikipedia articles of importance to the institution, reporting of new articles created, reporting of Did You Know (DYK) nominations, the names and project links for other cultural institutions whose projects are similar in size to PMML's, and other statistical items that may be of interest to the Museum & Library's stakeholders.

For example, in March 2017, the Museum & Library's internal report included the following:

The Museum & Library is one of the larger cultural partnerships with Wikipedia, according to Wikipedia's WikiProject Directory (https://en.wikipedia .org/wiki/Wikipedia:WikiProject_Directory). Comparable projects in size and scope include:

- GLAM/Archives of American Art
- GLAM/British Library
- GLAM/Smithsonian Institution Archives

The chart in table 3.1 shows the Wikipedia articles that have been edited as a result of the PMML project, with the quality being the quality of the article as defined by Wikipedia's standards and the importance being defined by the Pritzker GLAM project participants as they relate to the collection holdings of the Museum & Library.

TABLE 3.1

Pritzker Military Library-related articles rated by quality and importance

Pritzker Military Library-related articles by quality and importance							
	Importance						
Quality	Top	High	Mid	Low	NA	???	Total
★ FA		4	10	5			19
★ FL			1				1
Ⓐ A			2	1			3
⊕ GA	1	2	12	18			33
B	2	14	61	77			154
C		21	96	211			328
Start	3	38	169	952			1,162
Stub		1	43	719			763
List		1	6	21	1	1	30
NA			1		16		17
Assessed	6	81	401	2,004	17	1	2,510
Unassessed						1	1
Total	6	81	401	2,004	17	2	2,511
WikiWork factors (?)		ω = 12,248			Ω = 4.97		

In March 2017, new articles were created for Wikipedia on:

- Martha Baker, American Civil War nurse
- Lucy Fenman Barron, American Civil War nurse
- Mary Bell, American Civil War nurse
- Sophronia Bucklin, American Civil War nurse
- Caroline Burghardt, American Civil War nurse
- DeRosey Caroll Cabell, American Maj. Gen. during World War I
- Frank Merrill Caldwell, American Brig. Gen. during World War I
- Betsey Cook, American Civil War nurse
- Susan Cox, American Civil War nurse
- Mary Darling, American Civil War nurse
- Lois Dunbar, American Civil War nurse
- Mary Ellis, American Civil War nurse
- Delia Bartlett Fay, American Civil War nurse
- Elida Rumsey, American Civil War nurse
- Modenia Weston, American Civil War nurse
- Operation Jeb Stuart, a 1st Cavalry Division operation during the Vietnam War

Each month the Books and Library Services team reports the number of views Wikipedia has had for articles related to the Museum & Library's current exhibits. The Museum & Library hosted the exhibit *SEAL: The Unspoken Sacrifice* about the Navy SEALs in 2014. Before the exhibit launched, the main article on Navy SEALs was tagged with our Wikipedia Project tag on its talk page and the article was updated accordingly. Then, the Books and Library Services team reported the number of visits to the Wikipedia article on the Navy SEALs as part of our internal monthly statistics provided to institutional stakeholders. When the SEALs exhibit was running, several television episodes were taped with authors of books related to the topic. Those books saw heavy circulation, especially interlibrary loan transactions, as a result. The page views for the authors' Wikipedia articles had a correlational increase as well.

In 2017 the Museum & Library hosted two exhibits on the Vietnam War: *Hunting Charlie: Finding the Enemy in the Vietnam War* and *Faces of War: Documenting the Vietnam War from the Front Lines*. *Faces of War* explores the conflict through a unique collection of photographs, motion pictures, and artifacts from the Department of the Army Special Photographic Office (DASPO), which was in existence from 1962 to 1974. PMML staff created a Wikipedia article on DASPO in September 2015 before the exhibit launched.[16] Views of this Wikipedia article are reported internally each month. For example, the report for February 2017 stated that the "Department of the Army Special Photographic Office has been viewed 58 times in February with an average of 2/day." The article was viewed 71 times in March 2017, with an average of two views per day.

The Museum & Library participated in the 2016 and 2017 #11ib1ref ("one librarian, one reference") campaigns organized by Wikipedia. The campaigns encouraged librarians to add one reference citation to Wikipedia. For 2016, PMML librarians and interns added the hashtag string #11ib1ref to articles they worked on only in Wikipedia during the period of the campaign. For 2017, the librarians went one step further: They provided the Museum & Library's External Affairs team with the names of the Wikipedia articles recently created by the GLAM project for use on the institution's social media accounts. Most of these social media posts ran on Twitter in February 2017. The institution's top tweet for the month of February was from the #11ib1ref campaign. It was: "New ref on @Wikipedia has been added by PMML interns & librarians! Augustus Perry Blocksom, Maj Gen in WWI http://bit.ly/2jzzT0A #11ib1ref." It had 691 impressions (or number of displays to viewers). Overall, the #11ib1ref 2017campaign tweets generated 6,070 impressions and 84 engagements.

As project lead, I've begun to contribute articles to library and related trade publications on PMML's experience with Wikipedia in order to share with others in the field the best practices that PMML project participants have discovered.

MEASURABLE EFFECTS OF PARTICIPATION

The Museum & Library has been able to document measurable effects for its participation in Wikipedia. More than 10 percent of traffic to PMML's website comes from Wikipedia referrals each year. In March 2017, 13.5 percent of all referrals to PMML's website came from the English version of Wikipedia.

The Books and Library Services team has seen a steady increase in interlibrary loan transactions, especially from out-of-state libraries, since 2013. Some of these loan requests are for scarce resources (i.e., resources held by fifty or fewer libraries in OCLC) that were added as citations to articles on Wikipedia. This has made PMML a net-lender institution, despite the small size of our collection when compared to other research institutions in the Midwest.

Feedback from individuals has been very positive. Members of the military have e-mailed the librarians asking to have specific Wikipedia articles updated. In a few cases, the librarians were asked to create new articles on specific topics from reliable sources. One example of this was the request to have a Wikipedia article created/expanded on the Gray Team, more formally known as the Joint Neurosciences Inspection Team, which was a team investigating how to prevent traumatic brain injuries between 2009 and 2011.

Additionally, interns at PMML have reflected favorably on their experiences there. Many interns have reported that their participation has made them more confident in their communication abilities and/or prepared them for graduate school-level course work within their discipline. Some interns have used one of their Wikipedia articles in their writing portfolios. Another good indicator of the interns' experience with Wikipedia is how many have contributed to Wikipedia via editing since their internship ended. Eleven of the thirty-six interns have made such contributions.[17]

FUTURE INITIATIVES

Based on the project's success to date, PMML plans to increase its contributions to Wikipedia in 2017–2018. These contributions will likely include minor adjustments to PMML's internal acquisition workflows to further coordinate with Wikipedia efforts, adding more articles on World War I people and related topics, adding more articles on military women, adding more articles on World War I and World War II music, and adding more topics on noteworthy books. PMML will continue to seek interns as project participants in 2017–2018.

NOTES

1. "Mission Statement," Pritzker Military Museum & Library, 2017, www.pritzkermilitary .org/about/mission-personnel/mission-statement/.

2. Ibid.

3. "What Americans Don't Understand about Their Own Military," *Defense One*, 2017, www.defenseone.com/ideas/2015/05/what-americans-dont-understand-about-their-own -military/112042/.

4. "BRAC Finds Some Stable Ground in 2017," *FederalNewsRadio.com*, 2017, http://federal newsradio.com/defense/2017/02/brac-finds-stable-ground-2017/; "Congress Formally Begins the Process for a New BRAC," *Dayton Business Journal*, 2017, https://www.biz journals.com/dayton/news/2017/01/27/congress-formally-begins-the-process-for-a -new.html.

5. "Wikipedia:GLAM/Pritzker," Wikipedia, 2017, https://en.wikipedia.org/w/index.php? title=Wikipedia:GLAM/Pritzker&oldid=774802475.

6. "WikiProject," Wikipedia, 2017, https://en.wikipedia.org/wiki/WikiProject.

7. Tristan Bravinder, "Wikipedia Is Now a Reference Librarian's Job," *The Getty Iris*, 2017, http://blogs.getty.edu/iris/wikipedia-is-now-a-reference-librarians-job/.

8. "Wikipedia:WikiProject Military History/Notability Guide," Wikipedia, 2016, https:// en.wikipedia.org/w/index.php?title=Wikipedia:WikiProject_Military_history/Notability _guide&oldid=742164437.

9. The full citation for Davis's book is: Henry Blaine Davis, *Generals in Khaki* (Raleigh, NC: Pentland, 1998).

10. For more on the National World War I Centennial Commission, see National World War I Centennial, 2017, www.worldwar1centennial.org.

11. For more on the Illinois World War I Centennial Commission, see "Illinois and the Great War," 2017, Illinois World War I Centennial Commission, www.worldwar1centennial.org/ index.php/illinois-wwi-centennial-home.html.

12. The full citation for Pennington's book is: Reina Pennington, *Amazons to Fighter Pilots: A Biographical Dictionary of Military Women* (Westport, CT: Greenwood, 2003).

13. "Wikipedia:TWA/Portal," Wikipedia, 2015, https://en.wikipedia.org/w/index.php?title =Wikipedia:TWA/Portal&oldid=646728233.

14. "Wikipedia:Teahouse," Wikipedia, 2017, https://en.wikipedia.org/w/index.php?title =Wikipedia:Teahouse&oldid=775080926.

15. "Stephenhartsinternship: My Experience at the Pritzker Military Museum and Library," 2017, https://stephenhartsinternship.wordpress.com/.

16. To see the full Wikipedia article, "Department of the Army Special Photographic Office," 2017, Wikipedia, https://en.wikipedia.org/w/index.php?title=Department_of_the_Army _Special_Photographic_Office&oldid=759386365.

17. This statistic includes two interns whose internship ended within the last month.

4

Bringing Wiki(p/m)edians into the Conversation at Libraries

ALEX STINSON AND JASON EVANS

For hundreds of years libraries were the world's primary providers of knowledge and information, and while libraries continue to provide vital services, the landscape in which they operate has changed dramatically. One of the most dramatic components of this changing landscape is the advance in digital access to research materials and alternative public entry points, like Wikipedia, which have created challenges for libraries' strategy. To some, Wikipedia might seem like a librarian's nemesis, but there is in fact a growing collaboration emerging between Wikipedia and the library community: libraries and Wikipedia are increasingly working together toward their common goal of providing free and open knowledge to all.[1]

Many of the skills that make good librarians effective in reaching their patrons overlap with the skills of the most effective Wikipedia contributors: an interest in and understanding of quality research materials; an interest in effective citation and attribution of those research materials; and clear communication with the public. Moreover, Wikipedia's "sum of all human knowledge" mission also closely aligns with the service-focused goals of the library profession, and providing patrons with access to the best public knowledge drives both activities.

The big difference between the two communities is in their degree of formal responsibility: librarians are trained professionals working in institutions with public charges to provide information access, while Wikipedians are (for the most part) volunteers, whose interests align with their hobbies and values. But the closeness of the goals, skills, and interests of Wikimedians and librarians means that finding a common ground for collaboration is often not only a possibility, but actually quite easy. Finding the right people to collaborate with on this broad, and frankly never-ending, mission is an important first step to effective collaboration.

In this chapter, we will explore who the Wikimedia community is, and how to find the right allies in that community. Wikimedia-related initiatives work best when coalitions of different types of contributors—professionals and volunteers, experienced Wikimedians and local knowledge enthusiasts—come together to enhance public access to knowledge.

FINDING YOUR ALLIES IN THE WIKIMEDIA MOVEMENT

When you participate in Wikipedia and other Wikimedia platforms, such as Wikimedia Commons, Wikidata, or Wikisource, it's important to understand that these platforms operate as part of a vast and complex social movement. When approaching Wikimedia, it is important to account for a fundamental though rarely understood premise for Wikipedia and its contributor community: there is very little formal hierarchy or structure, and the many different segments of the community have different forms of power and varying levels of influence over the projects. Many activities and projects within Wikimedia communities are entirely volunteer-led: some of those volunteers may be working with support or funding from the Wikimedia Foundation or local Wikimedia chapters, and still others are working on projects developed by other stakeholder groups, such as educational institutions, research communities, or cultural heritage organizations—the last of which is the focus of this chapter.

Wikipedia's barriers for participation are fairly low: in most parts of the community, almost anyone can contribute to the content pages, discuss content policies, and even contribute patches to the software. Many of these spaces have checks and balances on this openness, such as the software itself, which has a

number of community and Wikimedia Foundation-controlled review mecha-
nisms, or the mechanism for controversial topics and high-visibility spaces, like
the front page of Wikipedia, which are blocked from editing except by more
experienced editors or elected administrators.[2]

The low barrier to entry means that every month nearly 20,000 new accounts
register on Wikimedia projects, and English Wikipedia alone has 130,000 to
140,000 accounts making at least one edit per month. In this context, even
the formal organizations that support the Wikimedia community, such as the
Wikimedia Foundation which controls the trademarks and servers that keep
the websites operating, have almost no control over the governance, editorial
practices, or decision-making that create the content on Wikipedia, Wikimedia
Commons, Wikidata, and other Wikimedia projects—except for defining the
terms of use for participation and a privacy policy.[3] This governance power is
distributed across the volunteer community through broad principles and practices of contributor-consensus, neutrality, and verifiability.[4]

If the power rests with the community, who is that volunteer community?[5]
Every month, 75,000 to 80,000 individual Wikimedia accounts contribute five
or more edits to one of about 285 language Wikipedias or other Wikimedia
projects, which are also available in a number of other languages. English Wikipedia, the most voluminous of these projects, includes about 30,000 of these
contributors each month. That seems like quite a large number, but in practice
five contributions to Wikipedia per month is actually a rather casual participation
in the project: most likely these are contributions to content pages, and those
contributors have very little participation in the actual community processes
that govern the projects.

To find the folks most invested in the broad maintenance of the projects, we
need to look at different numbers: folks who contribute 100 or more edits per
month, which includes about 14,000 people per month across the Wikimedia
projects. On English Wikipedia, which is still the biggest highly active community,
this includes about 3,500 individuals during any given month. For a top 10 website, this is actually a rather small community with relationships and community
dynamics that have evolved over the sixteen years of Wikipedia's existence. This
long history means that this relatively small community has its own practices,
cultural expectations, and social problems of similar complexity to those that
emerge whenever you ask groups of human beings to contribute time to an
intellectual effort. Moreover, multiple studies have found the community to not
be very diverse when examining specific cross-sections, including less than 15

percent of contributors identifying as female—so a lack of diversity complicates these broader social issues.[6]

With all of this social activity online, Wikipedia could be described as a social network of sorts: for example, different parts of the Wikimedia movement have developed offline or in-person methods of working together. Sometimes this takes the form of informal meet-up groups, where folks get together for beers, coffee, editing activities, or photo scavenger hunts. Increasingly, however, this organization takes the form of more formal working groups focused on outreach and participation campaigns, and community organizations formally recognized by the Wikimedia Foundation as representatives of a local community, called affiliates.

Though participating as an individual in the Wikimedia community has a low threshold for entry, doing more than common content contributions necessitates a certain kind of organization and relationship between contributors. For formal organizations, such as libraries, which may want to not just contribute small amounts of content, but also take advantage of and participate in the Wikimedia community, navigating the community and culture of the Wikimedia projects can be complicated. Working with affiliates or at least finding an individual Wikimedia contributor to help interface with other experienced volunteers lowers the barrier for participation in the community, allowing the Wikimedia-experienced partner to provide community expertise while the organizational partner brings its knowledge and network.

Historically, communities of Wikipedia editors have grown up organically and independently, with little intentional cohesion. However, there are increasing efforts around the world to grow local editing communities around specific interest groups, volunteer groups, and educational initiatives and turn them into more formal organizations, called "affiliates." Wikimedia affiliates principally come in two major types: user groups and chapters.[7] Both of these organization types function as conduits for building relationships between local Wikimedia volunteer communities and potential partners and collaborators, including libraries.

In certain parts of the world, Wikimedia communities have formed relatively strong Wikimedia affiliates, called chapters, which are nonprofit organizations—many of them are in Europe—that represent the aims of the Wikimedia Foundation, Wikimedia projects, and the local Wikimedia community, and frequently have small professional staffs that provide different kinds and levels of support to the local communities. Many of these organizations have formed in response to the need for the formal support of partnerships with educational or heritage organizations, but they also provide other kinds of support for those communities, from organizing events to supporting communications, from outreach or lobbying to providing funds used by local volunteer organizers.[8]

In parts of the world that are less homogenous in terms of culture, language, country, and geography, or in countries like the United States, Australia, and Canada where the contributors to one project might be spread across very wide distances, national affiliates or chapters have less cohesion or influence; where the volunteer community doesn't have organizational capacity, another solution is needed. Instead, there are often small meet-up groups, or the slightly more formal "user group"—an informal organization recognized as a gathering for developing specific activities and which is eligible for small grants and other support from the Wikimedia Foundation.[9] Examples include the regionally focused Cascadia Wikimedians (a user group that includes members from the Northwestern United States and British Columbia) and the Wikimedia and Libraries User Group (a global group that supports connections between Wikimedia projects and libraries).

However, many Wikimedia/pedia contributors are not aware of these organizations, or are satisfied contributing to Wikipedia or another Wikimedia project as individual volunteers who are independent of these organizations.[10] Wikipedia editors are as diverse as the encyclopedia; they edit and may or may not have any interest in collaborating on projects beyond the interests that originally brought them to the projects—for example, a subject area, or addressing specific grammatical errors. Therefore, libraries wishing to engage with Wikipedia contributors should not necessarily turn to the most active online editors, since they may have no desire to be part of formal projects or take on any additional responsibility.

For library organizations that want to get involved in Wikimedia projects, reaching out to one of these organized affiliates is frequently the best course of action: these affiliates often have technical experience organizing events or projects in their region, and they can find the right resources to provide guidance and training to cultural professionals.[11] But if you can't find a local affiliate, we recommend trying several tactics:

- First, search to find if local editors or contributors have hosted meet-ups via the Meetup listing page.[12] Organizers or participants of meet-ups can often also host events with local partners.
- Reach out through social media channels and/or other networks and ask for someone who has Wikimedia experience. Though having someone locally

available is often a good start, you may not find someone local who is also interested in supporting outreach or programmatic activities—increasingly, library communities have at least one or two library professionals in their own network who have run Wikipedia edit-a-thons or Wikipedia education assignments. Sometimes the best support will come from aligned professionals.

- Reach out to the closest affiliate in your language context and ask them to help you find a more local Wikimedian. They will likely use several tactics for searching out community members:
    - Local Wikimedia chapters often have a directory of trained or experienced volunteers who are capable of effectively training new editors—even in nearby regions that lie outside their scope.
    - The part of the Wikimedia community that does outreach is relatively well connected, as a social network, so they may know someone in your region through an unconventional method.
    - Use categories and user templates to find active users who either self-identify as being from a particular region, or participate in editing topics relevant to your context.[13]
    - If you are organizing an event or gathering, you can solicit a Geonotice, which places a banner on the Watchlist of people who sign in within your geographic area without exposing their location to the message sender.[14]

In most parts of the world, these requests will find someone who can connect you to Wikimedia contributors in your local context. If you don't find these networks responsive, there are an increasing number of Facebook groups and mailing lists that can connect you with the larger network working at the intersection of cultural heritage (GLAM—Galleries, Libraries, Archives, and Museums) and the Wikimedia community, including a Wikipedia + Libraries Group, that can help you find fellow librarians or supporters who can work with you remotely.[15]

CREATING WIKIMEDIANS IN YOUR COMMUNITY

Once you define the Wikimedia activity that you want to pursue, whether it's an edit-a-thon or the upload of open access content, or if you want to create a regular editing group to focus on a particular topic, it's important to bring volunteer capacity to the projects.[16]

Wikimedia's culture of bold volunteerism with a very low barrier to entry means that Wikimedia volunteers often have a range of motivations, capacities, and organizational skills that may or may not meet the needs of more formal institutions. Additionally, Wikimedia volunteers may invest a large amount of energy in projects which they feel passionate about, or which connect with the needs of other communities—but like all projects of passion, that enthusiasm can wane, or you might find that your local Wikimedians don't want to focus on the topics you are interested in. So what do you do then?

The best approach is to develop new interest in Wikimedia contributions from other volunteer communities in your local context, who can attend local events. Typically, these new contributors can come from hobbyists or volunteers who are already associated with your library or similar heritage organizations. Local community groups may offer some of the best allies: for example, local history societies and social, charitable, and educational groups of all sorts. There is also a growing number of individuals who are prepared to volunteer at libraries and other cultural institutions. These communities frequently are interested in communicating knowledge in your context, and many of them publish their own journals, newsletters, and books. For librarians looking to increase engagement with local communities, Wikipedia offers a ready-built platform, in multiple languages, where local communities can work with their local libraries to improve Wikipedia content relating to their interests or expertise.

CASE STUDY

Catalan Wikipedia has a relatively limited geography where it can expect to find volunteers for the project: in Catalan-speaking parts of Spain and France. By collaborating with the Public Library Network in Catalonia, the Catalan community has involved over 200 libraries in their Bibliowikis initiative.[17] The model for the collaboration is a simple one: librarians run programs that involve the local public, and those librarians train other librarians on developing that kind of programming in their own context. Program models include basic Wikipedia editing workshops, and a number of activities that promote local history and culture, such as photo-scavenger hunts and local book clubs writing about local authors and regional history. Amical Wikimedia (the Catalan Wikimedia affiliate) provides very little support to get the libraries started in activities: documentation and trying to find a regionally available volunteer for the librarians to collaborate with. Once the activities start at a local library, they typically develop other local volunteers who can help support and provide energy for local projects.

Unlike already committed Wikimedians, who will frequently show up at events just because they're Wikimedia-related, we have found that involving a broader volunteer community works best with thematic focuses. These focuses offer simpler communication strategies (i.e., "filling a gap on Wikipedia") and elicit better public interest than offering "learn about Wikipedia" programs.[18] These themes can fit closely the institutional objectives of the GLAM hosting the activities:

- Many institutions host what's called a "backstage pass" where they highlight an important topic in their collection as the theme—such initiatives allow volunteers and staff to share in the professional activities of the organization and rare parts of their collection.
- These themes might fit into the outreach programming goals of your institution—the Catalan Public Library network collaboration includes frequent book club or local author editing events, which focus on highlighting literary culture that is also subject to public library programming.
- The topic might be more political and draw from an activist or knowledge community that is interested in public understanding of that topic—for example, the Art+Feminism events are hosted by GLAMs around the world, and draw large numbers of women editors into the community because of the broad call for "feminist" participation in the projects.

Picking one of these tactics can excite an existing community and provide a motivating draw for volunteers to become engaged in the project and therefore with the library's collections. Moreover, thematic or project-focused communications provide platforms for highlighting the importance of institutional work in that field to local media.

Online programs for the Wikimedia community can also draw participation and collaboration with contributors outside of the geographical scope of the library, especially on topics of broader interest than local history and culture. Typically, contribution campaigns focus on a theme or topic that the library or other institution offers digital collections on, and require a fair amount of online Wikimedia community skills. For example, the National Archive of the Republic of Macedonia runs a multilingual competition for contributing content related to parts of its collections that it has uploaded to Wikimedia Commons; a similar strategy has also been adopted by the Bulgarian Archives State Agency.[19] Working closely with existing Wikimedia communities or online networks to find the right topics that will excite or engage volunteers helps ensure that these kinds of projects succeed.

CASE STUDY

Wicipop—an initiative funded by the Welsh government and managed by the Wikimedian in Residence at the National Library of Wales—used a blend of online and offline activities to achieve the project's goal of creating 500 new Welsh Wikipedia articles about Welsh pop music in three months. Three themed public edit-a-thon events were held, which drew new and experienced editors into the same physical space in order to create new content. Events like these are great for publicity, and several of the events attracted interest from the local media. The project also targeted active editors online by establishing a project landing page on Wikipedia itself. This led to a substantial contribution from experienced Wikipedians that the National Library of Wales hadn't previously engaged. A social media campaign also led to local publishers releasing content on an open license which editors could then reuse on Wikipedia—contributing to a broader cycle of increased public access to knowledge.[20]

PLANNING FOR NEW CONTRIBUTORS

Engaging new volunteers with Wikipedia and Wikimedia projects has its challenges. Some first-time editors lack the confidence to publish on such a visible and far-reaching platform as Wikipedia. Others struggle with the technical aspects of editing. Perhaps the biggest challenge, however, is the retention of editors following an initial training session or edit-a-thon event.[21]

The main challenge when introducing new volunteers to Wikimedia projects is frequently apprehension or lack of confidence: Wikipedia is a large website, is seen as an almost venerable institution, and is often misunderstood by the public; contributing to this large and mysterious project can be intimidating or simply unmotivating. Having a champion on hand to lend confidence to new contributors helps them to interpret the project's nuances and feedback systems. For example, it is very useful to have someone with Wikipedia experience in new-contributor events to serve as interpreters. When more seasoned Wikipedia volunteers have first interactions with new editors, sometimes they are rather abrupt or less than welcoming. Having an interpreter on hand to explain what a template means, or how to figure out if the critique of a new editor's work is valid, provides in-person opportunities for modeling and decoding what can often be a difficult to understand community/social dynamic of developing content.

If you are planning on hosting an event to edit Wikipedia, it is also useful to make contact with a few experienced Wikipedians via their Wikipedia profiles; if you can get hold of editors with administrative rights, that's even better. These editors will then be aware that a group of new editors is being trained and can offer appropriate online support—such as patrolling new content to ensure that it won't solicit poor responses from other editors.

In order to address these and other issues of building sustainable communities of local editors, most projects need at least one champion. Such champions come in many guises, from enthusiastic outreach staff within libraries and proactive local community leaders to Wikipedians in Residence and online Wikimedia volunteers. As the Wikimedia community has grown and become more effective at outreach, we have found that it's less important for these champions to fully understand Wikimedia projects; what's more important is for them to have strong teaching skills so that they can explain interactions to new contributors and be able to tap a network of supporters with deeper Wikimedia knowledge.

PROTIP

Initially Wikipedia editors had to have a basic grasp of wiki markup[22] in order to contribute to the encyclopedia. In recent years, Wikipedia has introduced a new "Visual Editor" which modernizes the process to act more like a word processor or contributes to a content management system like Wordpress. The introduction of this tool, since late 2012, has drastically cut training times and made Wikipedia editing accessible to a far wider audience. Those teaching new contributors how to edit Wikipedia can start volunteers in the Visual Editor, while providing a brief introduction to the wiki source code.

Another important component of maintaining volunteer communities is providing tangible feedback and demonstration of the impact of volunteer work. Wikipedia and its sister platforms provide a global environment for a hugely varied corpus of information, data, and media. Because of this reach and scope, some volunteers will find motivation from seeing the instant fruits of their labor, in the shape of new or improved Wikimedia content. However, providing sustained morale-building throughout the programming helps strengthen that initial value.

There are a number of tactics for sustaining morale that overlap closely with good library programming: for example, coordinating press and social media communications with volunteer activities, which highlights the value of individual volunteer work, or providing small benefits to participants in the events, like free refreshments or a "backstage" tour of your institution, which rewards volunteers for their participation with tangible benefits. Your local user group or Wikimedia chapter may also have a budget for merchandise such as badges, pens, stickers, and T-shirts which they can distribute for free, and these are usually well received by volunteers. Innovating on different kinds of motivation and moral support, and sharing what works help develop best practices for public knowledge projects more generally. For example, at West Virginia University, the Wikipedian in Residence is partnering with sororities to give sorority members service credit for their participation in Wikimedia activities in collaboration with the library and educators.

CASE STUDY

Many libraries coordinate small teams of volunteers who wish to work with them. At the National Library of Wales, volunteers who wish to work with the institution are all offered the chance to work with Wikipedia, and in March 2017 fifteen volunteers were working regularly on improving Wikipedia content. Tasks are tailored to every individual's needs and interests. The library holds an annual awards ceremony to recognize the achievements of its volunteers and offers free parking and refreshments to all members of the team. The scheme has been so successful that there is often a waiting list to volunteer.

GETTING THE RIGHT SUPPORT: INTEGRATING WIKIMEDIA CHAMPIONS INTO THE LIBRARY

As we described in the last section, you can bring many different types of people into an organization to work on Wikimedia projects. However, codifying the role of staff or volunteer advocates for these collaborations within your organization can greatly strengthen the effectiveness of projects: rather than having one-off editing events or data donations, if your champions have formal roles, they can develop a more strategic and integrated plan. This integration allows these champions to work more closely with library staff, the Wikimedia community, and other volunteers to identify common objectives and implement mutually beneficial programs. Moreover, this enables the library administration to recognize the work and its place within the organization. Integrating champions into your library and formalizing their roles also places faith in them as individuals, and this can motivate them to stay engaged with the project for longer times. This is particularly true when working with unpaid champions, who are often young graduates looking for work experience to bolster their curriculum vitae.

Staff Champions

The first, most obvious, and most cost-effective way to integrate Wikimedia projects into the strategy of a GLAM is to formalize the role of its staff for organizing activities and working on Wikimedia projects within the course of their regular work. Staff can allocate a certain amount of their work hours to work on Wikimedia projects, typically with a broader public access or outreach mission in mind. However, if the addition of Wikimedia is a side project (or just a tactic within someone's job), there are risks: the main one is that it's hard to get broad support across hierarchical organizations without some sort of strategic investment in Wikimedia contribution as an organization.

Two major tactics have been used by GLAMs in identifying the roles for existing staff members who contribute to Wikimedia:

- At the U.S. National Archives and Records Administration, the social media and digital innovation offices supported an informal Wikipedia editing guideline that is similar to the other social media use guidelines.[23]
- At the State Library of New South Wales in Australia, a staff committee created a formal policy on staff integrating Wikimedia projects into organizational workflows.[24]

The first tactic, a more informal one, gives permission for staff, whereas the second, which required a longer and more formal process, has been very effective at not only giving permission, but providing the rationale for integrating Wikimedia work into the organization's priorities—and it does so with a more inclusive organizational strategic buy-in. Generally, either mechanism, either a team strategically explaining the alignment of the work with broader organizational priorities or a cross-organizational recognition of the strategic priority, allows staff who act as Wikimedia champions to justify appropriate Wikimedia programming and roles within their jobs.

Within many organizations that don't formalize the strategic interest in Wikimedia projects, staff end up taking Wikimedia collaborations on as "volunteers" beyond their staff roles. In the face of the undervaluation of cultural heritage work more generally, expecting staff to do this work as an "extra" to their existing jobs leads to uneven focus, and in the long term, contributes to the under-recognition of something that is fundamental to organizational missions: a strategy for broader public access to collections and specialized knowledge. Many heritage organizations are not ready to invest large amounts of staff time in developing a case for or test of Wikimedia contribution tactics as part of a broader public-access strategy. Instead, many organizations will build another role into their staff, with either volunteers or term-based staff.

Wiki(p/m)edians in Residence

The best-described and commonest way of creating the "empowered champion" role in the Wikimedia community is the "Wiki(m/p)edian in Residence" (WIR). A WIR is tasked with integrating a strategy for Wikimedia projects and broader OpenGLAM into the workflows and practice of a library or other cultural institution. The WIR's role is not to edit Wikipedia on behalf of the institution (a common misconception), but rather to focus on projects that grow the understanding, skills, and capacity of the organization to successfully engage with Wikimedia projects and to improve their broader strategy for open, public engagement with institutional content.

This role usually includes a number of sub-activities, such as creating a free-licensing/open access policy for digital heritage assets; training staff in Wikimedia editing or open-licensing; organizing events, edit-a-thons, or other contribution activities which utilize institutional expertise; or facilitating the donation of media to Wikimedia Commons. Typically these residencies last at least six months, though some have been shorter; most organizations find that they need at least a year of a residency to fully integrate their capacity with a broader "public-access through Wikimedia" strategy—a handful of these roles have extended to semipermanent or permanent roles, as it has been at the U.S. National Archives and Records Administration.

The Wikipedian in Residence idea was first developed and tested at the British Museum by an experienced Australian Wikipedia editor named Liam Wyatt in 2010. Wyatt, who held the residency as a volunteer for five weeks, was able to demonstrate how enriching Wikipedia content relating to the museum's collections increased the number of linkbacks to the museum's website and led to an increase in its community engagement activities.[25] Since then residencies have been hosted by well over a hundred institutions within a number of different language and cultural contexts and structural arrangements.[26]

Early iterations of WIR roles were entirely unpaid (building on the idea that a "Wikimedian" is a volunteer, who can be "in residence" at an institution); in the last four or five years, however, many of these WIR roles have received at least some sort of compensation, acknowledging that an extended residency at a GLAM institution requires a certain caliber of organizer who should not have to sacrifice his or her well-being or career development in order to volunteer. Moreover, while the work of a normal Wikipedian might be seen as fun volunteerism (developing content on a topic of personal interest), the work of a WIR frequently requires participating in organizational development and dynamics—which is clearly not in the scope of full or part-time volunteer work. Compensation is usually in the form of a short-term contract, funded through either an outreach-focused budget, an external grant, or existing residency, fellowship, practicum, or internship programs for early professionals. That being said, small or under-resourced institutions may be able to build a close relationship with a Wikimedian or other volunteer who is willing to do a "Wikipedian in Residence" role without this much investment, or it might be appropriate for a coalition of institutions to resource a Wikipedian in Residence—as happened at the York Museums Trust or METRO library association in New York.[27]

Early WIR roles were recruited almost exclusively from experienced Wikimedia community members, who had a deep understanding of the social dynamics of different Wikimedia projects. However, this has changed with the proliferation of different Wikimedia outreach programs, which in turn has allowed Wikimedia communities to gain experience in developing relationships with GLAM institutions, resulting in better documentation that is understandable by cultural heritage professionals. Moreover, the deeply engaged online community only has so many volunteers who are capable of setting aside their careers for temporary employment and also have the right skills for effective program development at partner organizations. Instead, hiring individuals with little to moderate Wikimedia experience, but with demonstrated energy, experience, and alignment with digital communities alongside outreach and project management skills, has proven effective in a number of situations.

When supported by a broader community of Wikimedians through an affiliate or network, it's even possible to develop effective programs with someone who has no Wikimedia experience: for example, the West Virginia University Libraries hired Kelly Doyle, a community organizer and educator, who had no previous experience working with the Wikimedia community. Her ability to organize effective events, learn and teach about the social components of the Wikimedia community, and innovate on existing project models has empowered a wide group of stakeholders across the campus and the wider West Virginia community to address "gender equity" on Wikipedia: from local history communities, to sorority students, librarians, and faculty.

The outcomes from WIRs range widely, based on the organizational strategies, the project pursued, and the capacity within the organization to prioritize resources and open-license content for use in the partnership. But documented outcomes and descriptions of the experience by host institution staff tend to be very strong. The use of WIRs has resulted in positive organizational culture changes, theoretical public impact (through the increased visibility of topics of importance to the institution), and tangible metrics in terms of large numbers of page views of new content created on Wikipedia and media uploaded to Wikimedia projects, as well as an increase in referrals from Wikimedia websites to institutional resources.[28]

Residencies can be described as successful based on tangible metrics and impacts. However, evaluating and implementing the WIR model in isolation often fails to leave any lasting institutional impact on Wikimedia's projects and mission once the residency ends. Meaningful strategic impact, particularly in larger GLAMs, can take a very long time and may meet with resistance from staff who have conflicting priorities and targets. In order to aid a lasting Wikimedia collaboration, the WIR must work closely with the institution to build a sustainable model for engagement. This might involve establishing a volunteer community under the management of a permanent library staff member who acts as the champion after the residency, securing policy change within the time scale of the residency, expanding written job descriptions to include Wikimedia-related duties, or building content release or donation into digitization workflows.

Wikipedia Visiting Scholars

Wikipedian in Residence roles are high risk/high reward roles for institutions: they cost a fair amount of money, in terms of the role itself and supervising the role, but they ensure that someone on the staff has the energy and time to integrate Wikimedia, either through its projects or through its values of openness and public access, into the organizational strategy. However, when an organization isn't ready for this kind of strategic commitment, it's still worth designating an advocate from outside the organization to experiment within existing collections or resources. Increasingly, institutions are turning to the concept of a "Wikimedia Visiting Scholar": this is someone whose real expertise is on creating Wikimedia content and exposing the institution to the connections between the institution's mission and Wikimedia projects, while not focusing on increasing capacity by creating new Wikipedia editors.[29]

Visiting Scholars, like Wikipedians in Residence, usually have some experience with Wikimedia projects, but that experience must be targeted on developing high-quality content. To create such a role, an institution works in partnership with an affiliate or a champion to find a Wikimedian editing in a certain topic area that is relevant to the collection, and then the institution invites that Wikimedian to fill the "Visiting Scholar" position. This arrangement is modeled off "visiting scholar" positions at academic institutions. The Wikipedian gains some type of unique access arrangement, such as access to materials licensed by a research library or direct support from a handful of the staff, that allows him to more effectively research so that he can contribute to an agreed-upon field of knowledge. These Visiting Scholar roles provide an interface with the Wikimedia community: humanizing the activity, introducing staff to the creation of content on Wikimedia projects, and helping staff examine the relationship between organizational knowledge and Wikimedia projects.

Typically, Visiting Scholar roles are initiated for a window of time, usually for six months to a year and often remotely, to contribute a certain amount of content (i.e., 15–30 high-quality Wikipedia articles, or the integration of a dataset into Wikidata), with a presentation or collaboration with staff at the end which highlights the relationship of the Wikimedia content to the organization's goals. Some Wikipedia Visiting Scholars have asked for closer collaboration with their host institutions, creating the stepping-stone for a Wikimedian in Residence type of position. In other situations, the temperament or interests of the Wikimedian don't lend themselves to deeper collaboration, but they sustain contributions to Wikimedia projects in collaboration with the institution.

CASE STUDY

The Wikipedia Visiting Scholar scheme offers more flexibility than the more formal Wikipedian in Residence role. It can be adapted to suit the needs of the host institution, as well as the skills and interests of the volunteer. In 2015 the National Library of Wales developed and invited applications for a Wikidata Visiting Scholar position. Working to the same principles as the Wikipedia Visiting Scholar position, the successful applicant was guaranteed access to otherwise closed-access datasets, as well as specialist advice from curatorial staff and technical support from the systems team. The successful candidate was able to work remotely, processing library data and combining it with other open data to create a rich linked open-data resource on Wikidata. This allowed the library to share its data openly for the first time, and to study the advantages of doing so, with little or no cost and no disruption to core library duties. While the library had clear goals (convert metadata to linked data and release via Wikidata), the Visiting Scholar was given the freedom to choose which data he would develop and how he would visualize and interpret the data later. This flexible approach can make all the difference in keeping key volunteers engaged, motivated, and focused.[30]

Student Interns, Practicum Students, or University Classes

One of the common patterns that emerges among Wikimedians who become Wikipedians in Residence or staff champions is that they often do so after being high-performing students (usually graduate students) in a field related to the institution's focus: either library science, museum studies, archival studies, or a related writing-focused program, such as art history, history, or a social science. Moreover, there have been a number of projects in which university libraries or archives engaged student workers to highlight institutional content by contributing new content on Wikimedia projects. These projects initially took the approach of "just adding links" to institutional collections on Wikimedia, a practice perceived as spam by some parts of the Wikimedia community; newer projects have focused on the win-win relationship between creating high-quality content on Wikimedia projects and increasing the visibility of not only the contributing institution's digital assets, but also the broader materials available on that niche subject area.

Employing students to get involved in Wikimedia contributions for the institution acts as a flip-version of the Wikipedia Visiting Scholar project: instead of a low-cost, low-risk contribution from a Wikimedian, student employees offer a low-cost, low-risk introduction in which the institutional supervisor and her student learn how to effectively participate within the guidelines put out by the Wikimedia community. Important to this process is creating the expectation that students not only add references to a digital institutional resource, but expand content using different kinds of cultural heritage research from beyond the institution. The Wikipedia Library team ran an experiment with several academic and research libraries in order to systematize these kinds of internships into cohorts. Outcomes were high, with a better quality of Wikipedia content than typical documented student work, but the cohort model was intensive to organize.[31] By building champions out of the students and their supervisors, the institution is able to do low-risk experiments while learning about Wikimedia projects, and testing whether the student can be a good long-term advocate, in the form of a staff champion or Wikipedian in Residence.

There are a number of examples of this kind of project. See chapter 3 in this book about the Pritzker Military Museum & Library, where they supported a continuous flow of student interns filling topically important gaps like World War I patriotic music.[32] Other institutions, such as the Smithsonian Freer/Sackler Gallery in cooperation with Smithsonian Libraries, have hosted interns who profiled Asian art topics that are systematically under-covered on Wikimedia projects.[33] All of these models find a champion either in the students themselves or in their supervisors or institutional instructors, and they allow the institution to test the broad potential of Wikimedia to fit in with existing efforts and staff priorities.

A well-documented and well-supported project model, the Wikipedia Education Program, can be a good way to extend this low-risk experimentation. Wikipedia Education Program assignments allow instructors, typically college-level, to assign students to write full articles which fill topical gaps on Wikipedia. This can be done with a focus on topics relevant to institutional collections, acting as a form of academic outreach and collaboration. Working with a full class of students at a local university might be an unusual form of outreach for public or non-university research libraries: however, for local history, public history, and GLAM professional programs, direct engagement with the collections held by institutions, and using Wikipedia as an example environment and platform for public access to heritage, provide ample learning opportunities.

Working with classes of students can also introduce a number of complications for libraries that have not previously worked with educational communities; for example, it may be necessary to plan around a semester, provide research skills support, and match projects against learning outcomes. In the United States and Canada, there is a fair amount of assignment design and student support available from the Wiki Education Foundation for curriculum development, online tracking, and community engagement support. Affiliates in other parts of the world also regularly support education assignments, and although they frequently can't provide the same amount of professional support as the Wiki Education Foundation, they are often able to provide curriculum development support and might be able to provide broader support (including workshops).

CASE STUDY

While working at Kansas State University, Stinson worked with the Beach Museum of Art to have students in an art history class write content that exposed particular parts of the museum's collection alongside the best external research for that topic. The Wikipedia article work acted as a first step towards adding bibliographic research to finding aids and catalog materials for the museum's actual collection.[34] Moreover, students were introduced to the difference between primary source research and secondary research, and the various venues in which this knowledge can be shared—among researchers, with the public, and into institutional catalogs where the project provides context.

INNOVATING, GROWING, AND SUPPORTING COMMUNITIES

The models for engaging volunteers, collaborators, and champions are still very fluid in the Wikimedia community—outreach with cultural heritage organizations has only been systematically approached within the international Wikimedia community since 2010 or 2011. As a community working with libraries, the Wikimedia community is still learning what consistently creates desired outcomes, and how to best serve the missions of both communities, institutions and Wikimedia. Within this shifting context and understanding of how these collaborations work, it behooves Wikimedia allies in the library community to continue iterating upon what we know about community engagement: public programming around access to knowledge is something that librarians have much more experience with than the Wikimedia community.

Iterating on other forms of volunteer and stakeholder development, and finding ways to make Wikimedia participation relevant to local stakeholder groups, are important for both communities in the long term. The Wikimedia community is at a critical point in time: a very slow decline in active contributors on Wikimedia projects, from a peak of participation during 2007–2009, has recently leveled off, but during that time, the content on Wikimedia projects has more than doubled.[35] Developing communities of knowledge seekers and preservers who are ready to build the next stage of quality improvements, as well as finding knowledge stewards who can ensure the long-term reliability of Wikimedia content, is a strategic investment in the broader availability of information for the public. Ultimately libraries and Wikimedia communities need to figure out how to bring the right participants into these collaborations for maintaining public access to this knowledge.

NOTES

1. As is best evidenced by the Opportunity papers produced by IFLA. "Presenting the IFLA Wikipedia Opportunities Papers," International Federation of Library Associations and Institutions, January 17, 2017, www.ifla.org/node/11131.

2. To find protected pages, look for various colored locks in the right top-hand corner of a page. By clicking on the lock, you can learn which of nearly a dozen criteria and protection strategies are being used on that page, as part of the "Page Protection Policy." Typically protected pages are high-profile pages (the main page, for example), or high-profile content that is prone to vandalism or debate (the Palestine-Israel conflict, the pages of recent U.S. presidents), or pages highly visible to prank-prone high school students (music or movie stars, subjects taught in school, etc.). To learn about the protection policy, see https://en.wikipedia.org/wiki/Wikipedia:Protection_policy.

3. In part this is a legal defensive mechanism that protects Wikipedia and the formal organizations behind hosting the content under Internet liability laws like the Digital Millennium Copyright Act, and in part it is a historical artifact from the open-Internet philosophy that attracted contributors to the projects.

4. The core values for Wikipedia are often described in the five pillars of Wikipedia: https://en.wikipedia.org/wiki/Wikipedia:Five_pillars. However, in practice, other values tend to take even more precedence, expanding on the pillar "Wikipedia is free content that anyone can use, edit, and distribute" to include other forms of "openness" and "freeness."

Additionally, the community has been placing increased importance on references and attribution for knowledge as a check on both plagiarism and copyright violations, and as a defensive mechanism against critics of the quality of Wikimedia content. (See Stinson's discussion in this talk: Wikimania Esino Lario, "File:Wikimania 2016—Verifiability of Wikipedia by Alex Stinson.webm," Wikimania 2016, https://wikimania2016.wikimedia .org/wiki/File:Wikimania_2016_-_Verifiability_of_Wikipedia_by_Alex_Stinson.webm).

5. To find out more about these statistics, see https://stats.wikimedia.org/.

6. See the chapters elsewhere in this book about the gaps in certain parts of the Wikipedia community and its knowledge. Moreover, like other radically open communities on the Internet, openness for participation also provides an open opportunity for abuse, which is currently a targeted focus of research and investment by the Wikimedia Foundation. (See, for example, Ellery Wulczyn et al., "Algorithms and Insults: Scaling Up Our Understanding of Harassment on Wikipedia," *Wikimedia Foundation blog*, February 7, 2017, https://blog.wikimedia.org/2017/02/07/scaling-understanding-of-harassment/.) Part of what can contribute to bad experience on Wikimedia projects is the fact that new contributors to Wikimedia projects often have a hard time distinguishing between experienced participants who speak for the Wikimedia community, and those participants who do not have the reputation or experience to represent the community's processes, yet declare the work of a new contributor bad (or act inappropriately for a welcoming community of practice). Working with allies or advocates for your project who can build more new contributor-friendly pathways to participation and act as interpreters of the community strengthens whatever programs you provide.

7. Though there is also a "thematic group" option—nonprofits without a geographical scope, but rather a thematic scope. However, there is only one such organization in the world (Amical Wikimedia in Catalonia). For more information about the structure of each of these movement organization models and their governance structure, see https:// meta.wikimedia.org/wiki/Wikimedia_movement_affiliates/Models.

8. For more description of the chapters, see https://meta.wikimedia.org/wiki/Wikimedia _chapters.

9. For more description of the user groups, see https://meta.wikimedia.org/wiki/Wikimedia _user_groups.

10. At the time of writing, the Wikimedia Foundation is in the process of developing a movement-wide strategic direction. One of the likely results of this more cohesive direction will be a clearer inspiration and objectives for this network of formal organizations in the Wikimedia movement—making it easier for contributors and heritage professional to identify if their needs can be met by movement organizations. For more information about the direction, see https://meta.wikimedia.org/wiki/Strategy/Wikimedia _movement/2017.

11. To find your local affiliate, we recommend starting at the portal at https://meta.wikimedia
    .org/wiki/Wikimedia_movement_affiliates. Some communities have designated particu-
    lar contacts for GLAMs; this list (not as well maintained) can be found at https://out
    reach.wikimedia.org/wiki/GLAM/Contact_us.

12. Find meet-up listings for English-focused projects at https://en.wikipedia.org/wiki/
    Wikipedia:Meetup.

13. Though this information is very public, most of it is going to be out of date, since it has
    accrued over the last sixteen years of the community. To find Wikimedians who identify
    in your geographical location, check out https://en.wikipedia.org/wiki/Category:Wiki
    pedians_by_location. To find Wikimedians active in a geographically focused editing
    project, see https://en.wikipedia.org/wiki/Category:Geographical_WikiProjects. Also,
    you may be able to find editors by looking at the history of articles relevant to your local
    context.

14. The Instructions for Geonotices can be found at https://en.wikipedia.org/wiki/Wiki
    pedia:Geonotice.

15. For the active communication channels, see the listing at https://outreach.wikimedia.org/
    wiki/GLAM/Mailing_lists.

16. For an overview of various models of projects pursued by previous GLAM contributors,
    see https://outreach.wikimedia.org/wiki/GLAM/Model_projects.

17. For the program page, see https://ca.wikipedia.org/wiki/Viquiprojecte:Bibliowikis. A
    broader case study can be found at https://outreach.wikimedia.org/wiki/GLAM/Case
    _studies/Catalonia's_Network_of_Public_Libraries.

18. Broad illiteracy about how Wikipedia works leads to a general lack of knowledge about
    what it means to "learn how to contribute to Wikipedia." Additionally, these kinds of
    overbroad calls tend to solicit people who want to use Wikipedia for cross-purposes
    with the general knowledge interest of Wikimedia and libraries, such as folks interested
    in promoting businesses or who want profiles of their friends on Wikipedia, leading to
    conflicts of interest and challenges with other Wikimedia policies.

19. See the second iteration of this contest at https://meta.wikimedia.org/wiki/DARM
    _Challenge_2 and the documentation of the Bulgarian Challenge at https://outreach
    .wikimedia.org/wiki/GLAM/Newsletter/October_2016/Contents/Bulgaria_report.

20. See the Wicipop project final report at https://en.wikipedia.org/wiki/User:Jason.nlw/
    Wicipop_Project.

21. A 2015 report from the Wikimedia Foundation shows that this number could be as low
    5 percent at six months. See the report at https://meta.wikimedia.org/wiki/Grants:Eval
    uation/Evaluation_reports/2015/Editathons/Outputs. As the report notes, this does not
    represent all events—only ones described through Wikimedia Foundation grant report-
    ing—and our measuring strategies for generating these numbers may be inaccurate. We

do have some evidence that sustained community activities have better retention results: in the Czech Republic, the public library did a training activity with senior citizens which used regular weekly trainings to get a 50 percent retention rate at three months: Dostál, Vojtěch, "Senior Citizens Learn to Edit Wikipedia in the Czech Republic," *Wikimedia Blog*, January 12, 2015, https://blog.wikimedia.org/2015/01/12/czech-senior -citizens-learn-to-edit/. Librarians and other knowledge professionals also have higher retention rates, often returning to Wikimedia contributions after long periods of time to host events and do information literacy work alongside their contribution. A number of projects since 2015 have shown a continuous ability to bring repeated attention and participation from large communities, including Art+Feminism, Black Lunch Table and Afrocrowd in New York City, and #1lib1ref.

22. Wiki markup, also known as wikitext or wikicode, consists of the syntax and keywords used by the MediaWiki software to format a page. In addition to Wiki markup, some HTML elements are also allowed for presentation formatting.

23. For the NARA guidelines, see https://en.wikipedia.org/wiki/Wikipedia:GLAM/National _Archives_and_Records_Administration/Guidelines.

24. For the State Library of New South Wales guidelines, see https://en.wikipedia.org/wiki/ Wikipedia:GLAM/State_Library_of_New_South_Wales#State_Library_of_New_South _Wales_Staff_guidelines_for_editing_Wikipedia.

25. British Museum Wikipedia project page: https://en.wikipedia.org/wiki/Wikipedia: GLAM/British_Museum.

26. For an incomplete list, see https://outreach.wikimedia.org/wiki/Wikipedian_in_Residence.

27. See the program page for York at https://en.wikipedia.org/wiki/Wikipedia:GLAM/YMT and a reflection on the METRO role on the *Wikimedia Blog*: Dorothy Howard, "On Consortium-Based Wikipedian in Residence Positions," *Wikimedia Blog*, November 15, 2013, https://blog.wikimedia.org/2013/11/15/wikipedian-in-residence/.

28. The most thorough evaluation of this has been by Wikimedia United Kingdom, which did a review of their program in 2014: Chris McKenna and Daria Cybulska, "Wikimedian in Residence Programme Review," Wikimedia UK, July 22, 2014, https://commons.wiki media.org/wiki/File:Wikimedian_in_Residence_Programme_Review_-_WMUK_2014 .pdf. Though the report has some findings specific to Wikimedia organizations within the Wikimedia community, the examination showed that the overall impact from an institutional perspective has been positive.

29. Documentation for this model of collaboration can be found at https://en.wikipedia.org/ wiki/Wikipedia:Visiting_Scholars.

30. Jason Evans and Simon Cobb, "How the World's First Wikidata Visiting Scholar Created Linked Open Data for Five Thousand Works of Art," *Wikimedia Blog*, November 5, 2016, https://blog.wikimedia.org/2016/11/05/wikidata-visiting-scholar-art-dataset/.

31. Though they are not running the program any longer, the curriculum is still a valuable tool: https://en.wikipedia.org/wiki/Wikipedia:TWL/I.

32. For example, the recent work by the Pritzker Military Museum & Library: Theresa A. R. Embrey and Andrew H. Bullen, "Music of World War I: Turning a Static Collection into a Vibrant Resource," *Information Today* 37, no. 4 (May 2017), www.infotoday.com/cilmag/may17/Embrey-Bullen—Music-of-World-War-I-Turning-a-Static-Collection-Into-a-Vibrant-Resource.shtml.

33. See the blog post: Eirn Rushing, "Mughal Art for the Masses," *Smithsonian Libraries Unbound*, September 21, 2016, https://blog.library.si.edu/2016/09/mughal-art-masses/.

34. See the outcome of their work at https://en.wikipedia.org/wiki/List_of_artwork_by_John_Steuart_Curry.

35. For this information, see https://stats.wikimedia.org/EN/SummaryZZ.htm.

Minding the Gaps
Engaging Academic Libraries to Address Content and User Imbalances on Wikipedia

KELLY DOYLE

Who run the world? Girls
—BEYONCÉ KNOWLES-CARTER

WIKIPEDIA CONTENT AND "SYSTEMIC BIAS"

Wikipedia has been praised as a global archive for the sum of all human knowledge. This is both a worthy cause and a worthwhile aspiration. While great strides have been made in the last sixteen years toward these goals, given the ambitious scope of the project, it is likely fair to say that it is still in a state of relative infancy. Indeed, it may be impossible to collect all knowledge, past and present, and already certain gaps and omissions, due to systemic bias, have begun to make themselves apparent in the structuring of Wikipedia as an archive and knowledge repository. These gaps in knowledge and knowledge types cannot be seen as benign or dismissed as incidental if Wikipedia is to be considered the preeminent global knowledge resource now and in the future.

Wikipedia is centered around facts, and it places value on the verifiability of information. However, as a repository, it needs to strive not just for accuracy of content, but for relative completeness in terms of its structuring as well. Therefore, if the structuring of the knowledge base of Wikipedia is just as important as the information itself, then as responsible human beings seeking to improve conditions for all of humanity, we need not only to ensure that the knowledge housed on Wikipedia is equally accessible and usable by all, but also that the wide breadth of knowledge is recorded completely.

As the Wikipedian in Residence for Gender Equity at West Virginia University, my role is not just about increasing the raw numbers of editors and bytes on Wikipedia, but rather to try to affect the underlying structure of the encyclopedia as a whole by advocating to close the gender gap and achieve gender equity on Wikimedia projects. Wikipedia is overwhelmingly edited by educated Western males, typically of the middle class, situated in the Western world.[1] The reason for this lopsided demographic is not just because of leisure time but because as males with social and economic power, Wikipedia editors have been socially and culturally trained to believe that what they have to say is important and worthwhile, in a way that women and minorities have not been enculturated to do. This then leads to the creation of a high volume of content particularly geared towards topics that they, and others like them, are interested in while topics of specific interest to other groups remain underrepresented. This systemic bias creates the gaps in Wikipedia coverage that my role is attempting to address: my role exists because these knowledge and content gaps create systemic issues that affect the way that we, as a society, view and understand the world. Inherent in the gaps is the omission and obscuration of information that subtly influences Wikipedia users' and readers' perceptions and worldview.

While, given the scope of its ambitions, it is inevitable that Wikipedia has gaps, nevertheless Wikipedia is considered by large swaths of society to be a totalizing body of knowledge. Consciously or unconsciously, these gaps reveal a certain perception of what knowledge is valuable enough to be recorded, retained, and written about. Historically, a mainstay of dominant groups in unequal power relationships has been maintaining control, either intentionally or unintentionally, over the archive of knowledge, therefore having power over what is recorded and preserved. Wikipedia's systemic bias could be used to reinforce this hegemonic power by regulating whether or not certain knowledge is deemed worthwhile or notable.

This is not, of course, to imply that Wikipedia is a totalitarian global cabal, aiming to regulate knowledge validation throughout the globe—in the case of Wikipedia, these gaps are largely unintentional and are at least partially informed by the demographics of those participating in the Wikipedia community. In this environment, then, what is important is that a Wikipedian in Residence for

Gender Equity draw attention to the fact that these gaps exist, and to the deeply troubling implications of those gaps so that the community as a whole can come together to close them. When there is a preponderance of articles in Wikipedia about men featured as notable while much more notable women are omitted, it can send a very clear, if unintentional, message about what knowledge is (and which people are) valued. For this and many other reasons, the gaps in Wikipedia should be the main focus of engagement within both the Wikimedia community and the information profession while we continue to critically consider the types of diverse narratives we are excluding through the use of Eurocentric ("Western") sourcing standards.

ADDRESSING GAPS

So what exactly is at stake when Wikipedia's content is constructed largely by white males?[1] How is Wikipedia's content, in terms of quality and representation, impacted by this simple fact? Why should the Wikimedia community and the greater general population be concerned? If gender plays no significant difference in the readership rates of Wikipedia, why then does the content not reflect this?[2]

Only an equitable approach to knowledge can provide a clear picture of history and the present for global audiences. In omitting notable figures, movements, and topics we are signaling their insignificance. The cultural capital of Wikipedia is such that existence within it denotes a level of power and importance. The phenomenon of considering something or someone truly significant or insignificant, through its presence or absence on Wikipedia, can be a damaging one. The inherent gaps in both subject matter and editorship serve to reinforce historic, unequal patterns of knowledge validation and valuation. As Wikipedia develops, all of us should have a vested interest in filling in these gaps and the flow of information, especially among information professionals. We, as volunteers and purveyors of content, should be mindful about ensuring an equitable control of information flow and how we bestow legitimacy on certain types of knowledge and worldviews. A global resource in which women and women's issues as well as minorities and minority issues are sparse is not a fully formed global resource. We should challenge the notion of Wikipedia as a complete resource, and rather consistently and repeatedly raise awareness instead about its current gaps. Not only are Wikipedia articles themselves narratives, but which articles get written, and to what level and quality, is a narrative to take into consideration as well.

Wikipedia editors, as part of a wholly volunteer movement, can be anyone, which then places the onus upon each of us to edit or advocate. The role of Wikipedians in Residence in all forms should be to seek revolutionary ways to fill content and editor gaps across Wikimedia projects. While Wikipedia strives to be apolitical, it's not immune to societal and systemic structures, in particular the types of individuals who currently edit Wikipedia. The Wikimedia Foundation has conducted several gender participation surveys, all of which point towards a systemic bias that manifests itself as a pattern of male-centric participation that has several culprits: harassment, available leisure time, confidence gaps, and more.[3] While Gamergate[4] has made the problems of harassment for women participating in online communities common knowledge and the importance of leisure time in general should be fairly obvious, solving problems such as confidence gaps is a much more difficult proposition. Creative problem-solving to increase the ease of engagement for women and minorities is required to effectively close these gaps.

It makes sense, then, in trying to combat this systemic bias, to begin to look towards higher education and academic libraries as partners in correcting the knowledge and participation gaps in Wikipedia. Librarianship is an overwhelmingly female profession, and with women comprising larger swaths of undergraduate and graduate populations, higher education seems to be a natural point to begin effecting change on Wikipedia.[5]

PROJECT FOUNDATIONS

In 2015 Jon Cawthorne, who was then dean of libraries at West Virginia University (WVU), began the process of instituting the first Wikipedian in Residence for Gender Equity. I was hired by West Virginia University Libraries (WVUL), with the aid of an Inspire Grant from the Wikimedia Foundation.

When seeking to create and fill this position, Cawthorne was inspired by the work of the late Adrianne Wadewitz after viewing a PBS broadcast about her work. Wadewitz was a scholar of eighteenth-century British literature whose work brought together Wikipedia and academic pedagogy. Since her work straddled both Wikipedia and libraries and considered how partnerships could be formed in order to close the previously discussed gaps, it sparked the idea of a Wikipedian in Residence for Gender Equity at West Virginia University Libraries, a WIR whose sole focus would be on gender-based solutions from within higher education, embedded specifically in the academic library. With roughly 80 percent of the librarian workforce identifying as women, Cawthorne sensed he could encourage the adoption of Wikipedia within the WVUL and address the gender gap at the same time,[6] continuing Wadewitz's work and efforts to diversify Wikipedia and bring awareness to its gender-based problems.

In March 2015, West Virginia University held an event entitled "Where Are All the Women? Wikipedia's Gender Gap." Shortly afterwards, WVU initiated a search to fill the newly created position of Wikipedian in Residence for the WVU Libraries, funded by the Wikimedia Foundation. Since filling the position in October 2015, I have been successful in creating the envisioned partnerships, and currently 75 percent of WVU librarians are registered Wikipedia users who can competently instruct students on "Wikipedia literacy" and advocate for the foundational work of the WIR.

THE GENDER GAP

The content gaps on English Wikipedia are glaring, with significant absences in articles relating to gender, race, and the global south, in addition to the implicit biases within articles that influence the understanding of a topic. The gender gap in particular is the focus of my Wikipedian in Residence role at WVU. With less than 17 percent of English Wikipedia content relating to women and less than 10 percent of Wikipedia editors identifying as women, the work to be done is considerable.[7] While libraries and Wikipedia are natural allies in the aim for access to information, creating these institutional relationships takes significant infrastructure and culture-building, and my project is one piece of that larger process.

The Wikimedia Foundation, aware of this imbalance and the long-range implications of continued gaps, created a round of funding in 2015 dedicated to addressing the gender gap. These Inspire Grants funded sixteen unique projects to promote gender diversity on Wikimedia projects. The WIR role at WVUL was included in this round of funding, with the position beginning in October 2015.[8]

Typically, WIRs are editors who have long-term Wikipedia experience and positive standing in the Wikimedia community. As a newcomer to the Wikipedia world, there was much for me to learn, but my skills in community organizing within higher education allowed me to understand the necessary steps needed to harness the WVU campus community around the aims of the project. Wikipedia has a mixed reputation within higher education, and before I could promote the importance of filling gender gaps in Wikipedia, I first had to overcome a lack of understanding of how Wikipedia works. I define "Wikipedia literacy" as a reasonable competency level about Wikipedia's functions, uses, community, and construction. It was clear that as a first step these Wikipedia literacy skills of all types needed to be learned throughout all levels of the campus community, from students to academics to administrators.

WIR positions hinge on the notion that an embedded Wikipedian can develop sustained partnerships with an institution in the service of both the institution and Wikipedia, building both content and community. The genesis of my particular WIR position came from asking a similar question: what if the gender gap on Wikipedia could be tackled through partnerships within higher education? Many adaptable models for success in building community and content around the gender gap have been created and tested through the WIR position; namely, a service model that combines student life and library services in ways that benefit academic institutions, students, and librarians. Without the opportunity to explore the avenues for partnership within higher education and academic libraries, this and other areas for growth would still be waiting to be discovered.

Harassment, or even fear of harassment, is an impediment to editing Wikipedia that many women face. From edits being reversed by veteran editors to being on the receiving end of disparaging or hateful comments, women report disillusionment with the process. In this atmosphere, women must choose between gender-neutral user identities or outing themselves as female on their user pages or in interactions on talk pages. The students recruited at WVU have experienced relatively little overt harassment, but instead have seen passive harassment in the form of large numbers of articles on notable women (for example, female photojournalists who have won Pulitzer Prizes) being labeled as non-notable and nominated for deletion. While these articles have eventually been allowed to remain, it took continual interventions and a not-insignificant amount of time from both the WIR and the students, leaving the students discouraged and disappointed. Any culture shift naturally requires a certain amount of time—in order to effect this change, the Wikimedia Foundation has worked on tools to combat harassment across its projects, but we are nevertheless losing valuable editors to harassment in the meantime.

WIKIPEDIAN IN RESIDENCE FOR GENDER EQUITY

The aim of my project was to professionalize and normalize the WIR position within academia and gain access to administrators, faculty, and students within the university in order to develop creative solutions to gender-based problems in Wikipedia. The hope was also to establish a model in which WIRs in academic libraries can work towards institutionalization in the service of closing the gaps in Wikipedia. While some WIR positions are focused on content creation by the WIR, others fill outreach and advocacy roles. My position falls firmly in the latter category: an outreach-based role allowed for harnessing the potential of the academic system and developing a sustainable model for WIRs in academic institutions, rather than individual contributions. The individual contributions made by students and librarians far surpass what one WIR at one university could possibly accomplish by individually creating or editing articles. Raising awareness and developing programming across the university system provides the Wikimedia community with a constant stream of new voices and perspectives that adds to the diversity of the users and content.

It became apparent that libraries are natural allies in helping to disseminate Wikipedia skills. By discovering the needs of librarians in an academic institution, how librarians function within that network, and their relationship to Wikipedia, a pattern developed. Overwhelmingly, librarians at WVU emphasized the users, students, and how these users interact with and utilize library collections. It's natural for students to start their research with Wikipedia, but how do they get to their end point, a credible source that will help support their academic work? How can librarians advocate for students to develop competency skills when searching for those sources? Wikipedia is that advocacy tool. Beginning library instruction with Wikipedia takes the user from start to finish in a research framework, mapping out the process students would take on their own. From this beginning point with university librarians, the issue of gaps could then be assessed once a baseline understanding of Wikipedia has been established. Since librarians manage the implications of content gaps within their profession (collection development, access, etc.) my role, and the gaps on Wikipedia more broadly, have concrete meaning. Similarly, professors within the university have taken to the possibility of incorporating Wikipedia into student learning and have begun actively pursuing a pedagogical approach.

The response to embracing Wikipedia as an important part of student learning has been overwhelmingly positive on campus and at other institutions. From

the Wikimedia Foundation to public libraries, and even to secondary education educators, the implications of effective instruction through Wikipedia are
far-reaching. What students, at all levels, can learn and give through contributing
to Wikipedia is indeed vast. At various levels of the university, there is excitement
about the implications of the role that Wikipedia can play in changing the way
students learn and think. What can students learn about knowledge production
and their role in that process from identifying gaps in Wikipedia? But the benefits go both ways. What can Wikipedia gain and learn from students and the
contributions of higher education as a whole?

THE MODEL

Obvious collaborators outside of the library presented themselves through faculty
and staff in the Women's and Gender Studies Department, other humanities
disciplines, and faculty organizations. These partnerships resulted in a multitude
of on-campus lectures, student training, and cohosted edit-a-thons, all of which
helped to raise visibility about both my WIR position and the problem of gender
gaps in Wikipedia. Students were excited to admit freely, in front of their professors, that they use Wikipedia regularly and enthusiastically. Students were further
excited by the prospect of participating in Wikipedia not only for a grade, but also
in service of their individual interests, especially social justice-oriented interests.

Students are increasingly seeking on-campus opportunities to hone their
skills for the job market while also dedicating time to causes they are passionate
about, and Wikipedia-related projects offer the opportunity to fulfill both needs.
The students I encounter depend on Wikipedia; it's all they've known in terms
of encyclopedias and thus reliable, accessible information on the Internet. University students are also involved in activist activities that relate to political and
social justice issues.[9] Students are more engaged and globally minded than ever,
fueled by access to the Internet and free information resources like Wikipedia.
And this is where the true change can start to be found. Students readily realize
both the implications of the gender (and other) gaps in Wikipedia and their
ability to correct those imbalances.

As a result of this, students at WVU have eagerly participated in learning
"Wikipedia literacy" skills and adapting those skills into social justice projects
on Wikipedia itself, in service of their particular interests. Students involved in
activities ranging from student government to LGBTQ advocacy groups see the
potential for increasing the visibility and reliability of information about causes

they care about by contributing to Wikipedia. This then becomes a self-perpet-uating cycle: as students see more gaps and omissions about various topics, the more passionate they become about editing the encyclopedia. This is the model that ensnares most active Wikipedia editors as well, but students learning about the gaps at a young age, through the advocacy of WIR positions, sets Wikipedia in good stead for continued engagement from these groups.

At WVU students can gain required service credit for editing Wikipedia. Students quickly learn that editing Wikipedia competently is no easy feat, and is rather something that takes dedicated time and effort to do correctly. The 29,000 students who attended WVU in 2016–2017 performed 10,236 hours of service in the spring 2017 semester. Some of this service was community service or was required for various coursework, or it was required of students on graduate fellowships. Wikipedia editing counts as service credit in all of these categories. While the hours logged for editing are minimal compared to the 10,236 hour figure, there is vast potential to leverage this aspect in university life throughout the United States. The next step would be to develop standardized programs and metrics to encourage other universities to develop similar programs.

The two main categories of students who edit Wikipedia for service credit at WVU are graduate students and sorority students. Graduate students, who are increasingly interested in open access across disciplines, view Wikipedia as an avenue to support accurate, mainstream understanding of their field or chosen area of study. Meanwhile, graduate students can edit Wikipedia in tandem with research conducted for theses or dissertations and simultaneously earn required service credit. Sorority students are required to participate in community service activities each semester in order to remain within their organization. This is a common practice at nearly all universities in the United States that have Greek organizations. The involvement of sorority members is quite exciting because it has the potential to contribute to addressing a range of issues associated with the gender gap in numerous ways. Not only will sorority students contribute to the closing of the editor and content-based gender gaps, but these groups also provide a counter to harassment and confidence issues that impede women's success and contributions on Wikipedia and Wikimedia projects.[10] Sororities also have well-organized alumni relations and connections across universities through their chapter systems, and these networks will likely contribute to the spread of Wikipedia editing among these groups.

The most exciting part about all of this engagement is that it resides in the academic library. Without librarians supporting research that starts in what is a natural place for college students (Wikipedia), without library collections and space, and without the dedicated librarians at WVUL who have leveraged their partnerships with departments on campus, this project could not run as smoothly. In addition, without the competency and Wikipedia literacy skills gained in the early stages of this initiative, librarians couldn't begin to consider hosting and organizing edit-a-thons independently, which will allow this model to grow.

COMMUNITY OUTREACH

With the support of the WIR position, this project has matured. As librarians at WVUL have developed their own Wikipedia skills, they can begin to advocate for both expanding Wikipedia literacy on campus and addressing the various content and editor gaps that exist on the website. The outreach model is simple: train for Wikipedia literacy skills and make the gaps in Wikipedia both obvious and personal by pointing out that women and other groups are underrepresented in the encyclopedia. A simple and straightforward approach guides newcomers through what can arguably be a complicated process of learning the ins and outs of Wikipedia editing and culture. Campus communities are rife with academic and social groups that represent unique research interests that Wikipedia can benefit from. Emeritus faculty to graduate assistants all have a place and value in the Wikimedia community.

Because of the infrastructure that was built and tested by WVUL, outreach at other universities and colleges is now possible in order to grow the model of academic engagement with Wikipedia that puts the library at the center. Similarly, training materials created specifically for librarians, students, and university administrators to support their understanding of Wikipedia initiatives on our campus are being created so that other interested academic libraries can test this model at their institutions.

VISION FOR WIKIPEDIA AND ACADEMIC LIBRARIES IN THE TWENTY-FIRST CENTURY

If we deem women as insignificant as represented in articles and within the culture of Wikipedia, the cycle of gender inequities is self-perpetuating precisely because of the wide-scale readership of the encyclopedia. Fully including women in the process and content of Wikipedia will help to fulfill Wikipedia's global mission to empower and enlighten everyone.

The global impact of full participation in the knowledge economy of Wikipedia has yet to be seen. Wikipedia's standing as the most up-to-date encyclopedia warrants the complete inclusion of women and minorities, which is both a realistic expectation and an aspiration. As initiatives like this one continue to grow and new ones are created, the possibility of reaching even an aspirational goal grows. We have a responsibility as a society to include articles on everything from rivers in Africa to biographies of seventeenth-century women writers. Omitting articles on important topics disparages their significance in history and influences our understanding of the present. We should consider what we want to signal to (young) learners across geographic and economic spectrums—they should see themselves reflected in Wikipedia. Libraries, as the historic stalwarts of knowledge, stand to participate in increasing access to equitable, quality information for all.

NOTES

1. "Wikipedia:Wikipedians," Wikipedia, https://en.wikipedia.org/wiki/Wikipedia:Wiki pedians#Demographics.

2. "Gender Bias on Wikipedia," Wikipedia, https://en.wikipedia.org/wiki/Gender_bias_on _Wikipedia.

3. "Harasssment Survey Results," Wikimedia, 2015, https://upload.wikimedia.org/wiki pedia/commons/5/52/Harassment_Survey_2015_-_Results_Report.pdf; "Editor Survey Report," Wikimedia, 2011, https://upload.wikimedia.org/wikipedia/commons/7/76/ Editor_Survey_Report_-_April_2011.pdf.

4. Caitlin Dewey, "The Only Guide to Gamergate You Will Ever Need to Read," *Washington Post*, 2014, https://www.washingtonpost.com/news/the-intersect/wp/2014/10/14/the-only -guide-to-gamergate-you-will-ever-need-to-read/?utm_term=.cca76f6d0e4f.

5. Matt Rocheleau, "On Campus Women Outnumber Men More Than Ever," *Boston Globe*, 2016, https://www.bostonglobe.com/metro/2016/03/28/look-how-women-outnumber -men-college-campuses-nationwide/YROqwfCPSlKPtSMAzpWloK/story.html.

6. Tracy Wholf, "'Wikipedian' Editor Took on Website's Gender Gap," *PBS*, 2014, www.pbs .org/newshour/bb/wikipedian-editor-took-wikipedias-gender-gap/.

7. "ALA Fact Sheet," American Library Association, http://ala-apa.org/files/2012/03/Library -Workers-2011.pdf.

8. Siko Bouterse and Alex Wang, "Meet the Inspire Grantees," *Wikimedia Blog*, 2015, https://blog.wikimedia.org/2015/05/01/meet-the-inspire-grantees/.

9. Alia Wong, "The Renaissance of Student Activism," *The Atlantic*, 2015, https://www.the atlantic.com/education/archive/2015/05/the-renaissance-of-student-activism/393749/.

10. Jessica Bennett, "When a Feminist Pledges a Sorority," *New York Times*, 2016, https://www.nytimes.com/2016/04/10/fashion/sorority-ivy-league-feminists.html.

REFERENCES

Alcantara, Chris. "The Most Challenging Job of the 2016 Race: Editing the Candidates' Wikipedia Pages." *Washington Post*. 2016. https://www.washingtonpost.com/graphics/politics/2016-election/presidential-wikipedias/.

Bayer, Tilman. "How Many Women Edit Wikipedia." *Wikimedia Blog*. 2015. https://blog.wiki media.org/2015/04/30/how-many-women-edit-wikipedia/.

Bear, Julia and Benjamin Collier. "Where Are the Women in Wikipedia? Understanding the Different Psychological Experiences of Men and Women in Wikipedia." *Sex Roles* 74 (January 2016): 254–65. https://link.springer.com/article/10.1007%2Fs11199–015–0573-y.

Bennett, Jessica. "When a Feminist Pledges a Sorority." *New York Times*. 2016. https://www.nytimes.com/2016/04/10/fashion/sorority-ivy-league-feminists.html.

Blanding, Michael. "Wikipedia or Encyclopedia Britannica: Which Has More Bias." *Forbes*. 2015. https://www.forbes.com/sites/hbsworkingknowledge/2015/01/20/wikipedia-or -encyclopaedia-britannica-which-has-more-bias/#6e2bbc487d4a.

Cohen, Noam. "Define Gender Gap? Look Up Wikipedia's Contributor List." *New York Times*. 2011. www.nytimes.com/2011/01/31/business/media/31link.html.

Dewey, Caitlin. "The Only Guide to Gamergate You Will Ever Need to Read." *Washington Post*. 2014. https://www.washingtonpost.com/news/the-intersect/wp/2014/10/14/the-only -guide-to-gamergate-you-will-ever-need-to-read/?utm_term=.cca76f6d0e4f.

Ford, Heather, and Judy Wajcman. "'Anyone Can Edit,' Not Everyone Does: Wikipedia and the Gender Gap." *Social Studies of Science*. Vol 47, Issue 4, 2017 . http://eprints.lse.ac.uk/68675/.

Garrison, Lynsea. "How Can Wikipedia Woo Women Editors." *BBC*. 2014. www.bbc.com/news/magazine-26828726.

Lih, Andrew. "Can Wikipedia Survive?" *New York Times*. 2015. https://www.nytimes.com/2015/06/21/opinion/can-wikipedia-survive.html?_r=0.

Meyer, Robinson. "90% of Wikipedia Editors Are Male—Here's What They're Doing About It." *The Atlantic*. 2013. https://www.theatlantic.com/technology/archive/2013/10/90-of -wikipedias-editors-are-male-heres-what-theyre-doing-about-it/280882/.

Paling, Emma. "Wikipedia's Hostility to Women." *The Atlantic*. 2015. https://www.theatlantic .com/technology/archive/2015/10/how-wikipedia-is-hostile-to-women/411619/.

Reagle, Joseph. "'Open' Doesn't Include Everyone." *New York Times.* 2011. https://www.ny times.com/roomfordebate/2011/02/02/where-are-the-women-in-wikipedia/open -doesnt-include-everyone.

Reagle, Joseph, and Lauren Rhue. "Gender Bias in Wikipedia and Britannica." *International Journal of Communication* 5 (2011): 1138–58.

Simonite, Tom. "The Decline of Wikipedia." *Technology Review,* November/December 2013. https://www.technologyreview.com/s/520446/the-decline-of-wikipedia/.

Torres, Nicole. "Why Do So Few Women Edit Wikipedia?" 2016. https://hbr.org/2016/06/ why-do-so-few-women-edit-wikipedia.

"Wikimedia Foundation Editor Survey Report: 2011." Wikimedia. https://upload.wikimedia .org/wikipedia/commons/7/76/Editor_Survey_Report_-_April_2011.pdf.

"Wikimedia Foundation Harassment Survey Results: 2015." Wikimedia. https://upload.wiki media.org/wikipedia/commons/5/52/Harassment_Survey_2015_-_Results_Report.pdf.

Wong, Alia. "The Renaissance of Student Activism." *The Atlantic.* 2015. https://www.the atlantic.com/education/archive/2015/05/the-renaissance-of-student-activism/393749/.

The Wikipedia Library

The Largest Encyclopedia Needs a Digital Library and We Are Building It

JAKE ORLOWITZ

I have always imagined that Paradise will be a kind of library.
—JORGE LUIS BORGES

Wikipedia is positioned to become the virtual front page of every library in the world—a ubiquitous starting point for public information gathering, a jumping-off point for deeper learning—and a natural ally of libraries, in partnership to complete a virtuous circle of research and knowledge dissemination. With over 45 million articles and 40 million free images, Wikipedia is the fifth most-visited website in the world: over 500 million readers each month view it a total of 8,000 times per second. And Wikipedia's readers don't stop their learning at Wikipedia articles—there are many indications that people use Wikipedia as a holistic research platform. A striking example is that Wikipedia refers the sixth most traffic to all DOIs (Digital Object Identifiers) to online scholarly materials including journal articles, books, and ebooks made available through CrossRef,

The Wikipedia Library (TWL) aims to deliver library and research services to every editor and reader of the site, making possible access to the references which support the "sum of all human knowledge." TWL is a global program supported by the Wikimedia Foundation to develop shared library infrastructure and services for Wikipedians and Wikipedia readers. We partner with scholarly publishers to increase access to research, build community-run support hubs and tools to improve reference, and reach out to publishers and libraries.[1] The program's focus has been to give the Wikipedia editing community of 100,000 monthly volunteers free access to paywalled research material, so they can cite reliable content and provide accessible summaries to the public in Wikipedia articles.

Since its inception in 2011, TWL has established partnerships with nearly seventy publishers, including the largest and most scholarly collections, to provide free access for Wikipedians to over 80,000 unique periodicals and an even greater number of books.[2] TWL expanded its scope as we developed other relationships focused on references: for example, working with the Internet Archive to fix over one million dead citation URLs, developing OABot to link to versions marked as free-to-read alongside paywalled content in citations, and integrating WorldCat's 380 million ISBNs into our automatic citation generator tool.

The success of the program grows from what we learn in partnership with library professionals. The TWL team cowrote two International Federation of Library Associations and Institutions (IFLA) white papers on Wikipedia collaboration with academic and public libraries, and we have presented at the American Library Association's Annual Conference, the Coalition for Networked Information's Membership Meeting, Internet Librarian, the Frankfurt Book Fair, OpenCon, the Open Scholarship Initiative, and the Digital Library Federation Forum, among many other conferences.

When we began speaking about our work in library venues in 2012, the reception was curious but cool; five years later, Wikipedia's role in the library ecosystem is often met with enthusiasm and excitement. It has moved from "What are you doing here?" to "How can we get involved?" This transition, from being on the fringes to being in the center, reflects the broader acceptance of Wikipedia and the recognition of its central role in the public's quest for useful information.

Looking forward, TWL has several priority areas and projects to pursue, as described below.

For editors, TWL is working on technical solutions and infrastructure. Chief among these is the Library Card Platform, a central application system for tracking signups and delivering access to high-quality research material. The aim is to provide many of the features that are expected from a research library: direct proxy authentication to sources, full-feature search discovery, and integrated reference service. Another project involves supporting the development of Librarybase, an environment which stores Wikipedia's citations as structured metadata, with an API that can give research recommendations based on bibliographic structure.

For readers, our focus includes developing information and research literacy resources, as well as a universal reference service for all readers regardless of location or affiliation. We hope to reach a day when Wikipedia provides on-demand access for all Wikipedia readers to citations in research, as well as OpenURL referral to library resources, and links to full-text open access (OA) versions of paywalled content.

With libraries and librarians, TWL wants to engage reference experts to help us improve our shared digital research ecosystem. Since many library patrons use Wikipedia and its sister sites, librarians should have strategies for supporting Wikimedia projects, including understanding how content is created and maintained by becoming editors themselves. To this end, engagement with professional networks such as IFLA and the Association of Research Libraries will help librarians work with their patrons in knowledge discovery and curation, as will expanding the popular #1lib1ref (One Librarian, One Reference) global micro-contribution campaign.

The future of collaboration and integration between Wikipedia and libraries and Wikipedians and librarians looks very bright. We hope that our organization and programs have extended the dialogue and sparked new conversations among two natural allies in the realm of free knowledge.

BEGINNINGS

> *Bad libraries build collections,*
> *good libraries build services,*
> *great libraries build communities.*
> —R. DAVID LANKES

Wikipedia is the world's largest free online encyclopedia, with over 45 million articles across almost 300 languages, all written and edited by volunteers. Because of its requirement of *verifiability*—which states that facts and their interpretations should be accompanied by a citation to a reliable source verifying them—the quality of Wikipedia depends on the ability of its volunteers to access the best and most reliable scholarship on a topic. Ultimately, the website's efficacy depends on readers understanding this premise, so that they use Wikipedia as a starting point and not an ending point for their research, and so that they also understand how to contribute relevant content to the project. These are the fundamental issues The Wikipedia Library was inspired to advance.

The Wikipedia Library started in 2010 as an English Wikipedia community-based volunteer effort, to address the lack of access to reliable sources for editors to build Wikipedia articles. TWL's first initiative was to seek account donations from publishers and aggregators to provide access to editors so they could summarize and cite this research on Wikipedia.

An anecdote reveals the simple but powerful alignment between the interests of Wikipedia's editors and the publishers of reliable sources. When I founded The Wikipedia Library, one of my very first calls was to the news and magazine aggregator HighBeam Research, to gain a few additional resources for a minor biography I was writing. Upon being asked "for an account for me . . . and maybe a few for my close editing friends," HighBeam's head of customer service remarked, "*How about 1,000?*"

Credo Reference was the earliest partner, providing 500 free accounts to top article writers in 2011. HighBeam, Questia, Cochrane, and JSTOR followed in 2012.

The project received funding for a pilot experiment from the Wikimedia Foundation in 2013 in the form of an Individual Engagement Grant, broadening its outreach efforts and developing community capacity to scale.[3] The editing community's enthusiastic reception and positive participation in the program led to TWL being incorporated into the Wikimedia Foundation in 2014 as part of what is now the Community Engagement Department.

From the beginning, The Wikipedia Library set ambitious and broad goals:[4]

- Connect editors with their local library and freely accessible resources.
- Facilitate access to paywalled publications.
- Build relationships among editors, librarians, and cultural heritage professionals.
- Facilitate research for Wikipedians and readers.
- Promote broader open access in publishing and research.

TWL advances these efforts through a global branch strategy: twenty-two different Wikipedia language projects now have TWL branches, including French, German, Arabic, and Finnish.[5] Global efforts are driven by a core team of staff, contractors, and over 100 volunteer coordinators, which allows insights from one branch to be promulgated to others.

The Wikipedia Library works in tandem with the broader GLAM-Wiki movement. The budding community of practice around Wikipedia and libraries is a sign of a radical shift in the nature of authority and knowledge production: from scholarly credentials and expertise to literate evaluation of myriad references, from individual authors imbued with the authority of the academy to diverse crowds of contributors with varying levels of expertise. Three reflections illustrate the profound transition in which Wikipedia has come to be seen as an essential part of the information and research literacy ecosystem:

> Wikipedia is increasingly becoming the go-to reference resource for the newest generation of students . . . Librarians and faculty should help remove the stigma associated with Wikipedia by embracing this Website and its imperfections as a way to make information literacy instruction valuable for the twenty-first-century student.[6]
>
> When asked to contribute to a wiki—a space that's highly public and where the audience can respond by deleting or changing your words—college students snapped to attention, carefully checking sources and including more of them to back up their work . . . Instead of blindly consuming the content, they understand where the research comes from and how it gets there. In the past, we've told them not to use Wikipedia. That's insane. Rather than saying, "It doesn't have a place in the academy," let's explain to students how it can be used as a tertiary resource. It's not the end-all and be-all of research, but it's incredibly useful.[7]
>
> Producing information for others in online environments can give young people a starting point for reflecting on where information comes from; such experiences support second-order information literacy skills, which require students to reflect on the nature of information production . . . If we want to develop a more local, shared sense of responsibility, continuing efforts to incorporate public information production in classrooms should include opportunities for students to support and challenge one another in justifying and critiquing claims, as is done by co-authors on Wikipedia.[8]

The Wikipedia Library did not create this trend, but it has helped accelerate it through efforts to improve the work and lives of Wikipedia's editors, readers, and the network of librarians that support them. TWL's annual #1lib1ref campaign built on that momentum with a simple social media-friendly call to action: *imagine a world in which every librarian added one more reference to Wikipedia.* Imagine a world in which librarians were as much contributors to Wikipedia as they are critical consumers of its content.

FOR EDITORS: A WIKIPEDIA LIBRARY CARD

When I got my library card, that's when my life began.
— RITA MAE BROWN

The founding mission of The Wikipedia Library is to connect content editors on Wikimedia projects with the reliable sources they need to develop articles—to ensure that the content is supported by the highest-quality sources, and to open up topics that are not covered by locally available or free online references.

One Iranian recipient of TWL access from JSTOR wrote:

> Things changed when the international sanctions against Iran expanded
> and included banking transactions. Subscription fees could not be paid
> and the growing difficulties reduced my motivation to work on Wikipe-
> dia for free. However, thanks to the Wikipedia Library, I received JSTOR
> access, which incorporates Iranian Studies; this new access allowed me
> to continue my work on articles like *Kelidar,* the longest Persian novel.
> Subscription access is a must for Persian Wikipedia editors, not just due
> to the lack of reliable sources in Iran or Afghanistan, but because of the
> systematic bias and censorship that is so prevalent among books published
> in these countries. I even consider the Wikipedia Library a helpful project
> to counter the systemic bias in English Wikipedia itself. While every river
> or hill in North America or Europe has its own article, many vital issues
> concerning developing countries have not been covered. By getting global
> editors like me free access to rich digital libraries, we will be even more
> encouraged to write decent articles about our culture and geography in
> your language.[9]

Serving individual editors, "arming them with reliable sources," has long been an aspiration for The Wikipedia Library. This partnership model has grown to nearly seventy publishers and aggregators—including EBSCO, SAGE, Taylor & Francis, Elsevier, Oxford University Press, and Project MUSE—providing access to over 80,000 unique periodicals and a greater number of books to thousands of editors for a year per partner per signup.

The standard distribution process for this access has not been elegant. It has required editors to apply individually for each partnership they want access to, for applications to be vetted against account activity and experience criteria, to be approved and processed individually by dozens of coordinators, and for per-editor access codes to be delivered or accounts created by the publisher such that they expire one year after activation. This time-consuming process involved unnecessary duplication of effort and inefficiency in workflows, resulting in a multi-week wait between application and receipt of access. While this is certainly better than no access at all, we recognized quickly that there was obvious scope for improvement.

In an effort to solve these problems, TWL is currently developing a Wikipedia Library Card platform (https://wikipedialibrary.wmflabs.org/) to streamline application processes for database access and to deliver an access experience more similar to that of research libraries. It provides a centralized interface through which editors can apply for access to resources and volunteers can process those applications. This central platform greatly improves the efficiency of the access grant process—projections suggest an eventual wait time of only a few days rather than a few weeks for most resources.

The Library Card system supports a wider variety of resource provision modes than previously available under TWL. The application process is streamlined and can be partially or fully automated, depending on the approach preferred by the publisher. Foremost, it can support a proxy-based authentication system with a single sign-on for users. This will rapidly improve access to research for content editors.

An instantaneous access system is also being developed called the Library Card Bundle. In this iteration, access is approved through the system automatically rather than manually, so it can be granted on an as-needed basis to tens of thousands of editors instead of just hundreds at a time. The bundle approach solves the problem of users requesting access to a source simply to read a few specific articles rather than do long-term research in the topic area. Now, instead of occupying one of a limited number of slots for an entire year, a far greater number of users can simply gain access to what they need when it is needed.

Once this initial phase of authorization and development is completed, the next step is to integrate additional digital library services. A key component of the system will be a web-scale discovery service to allow users to find content across all publishers from a single search box. The service will index, in full text wherever possible, the resources available through the various partnerships that The Wikipedia Library has established, as well as open access content. Instead of visiting a series of individual publisher or database sites to search for resources, editors will be able to search centrally and discover most of the available sources on their topic of interest. Link resolvers will allow users to move seamlessly from search to the full text, further improving search efficiency. Integrated online reference support can also be delivered through the proposed system to assist users in locating content relevant to their research, and potentially to provide practical learning opportunities for library and information students in the model of the Internet Public Library.

The Library Card system also has the potential to greatly enhance the acquisitions process used by The Wikipedia Library. Currently, major publishers are frequently requested, whereas still-valuable alternatives with a lower profile are often overlooked. A discovery service can enhance the usage of niche publications by exposing them to unfamiliar users. The implementation of a discovery service generally increases full-text downloads of indexed publications.[10] An A-Z list will educate readers on which databases index a particular journal of interest, allowing them to be better informed on which partnerships they would want to request. This would replace a manually curated list, which is cumbersome to search and update.

The Wikipedia Library Card is a novel and challenging solution. It is effectively a global library, open to qualified Wikipedia editors from any country or region on the planet, and without any daunting subscription costs.

FOR READERS: FROM INFORMED ACCESS TO OPEN CITATIONS

A library implies an act of faith . . .
— VICTOR HUGO

Half a billion people each month use Wikipedia for research, but many may not understand how it is constructed and how to best make use of it. Wikipedia's principle of verifiability institutes an ideal that all knowledge in the encyclopedia, whether facts or outside opinions, is supported by a reliable secondary source—but sources that readers cannot access and use are of limited usefulness in furthering research.

The Wikipedia Library is developing research literacy materials to help support readers to understand how Wikipedia is built and how to explore its underlying sources. This ranges from supporting instruction on how Wikipedia works, to tools that help readers get from citations to sources, to help pages about locating a local library. These initiatives will contribute to the development of a more informed citizenry that is able to use Wikipedia (and other information sources as well) in a responsible manner, by examining the original sources to assess the validity of an article's claims.

The Wikipedia Library has also piloted open-referencing strategies. For example, Newspapers.com encouraged Wikipedia editors to use their *clippings* feature (https://www.newspapers.com/clippings/) for references on Wikipedia. Each clipping creates a free-to-read, openly available excerpt of sections of News papers.com articles which allow readers to see the same content as the editors researching for Wikipedia.[11]

We would like to eventually transition key publisher partners to a *toll-free access referral* program that could drastically enhance reader access to sources. Under this model, a reader clicking on a paywalled link on Wikipedia could gain full-text access to the source without needing a log-in or affiliation, solely because the traffic is referred from Wikipedia. This would open to readers the scholarly resources on which Wikipedia is built, allowing them to truly use it as a starting point for research even if they are unaffiliated with well-resourced libraries or do not meet the criteria for access in the Library Card.

Another factor blocking access to sources is linkrot—when content at a particular URL is moved or deleted—which leads to the previously live link becoming a *dead* link. A partnership with the Internet Archive (IA) and volunteer community members led to more than one million outbound broken links on English Wikipedia being replaced with archived versions, ensuring that readers are still able to access the original sources cited.[12] Using a Wikipedia bot and IA's Wayback Machine, Wikipedia articles are scanned to test if they are dead; if they don't properly resolve, then the Internet Archive version most closely dated to when the original link was added is inserted if available. Continued work in this area will expand the process to other language Wikipedias and implement methods to fortify our online citations against linkrot problems from the very moment when those citations are first added to Wikipedia.

While editors benefit directly from TWL's publisher relationships, readers face the same obstacle of closed-access paywalls that TWL was created to overcome for editors. OABot (https://en.wikipedia.org/wiki/Wikipedia:OABOT) is a tool that finds open-access versions of references in Wikipedia articles. If no URL is included in the citation, the tool adds one that points to an open-access repository version of the source; if one is available, OABot uses the Dissem.in service (http://dissem.in/) to find these versions from sources like CrossRef, BASE, DOAI, and SHERPA/RoMEO. On an article like "cancer," which has 200 citations, 15 percent of those citations will have free-to-read links to repository versions added. Those links will be accompanied by a green open lock icon broadcasting their availability to readers. This expands on previous efforts led by Daniel Mietchen and other open-access advocates to present icon-based indications of open-access sources as part of the OA Signalling Initiative (https://en.wikipedia.org/wiki/Wikipedia:WikiProject_Open_Access/Signalling_OA-ness). The growing prominence of both open-access publishing and article-level metrics (altmetrics) amplify each other on Wikipedia:

> The odds that an open access journal is referenced on the English Wikipedia are 47% higher compared to closed access journals. Moreover, in most of the world's Wikipedias, a journal's high status (impact factor) and accessibility (open access policy) both greatly increase the probability of referencing. Among the implications of this study is that the chief effect of open access policies may be to significantly amplify the diffusion of science, through an intermediary like Wikipedia, to a broad public audience.[13]

Part of supporting readers is making the creation of accurate and thorough citations easy in the first place. Through a TWL partnership with OCLC, editors can now use the WorldCat API to automatically generate book citations in Wikipedia articles. They need only enter the ISBN in a citation tool, which then draws from WorldCat to return fully formatted bibliographic metadata, including an OCLC identifier that links to libraries in which the book can be found.[14] This service, alongside similar services offered by Crossref for DOIs and using the PMID database, ensures that citation information provided in an article points readers to a deeper resource on the topic.

Lastly, TWL is working on the frontiers of meta-knowledge about our project's content. Wikidata (https://wikidata.org/) is a newer Wikimedia project created to store structured data. It is a language-independent, linked, open, structured database that is openly editable by both humans and computers. Since 2012 it has grown to include over 25 million items, each with a unique Wikidata identifier. TWL participates in WikiCite (https://meta.wikimedia.org/wiki/WikiCite), the collaborative community effort that aims to take advantage of Wikidata in order to build a repository of all the citations in Wikipedia and to design tools to take advantage of this rich data.

WITH LIBRARIANS: COLLABORATION ON A SHARED VISION

My library
Was dukedom large enough.
—WILLIAM SHAKESPEARE

The Wikipedia Library envisions librarians and Wikipedians as natural allies in working towards a goal of access to reliable information.

An early effort pioneered by TWL, in partnership with OCLC, was the creation of the first-ever Wikipedia Visiting Scholar (WVS) roles.[15] Through the WVS program, Wikipedia editors gain online access to an educational institution's library resources like databases, journals, e-books, and special collections. A WVS, like a Wikipedian in Residence (WIR), works in partnership with an institution to help expose its content on Wikipedia. The WVS role differs in that it is remote, unpaid, and primarily focused on creating content rather than building institutional capacity. Libraries get involved because of a desire to see their collections put to good use and to make a difference in public knowledge in one or more topic areas. Wikipedians receive access to specialized and paywalled content in order to expand and improve articles in topic areas they already care about. A Wikipedia Visiting Scholar at Rutgers University said:

> This was both Rutgers University's first collaboration with Wikipedians, as well as [my] first collaboration of this type with an organization. The initiative from Rutgers's side was directed by . . . Grace Agnew, who has been accessible, friendly, and resourceful throughout the whole exchange. As part of this initiative, twelve members from the Rutgers University team have learned more about how to add content to Wikipedia. Aside from teaching librarians and students about Wikipedia, I have also been the student.

> Graduate students Yingting and Yu-Hung jointly held a video conference
> with me on how to access the library resources of Rutgers remotely and how
> to use Medical Subject Headings (MeSH) to investigate healthcare-related
> subjects.[16]

While the WVS program is focused on content creation, it also clearly opens a channel for exchange of ideas, making it an ideal entry point for institutional partnerships. The Visiting Scholars program was piloted by TWL in 2014 and was passed off to the Wiki Education Foundation for all North American positions in 2016.

The #1lib1ref campaign (http://1lib1ref.org) goes further, calling upon librarians all over the world to add a single citation to Wikipedia themselves. It was created by TWL to offer a low-barrier-to-entry option for engagement, using a combination of a micro-contribution, a semi-automated interface, and a viral hashtag. The #1lib1ref campaign took advantage of the volunteer-developed Citation Hunt tool (https://tools.wmflabs.org/citationhunt), which automatically isolates sentences flagged with a "citation needed" tag, and presents them to the user for fixing. This simple workflow fostered significant participation rates in both English Wikipedia and other language Wikipedias.

#1lib1ref was conceived in fall 2015 by TWL project manager Alex Stinson, who recognized the potential of Citation Hunt. He took the functionality and connected it to an opportunity: other GLAM communities had not yet developed a way to celebrate the upcoming fifteen-year anniversary of Wikipedia in January 2016. Inspired by the changing conversation about the role of Wikipedia in research and among libraries, the TWL team developed the campaign with the goal of developing increased literacy and understanding among librarians about how Wikipedia's content is created and improved through verifiability, while generating awareness that other libraries are taking advantage of Wikipedia as an environment in which to further public programming. "Give Wikipedia the gift of a citation. Because facts matter #1lib1ref" was seen widely throughout social media platforms.

The campaign's first two years have proven to be quite successful. In 2016, there were over 29,000 views of the campaign page, coverage of the event in over 50 different venues (blogs, professional newsletters, etc.), over 1,100 Twitter posts using the hashtag, and at least 1,232 edits to Wikimedia projects. Though 1,232 citations barely makes a dent in the number of citations needed for Wikipedia

(English Wikipedia has over 300,000 "citation needed" tags), it did generate broad interest.[17]

In 2017, the campaign expanded by a factor of three to over 4,171 contributions in 18 languages, with continued positive press, and more events and support from local language Wikimedia communities.[18] One particularly motivating story: the State Library of Queensland committed to and accomplished contributing 1,000 references during the campaign from among its staff. This kind of campaign builds awareness and interest among the library community and allows for a dialogue that further shifts the Wikimedia community closer to the needs of libraries, and libraries closer to the goals of the Wikimedia community.

TWL, recognizing a need for persistent meeting and conversation spaces, has developed two new venues to further dialogue between Wikipedians and librarians: 700 members have joined the Wikipedia + Libraries Facebook group, and over 125 participants are signed up to the newly formed Wikipedia Library User Group. These forums spark regular mingling, noteworthy updates, and cross-pollination of ideas among Wikipedians and librarians, fostering a shared sense of identity and belonging in a community of practice around Wikipedia and libraries.

The capstone of advocating for such a mutually beneficial and interconnected relationship came when TWL worked with the International Federation of Library Associations and Institutions (IFLA) to publish two seminal white papers (www .ifla.org/node/10871): one on the opportunities for academic and research libraries to engage with Wikipedia, and a similar paper aimed at public libraries. These papers outline multiple areas of potential collaboration. For example, Wikimedia projects provide a venue to showcase cultural heritage resources in order to convey diverse perspectives to a diverse audience. Another path forward lies through structured data on Wikimedia's multimedia repository site Wikimedia Commons and the sister project Wikidata, which can enhance linkages between items and collections to support research across multiple semantic frameworks. The papers also express opportunities for professional development within library communities, in which Wikipedia editing skills can benefit a librarian's ability to grasp popular contemporary research practices, teach about digital information literacy and collaborative knowledge production, initiate community programs, and highlight a library's collections to the world.

CONCLUSION

The only thing that you absolutely have to know, is the location of the library.
—ALBERT EINSTEIN

It's said that "discovery happens elsewhere."[19] Less often said is that elsewhere is increasingly Wikipedia. As a top-5 website, Wikipedia is the sixth highest referrer to all DOIs online. With this position, The Wikipedia Library tackles the biggest challenges facing information professionals today: discovery, access, literacy, and participation.

Wikipedia's wealth of users means that it is an unparalleled opportunity for exposure and dissemination of content. Our goal is to make Wikipedia not an end point for research, but a starting point for deeper learning and research literacy—one where Wikipedia leads its 500 million monthly readers back to information professionals, scholarly resources, and full texts.

For our editors, this means access to world-class library and reference services comparable to a leading university library. For our readers, who often do not have access to journals or databases, Wikipedia has become a ubiquitous gateway: not all information is free, but most information can at least be summarized and cited on Wikipedia—and we are working to make every citation lead to where full text can be obtained. With libraries and publishers, this means having their resources found and used through contribution and content production—as participants, as experts, as builders in an "intellectual makerspace," and as natural allies in the common humanitarian mission to share knowledge with the world and all of its people.[20]

Acknowledgements: The Wikipedia Library is made possible by many hands. The TWL team deserves full credit: Alex, Nikki, Sam, Aaron, Felix, Jason, Twila, Patrick, and Andromeda. Special thanks to early readers of this draft Nick Wilson and Kelly Doyle—and to Nikki for her phenomenal research for this entire chapter. We're indebted to the historic support of Siko Bouterse and Anasuya Sengupta from Wikimedia Foundation grantmaking; Cindy Aden, Bill Carney, and Merrilee Proffitt from OCLC; Mark Graham and Wendy Hanamura from the Internet Archive; Elliott Shore from ARL; pioneering Wikipedia librarians in the form of Phoebe Ayers, Andrea Zanni, Robert Fernandez, and Alex Hinojo; ardent open-access supporters Megan Wacha, Nick Shockey, Antonin Delpeuch, and John Willinsky; and to dozens of others who have guided and aided our work, the thousands of librarians who have taken on improving Wikipedia in their professional careers, and the tens of thousands of tireless editors in the Wikipedia community—we do it for you.

NOTES

1. Bruce Murray, "The Wikipedia Library: A Partnership of Wikipedia and Publishers to Enhance Research and Discovery," *CrossRef,* April 4, 2016, http://blog.crossref.org /2016/04/the-wikipedia-library-a-partnership-of-wikipedia-and-publishers-to-enhance -research-and-discovery.html.

2. "Publishers," Wikipedia, https://en.wikipedia.org/wiki/Wikipedia:The_Wikipedia_ Library/Publishers.

3. "Grants:IEG/The Wikipedia Library," *Meta-Wiki,* https://meta.wikimedia.org/wiki/ Grants:IEG/The_Wikipedia_Library.

4. Jake Orlowitz and Patrick Earley, "Librarypedia: The Future of Libraries and Wikipedia," *The Digital Shift,* January 25, 2014, www.thedigitalshift.com/2014/01/discovery/library pedia-future-libraries-wikipedia/.

5. "Global," *Meta-Wiki,* https://meta.wikimedia.org/wiki/The_Wikipedia_Library/Global.

6. Eric Jennings, "Using Wikipedia to Teach Information Literacy," *College & Undergraduate Libraries* 15, no. 4 (2008): 432–37, doi:10.1080/10691310802554895.

7. Jimmy Daly, "Wikipedia: When College Students Have an Audience, Does Their Writing Improve?" *EdTech,* October 23, 2013, www.edtechmagazine.com/higher/article/2013/10/ wikipedia-when-college-students-have-audience-does-their-writing-improve.

8. Andrea Forte, "The New Information Literate: Open Collaboration and Information Production in Schools," *International Journal of Computer-Supported Collaborative Learning* 10, no. 1 (2015): 35–51, doi:10.1007/s11412–015–9210–6.

9. "Global Impact: The Wikipedia Library and Persian Wikipedia," *Wikimedia Blog,* December 11, 2014, https://blog.wikimedia.org/2014/12/11/global-impact-the-wikipedia -library-and-persian-wikipedia/.

10. David Pattern, "'I Wouldn't Start from Here.' Overcoming Barriers to Accessing Online Content in Libraries," UKSG 35th Annual Conference and Exhibition, March 26–28, 2012, SECC, Glasgow, http://eprints.hud.ac.uk/13220/.

11. Alex Stinson, "Expanding Local History with The Wikipedia Library," *Wikimedia Blog,* July 22, 2014, https://blog.wikimedia.org/2014/07/22/expanding-local-history-wikipedia -library/.

12. Mark Graham, "Wikipedia Community and Internet Archive Partner to Fix One Million Broken Links on Wikipedia," *Wikimedia Blog,* October 26, 2016, https://blog.wikimedia .org/2016/10/26/internet-archive-broken-links/.

13. Misha Teplitskiy, Grace Lu, and Eamon Duede, "Amplifying the Impact of Open Access: Wikipedia and the Diffusion of Science," *Journal of the Association for Information Science and Technology*, October 13, 2016, doi:10.1002/asi.23687.

14. Jake Orlowitz, "You Can Now Add Automatically Generated Citations to Millions of Books on Wikipedia," *Wikimedia Blog*, May 11, 2017, https://blog.wikimedia.org/2017/05/11/wikimedia-oclc-partnership/.

15. "Visiting Scholars," Wikipedia, https://en.wikipedia.org/wiki/Wikipedia:Visiting_Scholars.

16. Alex Stinson and Jake Orlowitz, "What Happens When You Give a Wikipedia Editor a Research Library?" *Wikimedia Blog*, March 17, 2015, https://blog.wikimedia.org/2015/03/17/wikipedia-research-library/.

17. "Lessons," *Meta-Wiki*, https://meta.wikimedia.org/wiki/The_Wikipedia_Library/1Lib1Ref/Lessons.

18. "*Books & Bytes* Issue 21, January–March 2017," Wikipedia, https://en.wikipedia.org/wiki/Wikipedia:The_Wikipedia_Library/Newsletter/January-March2017.

19. Lorcan Dempsey, "Discovery Happens Elsewhere," *Lorcan Dempsey's Weblog*, September 16, 2007, http://orweblog.oclc.org/discovery-happens-elsewhere/.

20. Eleanor Diaz, "Wikipedia: The 'Intellectual Makerspace' of Libraries," *Programming Librarian*, August 2, 2016, http://programminglibrarian.org/articles/wikipedia-intellectual-makerspace-libraries.

REFERENCES

"*Books & Bytes* Issue 21, January–March 2017." Wikipedia. https://en.wikipedia.org/wiki/Wikipedia:The_Wikipedia_Library/Newsletter/January-March2017.

Daly, Jimmy. "Wikipedia: When College Students Have an Audience, Does Their Writing Improve?" *EdTech*. October 23, 2013. www.edtechmagazine.com/higher/article/2013/10/wikipedia-when-college-students-have-audience-does-their-writing-improve.

Dempsey, Lorcan. "Discovery Happens Elsewhere." *Lorcan Dempsey's Weblog*. September 16, 2007. http://orweblog.oclc.org/discovery-happens-elsewhere/.

Diaz, Eleanor. "Wikipedia: The 'Intellectual Makerspace' of Libraries." *Programming Librarian*. August 2, 2016. http://programminglibrarian.org/articles/wikipedia-intellectual-makerspace-libraries.

Forte, Andrea. "The new Information Literate: Open Collaboration and Information Production in Schools." *International Journal of Computer-Supported Collaborative Learning* 10, no. 1 (2015): 35–51. doi:10.1007/s11412–015–9210–6.

"Global." *Meta-Wiki*. https://meta.wikimedia.org/wiki/The_Wikipedia_Library/Global.

"Global Impact: The Wikipedia Library and Persian Wikipedia." *Wikimedia Blog*. December 11, 2014. https://blog.wikimedia.org/2014/12/11/global-impact-the-wikipedia-library-and-persian-wikipedia/.

Graham, Mark. "Wikipedia Community and Internet Archive Partner to Fix One Million Broken Links on Wikipedia." *Wikimedia Blog*. October 26, 2016. https://blog.wikimedia .org/2016/10/26/internet-archive-broken-links/.

"Grants:IEG/The Wikipedia Library." *Meta-Wiki*. https://meta.wikimedia.org/wiki/ Grants:IEG/The_Wikipedia_Library.

Jennings, Eric. "Using Wikipedia to Teach Information Literacy." *College & Undergraduate Libraries* 15, no. 4 (2008): 432–37. doi:10.1080/10691310802554895.

"Lessons." *Meta-Wiki*. https://meta.wikimedia.org/wiki/The_Wikipedia_Library/1Lib1Ref/ Lessons.

Murray, Bruce. "The Wikipedia Library: A Partnership of Wikipedia and Publishers to Enhance Research and Discovery." *CrossRef*. April 4, 2016. http://blog.crossref.org/2016/04/ the-wikipedia-library-a-partnership-of-wikipedia-and-publishers-to-enhance-research -and-discovery.html.

Orlowitz, Jake. "You Can Now Add Automatically Generated Citations to Millions of Books on Wikipedia." *Wikimedia Blog*. May 11, 2017. https://blog.wikimedia.org/2017/05/11/ wikimedia-oclc-partnership/.

Orlowitz, Jake, and Patrick Earley. "Librarypedia: The Future of Libraries and Wikipedia." *The Digital Shift*. January 25, 2014. www.thedigitalshift.com/2014/01/discovery/librarypedia -future-libraries-wikipedia/.

Pattern, David. "'I Wouldn't Start from Here.' Overcoming Barriers to Accessing Online Content in Libraries." UKSG 35th Annual Conference and Exhibition, March 26–28, 2012, SECC, Glasgow. http://eprints.hud.ac.uk/13220/.

"Publishers." Wikipedia. https://en.wikipedia.org/wiki/Wikipedia:The_Wikipedia_Library/ Publishers.

Stinson, Alex. "Expanding Local History with The Wikipedia Library." *Wikimedia Blog*. July 22, 2014. https://blog.wikimedia.org/2014/07/22/expanding-local-history-wikipedia -library/.

Stinson, Alex, and Jake Orlowitz. "What Happens When You Give a Wikipedia Editor a Research Library?" *Wikimedia Blog*. March 17, 2015. https://blog.wikimedia.org/ 2015/03/17/wikipedia-research-library/.

Teplitskiy, Misha, Grace Lu, and Eamon Duede. "Amplifying the Impact of Open Access: Wikipedia and the Diffusion of Science." *Journal of the Association for Information Science and Technology*. October 13, 2016. doi:10.1002/asi.23687. http://onlinelibrary.wiley .com/doi/10.1002/asi.23687/abstract.

"Visiting Scholars." Wikipedia. https://en.wikipedia.org/wiki/Wikipedia:Visiting_Scholars.

Wikipedia and Education

A Natural Collaboration, Supported by Libraries

LIANNA L. DAVIS

W ikipedia and education have been interwoven since Wikipedia's beginnings.[1] Some of the earliest content contributors ("Wikipedians" or "editors") were students, librarians, and professors at higher education institutions worldwide. And perhaps not surprisingly, some of the earliest readers of Wikipedia were students: instead of having to visit the campus library to look up a topic in *Encyclopaedia Britannica*, students could find information in Wikipedia from the comfort of their dorm rooms with a simple Internet search.

In 2010, with the creation of the Wikipedia Education Program, Wikipedia's relationship with higher education became more formalized. In this now worldwide program, professors assign their students to edit Wikipedia articles on course-related topics as part of their class. In the United States and Canada, the program has expanded dramatically since its creation; in seven years, the program has expanded from 14 participating classes to 335 participating classes. We've empowered more than 28,000 students to add more than 29 million words to the English Wikipedia—that's the equivalent of two-thirds of the content in the last print edition of *Encyclopaedia Britannica,* or more than 52 full copies of *War and Peace.*

Along the way, university librarians have been some of our biggest champions, particularly thanks to Wikipedia assignments giving students better information and media literacy skills. In January 2000, one year before Wikipedia's founding, the Association of College & Research Libraries (ACRL) adopted the Information Literacy Competency Standards for Higher Education. The guidelines encouraged libraries and librarians to pivot at universities to a role facilitating information literacy pedagogy for students. ACRL adopted the more robust Framework for Information Literacy in 2016, maintaining the position that higher education institutions should include information literacy skills development in course curriculums. Librarians aim for students to graduate college with information literacy skills, and Wikipedia-editing helps students understand information and effectively use that information. This has made Wikipedia a natural ally for libraries.

WHEN STUDENTS EDIT WIKIPEDIA

Just what does it mean when students edit Wikipedia? Students are already doing research and writing their results up for their university faculty, as the literature review section of an analytical paper. These assignments strive to give students the grounding in a subject area that is needed in order to come up with critically interesting things to say about a topic. But whatever effectiveness these assignments may have had in earlier generations, they don't often accomplish these goals today. The availability of digital sources means that many university students never set foot in the physical library on campus, instead relying on Google and online scholarly journal databases. And do most students really take the initiative to seek out the premier sources? Or do they mostly rely on whatever appears in the first few search results, since the only person who reads their work is their professor?

A Wikipedia editing assignment turns these assumptions on their head: instead of a throwaway assignment, students are engaging in a meaningful service learning experience that others will use. For the instructor, this project offers an opportunity to discuss information and knowledge curation. The library offers books and journals that experts have deemed reliable and integral to the scholarship of that topic. While editing Wikipedia, students quickly learn how rigorous the citation requirements are, and the library's curated resources provide a superb starting place for their research. Some students will set foot in their campus library for the first time, seeking books, guidance from reference librarians, and exceptional sources for their Wikipedia article. Students survey what has been written on a topic, determine what the appropriate weight for each element of the subject is, and craft a neutral, fact-based encyclopedia article summarizing the topic area.

Here's an example: the article on the field of "geobiology" had been created on Wikipedia in 2005, but it lingered as what's known as a "stub" for more than ten years. It had five sentences about its definition and major geobiological events. And there was a list of five subfields.[2] Today, thanks to student editor Alice Michel from the California Institute of Technology[3], it is a 7,000-word description of a scientific field of study, with sections describing the history of the field, key concepts, methodology, and a detailed explanation of eleven sub-disciplines and related fields.[4]

Wikipedia assignments enable students like Alice to research and write articles on topics related to their courses, which makes their academic work meaningful. Today, thousands of students like Alice do so through a formal program that encourages university faculty to teach with Wikipedia.

PILOTING A FORMAL EDUCATION PROGRAM

By 2010, a trend had begun to emerge on Wikipedia, across language versions: Wikipedia editors who were university professors had begun to assign writing Wikipedia articles to their students. These professors began publishing articles calling for more engagement in Wikipedia from the academy. Adrianne Wadewitz, Anne Ellen Geller, and Jon Beasley-Murray published an article titled "Wiki-Hacking: Opening Up the Academy with Wikipedia,"[5] which highlighted why students could engage productively on Wikipedia, especially in the context of critiquing the production of knowledge by evaluating content gaps in academic subject areas.

At the same time, the Wikimedia Foundation (WMF), the nonprofit that supports Wikipedia, started noticing a precipitous decline in the numbers of editors. This trend was noticeable across the globe, but the decline was particularly stark on the English Wikipedia. WMF staff, led by the then-head of public outreach, Frank Schulenburg, identified engaging with university students in the United States in a structured program as a potential way to both fill content gaps on Wikipedia (this was a wild success) and recruit new editors to Wikipedia (it didn't). In the structured program, WMF staff would train volunteers, called "Wikipedia Ambassadors," to help students in the class, so instructors would not need to be longtime Wikipedia editors themselves.

Armed with a grant from the Stanton Foundation, a funder that was particularly interested in improving the quality of U.S. public policy articles on Wikipedia, WMF hired a team to run a yearlong pilot initiative to provide the support structure so public policy students could improve Wikipedia articles as a class project. (Disclosure: I was one of the people hired for the team.) We started with the Wikipedia article about the top public policy schools in the United States, looked up their faculty, and set out to cold e-mail professors until we had enough interest to move forward. We established the Wikipedia Ambassador program, recruited existing editors to help the students online, and sought out on-campus Ambassadors to help students in person.

Librarians were our biggest allies as we sought to provide this on-campus Ambassador support. Librarians volunteered to be Ambassadors, set up lab space for Wikipedia training sessions, helped bring more professors on board, and otherwise supported our program. Some librarians saw the value of the program, even in its pilot phase, and volunteered their time outside the structure of their jobs. Others convinced supervisors that helping with the Wikipedia pilot was a valuable part of their work, and they integrated Ambassador duties into their job description. At the level of the pilot—in its first term, we were supporting 200 students total, spread across ten different college and universities—we were still finding our way for providing good support, so we spent a lot of time in individual and small group conversations with the Ambassadors.

Some elements of the pilot phase worked really well. First, students added a lot of content, and the content was good. One of the staff members on our pilot team was tasked with conducting a research project to assess the quality of content that students added. Using a modified version of Wikipedia's internal assessment ratings, both public policy experts and Wikipedia editors evaluated student articles, comparing the version before a student's first edit to the version after they had finished their last edit for the class. The study[6] found that articles increased in quality by 64 percent on average. A second study,[7] replicating the first one a year later, found similar results. In other words, student work added to Wikipedia was overwhelmingly beneficial. And there was a lot of it: in the first year of the program alone, students added the equivalent of 6,000 sheets of paper, if the articles had been printed in a typical double-spaced page, to the English Wikipedia.

We also learned that the model worked: provided with support for the Wikipedia portion of the course, professors didn't need to be experienced editors themselves in order to have a successful class project. And professors were definitely interested in what we were doing; we jumped from 14 classes in the first term to 32 in the second and then up to 81 in the third. The increase was from word of mouth, media attention (we'd been featured on NPR's "All Things Considered," on the front page of the *Washington Post,* and in the *Chronicle of Higher Education* and *Inside Higher Ed*), and conference presentations we did at pedagogy conferences around the United States.

These pedagogy conferences also clued us in to another important aspect: student learning outcomes. Early on, we identified that the faculty participating in our program were motivated by the learning outcomes the Wikipedia assignment provided. Through surveys, focus groups, and student reflections,[8] we identified key learning objectives: media literacy, fact-based writing, research, and critical thinking. Wikipedia assignments were all rated equal to or better than traditional assignments at drawing out these skills in students. To this day, conveying how Wikipedia assignments provide these student learning outcomes remains a cornerstone of our outreach efforts.

Some elements of the pilot didn't work as well. We didn't stop the decline of editors on Wikipedia, since students didn't stick around after the term was over. Our volunteers provided wildly different levels of support to students. We spent a lot of staff time and money on in-person trainings for volunteers, which had only moderate success. And perhaps most challenging, our original goal was to establish a self-sufficient system that scaled up without much staff time after the conclusion of the pilot's grant.

We attempted a variety of volunteer structures to scale up the program without staff support, but these all had challenges. One primary issue of working with formal institutions like universities is that there are real consequences for students if a volunteer isn't able to meet a commitment. Coordinating volunteers by using other volunteers can work in certain situations, but our program simply wasn't well established enough to be in that situation. The idea that volunteers would run the program without staff support lasted only two months before we brought on a full-time staff person. For five terms, this model worked: with one full-time staff person overseeing it, the U.S. and Canada program could support around 65 to 75 classes each term, with varying levels of success in the volunteer support structure. In the spring 2013 term, we added an online student training; this was our first realization that training students directly was more effective, both in preparing students and utilizing volunteer time, than relying on Ambassadors to train them.

Because supporting students to edit Wikipedia as part of their coursework was so successful, WMF's goal for the education program shifted to a global focus. The education staff set out to support staff and volunteers in other countries to start education programs modeled on the U.S. pilot in their regions; learnings there influenced the growth of the U.S. program as well.

GOING GLOBAL

Education programs were being developed in other countries at the same time as the pilot program within the United States. Some closely mirrored the U.S. pilot, while others varied in key ways. Many programs worked in their native language Wikipedias, but one pilot in particular had significant implications for our work in the United States: that in Pune, India.

In the Pune Pilot, nearly 2,000 students in a handful of courses—many of them technical—were assigned to write Wikipedia articles on course-related topics as part of their work. The major problem, however, was that this was the first time most of these students had been asked to write original content, and the majority of students didn't have the necessary skills. Violations of U.S. copyright law abounded in the contributions that the Pune Pilot students added to Wikipedia, and the volunteer Wikipedia Ambassadors working with the students were unable to stem the tide of content being added by well-meaning students in the Pune Pilot, despite the Ambassadors' best efforts. Since WMF staff are prohibited from editing Wikipedia content, we had the additional challenge of relying on volunteers for the cleanup work required to remove poor-quality student work.

The ramifications from the Pune Pilot had ramifications for the U.S. education program. English Wikipedians began to question whether any student could make high-quality contributions to Wikipedia. Minor student mistakes became magnified as some editors pushed back on the student projects in general. The already strained volunteer mechanism within the U.S. program took an even bigger hit, as the reputation of education projects on the English Wikipedia eroded.

Nevertheless, during this time, WMF leadership recognized the potential of the U.S. program. The foundation created a working group of instructors,

Wikipedians, and librarians to determine a new home for the U.S. and Canada education program so that it could scale up. Out of this emerged a new nonprofit organization, spun off from the Wikimedia Foundation in November 2013. Called the Wiki Education Foundation, the organization focused exclusively on expanding connections between Wikipedia and higher education institutions in the United States and Canada.

INSPIRING LEARNING, ENRICHING WIKIPEDIA

The Wiki Education Foundation, or Wiki Ed, was formed as a mix of experienced Wikipedia and education veterans and some newbies. Board members included professors who had taught in our program, Ambassadors who had supported student editors, and others with nonprofit board and governance experience. Wiki Ed staff included three staff from the original pilot (myself included), the program manager hired in 2011, an Ambassador who had been with the program since the beginning as a volunteer, and some people new to the program, who provided fresh perspective. After one term of stabilization, we set out to start scaling up the program.

As Wiki Ed, we made some key changes to the program, in part as a reflection on lessons learned from the Pune Pilot. First, we invested heavily in technical projects. Second, we set out to reduce the reliance on volunteers. And finally, we set out to purposefully scale up through targeted recruitment.

TECHNICAL INNOVATIONS

Early on, we'd learned that one of the biggest predictors of the success or failure of a class was in the design of the assignment. If instructors assigned students the wrong thing, it didn't matter what we did; the course would go wrong. To be clear, we define failed classes as those that do more harm to Wikipedia than good. Common problems include students who write analytical essays rather than encyclopedia articles, students who repeatedly reinsert content that's been deleted for policy reasons before being blocked, or students who severely underestimate the amount of time it takes to write a good Wikipedia article, waiting until the night before to start, and ending up adding low-quality content. Good assignment design can overcome most of these problems: establishing expectations for both the instructor and students early; specifically calling out differences between Wikipedia assignments and traditional term papers; highlighting that students will be graded on their work, not on what sticks in Wikipedia; and using graded milestones throughout a multi-week period to ensure that students can't procrastinate, all help to overcome course challenges.

Because of this, our first tech project was to create an Assignment Design Wizard. In the Wizard, we ask instructors a series of questions about their class, their learning objectives, how many optional assignments they wanted to add, how they'd like to grade work, and so on; based on their inputs, we create a customized timeline for the Wikipedia portion of the course. In this way, we are able to provide the flexibility that instructors want (not everyone wants the same thing out of a Wikipedia assignment) while nevertheless establishing guardrails based on our best practices and ensuring that the assignment stays within those boundaries. Instructors are free to modify the assignment plan timeline that emerges from the Assignment Design Wizard, but many find that the customized timeline fits their needs perfectly, and they don't make any modifications to it.

The Assignment Design Wizard feeds the assignment timeline into our custom course management platform, the Dashboard.[9] Creating the Dashboard platform was the single biggest achievement in scaling up our program. We were able to have a system whereby we could monitor all the students' on-wiki activity, provide them with customized online training modules, and serve content based on the time frame (so, for example, if students are supposed to add images to their articles in a particular course this week, we suggest they take our online training module on adding images). It publicly tracks the work that students are doing on Wikipedia, making it much easier for instructors to see their students' work. And what was most highly motivating for students, we showcase how many people have read the articles they are working on since their first edits. By doing so, we highlight the impact students are having on Wikipedia content and the world, making the assignment much more real to the students.

We also launched a question-and-answer platform at ask.wikiedu.org. We populated it with most of the frequently asked questions our staff has received over the last few years, and every time we get a new question, we add it to the database. Search bars from the top of Dashboard pages enable students and instructors to search for answers when they get stuck, rather than having to send an e-mail to a staff member and wait for a reply. Providing more findable resources was key for scaling up our support to participating courses.

CONTENT EXPERTS

Another significant change we made was to stop engaging with the Wikipedia Ambassador program. While some Ambassadors had done exceptional work supporting classes, many struggled to provide adequate support for an entire course. Some just liked answering questions and weren't interested in reviewing drafts or mediating disputes, while others were happy to review drafts but didn't want to be bothered with questions. Inconsistency in support across classes resulted in a major challenge to scaling up the program. With the creation of the Wiki Education Foundation, we hired two longtime Wikipedia editors in staff positions as Content Experts. Rather than relying on great but sporadic volunteer help, we provide dedicated support for each class. Our Wikipedia Content Experts are able to monitor student activity, address any problems raised by community members, and better answer student questions.

Staff-facing features on the Dashboard alert Content Experts to which courses are active and when, provide a feed of activity from the courses they support, and provide automated flags for problems like plagiarism, students who haven't completed training, articles that are nominated for deletion, and more. And the ask.wikiedu.org question-and-answer platform provided self-discovered answers to many student and instructor questions. Through these technical services, we dramatically increased the number of students that each Content Expert supported. In the fall 2016 term, each Content Expert supported more than 3,000 students; in contrast, our Wikipedia Ambassadors each supported between 10 and 20 students. By moving the role into a staff position and empowering the staff with technical tools, we were able to scale up the program while heading off problems like those the Pune Pilot experienced and providing the same or better level of support for program participants.

TARGETED RECRUITMENT

It's one thing to have the capacity to increase our support for classes; it's another to actively recruit new instructors into our program. With the creation of the Wiki Education Foundation, we began purposefully recruiting new program participants for the first time since the pilot phase. In the pilot phase, we'd learned that two specific methods were the most effective: (1) peer recruitment, and (2) academic conferences. With the Wiki Education Foundation, we set out to replicate these successes while introducing new models.

In the peer recruitment model, we ask instructors who are currently teaching with us if they'd be willing to recruit a colleague to teach with Wikipedia. By colleagues, we can mean someone in their department, someone in a different department at their university, or perhaps a friend from graduate school. Social media and blog posts featuring the work of instructors are key in this recruitment method; when we ask instructors to guest blog for us about their experiences teaching with Wikipedia, they often share these posts to their networks, thereby raising our visibility in our stakeholder community. Peer recruitment remains one of our most effective models for bringing new instructors on board.

In the other most effective model, Wiki Ed travels to academic associations' annual conferences. In a handful of cases, we form official partnerships with academic associations;[10] as part of those partnership agreements, the associations provide reduced-cost or complimentary booth space and a speaking slot in the conference program. We collect names and e-mail addresses from interested instructors at the booth and presentation, and follow up with interested faculty after the conference. While these are expensive in relation to staff time and travel costs, conferences give us the opportunity to directly talk with faculty about how Wikipedia might fit into their courses and we acquire enough information to follow up with them in future terms, even if they're not interested in teaching with Wikipedia in the next term. If we don't have a partnership with an academic association but nevertheless think the subject matter is ripe for student work on Wikipedia, we will purchase booth space.

Often when we travel to an academic conference, we reach out to contacts at local universities to see if they will host us for a teaching workshop while we're in town. Librarians play a particularly crucial role in this element of our recruitment. Many of our university and college librarians enthusiastically embrace the opportunity to welcome us to campus, providing space for a workshop and spreading the word among faculty and other librarians.

With the creation of the Wiki Education Foundation, we were able to dramatically expand our travel schedule to accommodate significantly more academic association conferences and campus visits. We also started experimenting with new forms of outreach, including cold e-mailing faculty, social media ad campaigns, and pedagogy discussion list posts. Many of these worked remarkably well, and this targeted outreach has been successful in increasing our numbers of courses. Of course, we also maintain a fairly steady rate of "organic growth"— someone who has the idea and then stumbles across us when looking for support. See figure 7.1 for an illustration of our growth.

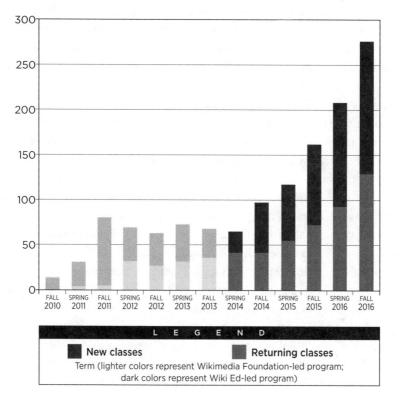

FIGURE 7.1

Growth in the number of classes participating in the program

Thanks to the targeted recruitment that brought on more classes, the Content Expert model for supporting those classes, and the technical platform that underlies our program, we've been able to scale up our impact on Wikipedia—and on the students' learning.

WHY OUR WORK IMPACTS LIBRARIANS

Since the pilot phase, librarians have been some of the biggest champions of the program. It's easy to see why: not only are we dramatically increasing the availability of free knowledge on academic subject matters by adding content to Wikipedia, but we're also improving the media literacy skills of college and university students across the United States and Canada.

Impact to Wikipedia

Librarians we work with appreciate Wikipedia. As an online encyclopedia with good search engine optimization, Wikipedia is often the first result in a web search for a topic. "Imagine a world in which every single person on the planet is given free access to the sum of all human knowledge," said Wikipedia founder Jimmy Wales. Access to the sum of all human knowledge is a laudable goal, and Wiki Ed's program is helping work toward this vision.

Because Wikipedia is written by volunteers, its content is reflective of the interests of its editors. Nobody is paid to contribute content to Wikipedia, Wikipedia entries are (generally) not accepted as publications on tenure applications so they usually are not written as part of an academic resume, and only a handful of initiatives like the Core Contest are specifically targeted at improving articles based on their importance. What all of this means is that the scope of Wikipedia's quality reflects the interests of its volunteers; and with a significant majority of editors being young males from the developed world, Wikipedia tends to have high-quality articles on subjects like video game characters, *Star Trek* episodes, and military history, while articles on women's studies, plant biology, and sociology lag behind in both quality and quantity. Of course, it's important to have articles available for people seeking information on video game characters, *Star Trek* episodes, and military history, but it's also important to have articles on women's studies, plant biology, and sociology. You might recognize the latter three disciplines in particular as those Wiki Ed has partnerships with; closing this content gap on Wikipedia is one of the major reasons why associations want to partner with us.

For example, our partnership with the National Women's Studies Association has brought nearly 2,500 women's studies students to Wikipedia. They've edited 2,400 articles, adding 1.72 million words of content related to women's, gender, and sexuality studies to Wikipedia. Along the way, they've filled countless content gaps, including creating new articles on feminist Audre Lorde's book *Sister Outsider,* Muslim women in sport, and women in law enforcement in the United States.

In 2016, Wiki Ed created the largest ever initiative to fill a content gap: the Wikipedia Year of Science. In this yearlong effort, Wiki Ed supported more than 6,300 students as they added nearly 5 million words to STEM (science, technology, engineering, and mathematics) and social science topics on Wikipedia. In one year, the students in Wiki Ed's program filled 11 percent of the last print edition of *Encyclopaedia Britannica* with new Wikipedia content in the sciences.

This wildly successful initiative demonstrates the impact students can have on improving content in broad subject areas like science.

In spring 2016, we set out to conduct a research project identifying what percentage of content added to academic articles was being added by our students, and the results were impressive. In the busiest part of the term, our students are adding 10 percent of all content to the previously underdeveloped academic-topic articles on Wikipedia (what are known as "start" or "stub" class articles).[11] That's a significant impact on Wikipedia—and it cements Wiki Ed's place as an important player in the Wikipedia space.

When student editors are engaged on Wikipedia through Wiki Ed's program, we're able to specifically target underdeveloped content areas in academic subject areas, and provide improvements to them. For librarians who want more free knowledge available to their patrons, Wiki Ed's program is a crucial way of filling content gaps in important subject areas.

Impact to Students

It's not just about the impact on Wikipedia, however: Wiki Ed's program also provides students with key media literacy skills. As recent research from Stanford University shows,[12] just because students are digital natives does not mean they are media-literate. Higher education students struggle to distinguish legitimate articles from advertorials, and as the rise of fake news sites has shown, people are surprisingly apt to believe an article which says something that matches their biases without any investigation into whether the source is trustworthy or not.

As libraries become increasingly digital, it's more important than ever to teach people media literacy skills. A librarian is not curating what's available on the Internet, only carrying the sources that meet a standard of reliability. The collection that is the Internet isn't curated at all, in fact: anyone can publish anything, thanks to the availability of free blogging platforms. As the Internet has shifted, digital literacy skills need to keep up. Education is just catching on to the fact that students need to be taught media literacy skills so they can successfully navigate this new sphere. And librarians are often tasked with providing these skills to students.

A lack of media literacy skills doesn't fly on Wikipedia, a website that's been successfully ousting fake news for years. Wikipedia's strict Reliable Source guideline requires that facts in articles must be cited to sources that (a) have a reputation for fact-checking, (b) have editorial oversight, and (c) are independent of the subject matter. When students enroll in Wiki Ed's Dashboard software to write Wikipedia articles, an online training walks them through what sources work for Wikipedia, and how to determine if the source they've found is acceptable or not.

What this means is that students cannot rely on the first Google hit to be their primary source. (And since they're improving Wikipedia, they also can't rely on Wikipedia!). We've had numerous students report that—ironically enough—the assignment to write a Wikipedia article was the cause of the first time they'd ever set foot in the campus library. Simple Google or even JSTOR searches aren't enough to find sufficient sources that meet Wikipedia's requirements; instead, students must consult the major sources in the field about the topic, and they often seek out reference librarians' help to find these. Writing for Wikipedia forces students to understand source evaluation, do in-depth research on their topic, and separate what they feel about a topic from what the published, reliable sources say about it. Students become media-literate consumers of information in the act of producing knowledge on Wikipedia.

What is the precise impact of a Wikipedia assignment on students' media literacy skills? In fall 2016, Wiki Ed brought a research fellow on board to conduct a study to measure this more precisely. More than 600 students took both a pre- and post-test in the term, using questions modeled on the Information Literacy Assessment & Advocacy Project (ILAAP), which maps to the Association of College & Research Libraries (ACRL) information literacy framework. An additional thirteen focus groups rounded out the study. By triangulating results, we determined that writing Wikipedia articles for class is a key way to teach students critical information literacy skills.[13] In particular, Wikipedia assignment skill development maps to four areas within the ACRL information literacy framework: authority is constructed and contextual, information creation is a process, information has value, and scholarship as conversation. The study also found that compared to a traditional assignment, 96 percent of instructors thought the assignment was more or much more valuable in teaching students digital literacy, and 85 percent of instructors thought the Wikipedia assignment was more or much more valuable for teaching students about the reliability of online sources. Wikipedia assignments also shift students' perceptions of Wikipedia's reliability to show more trust in Wikipedia. These research findings highlight the key role that Wikipedia assignments can play in teaching students necessary information literacy skills for the digital age.

Both the media literacy skills students acquire from writing a Wikipedia article and the improvement to open knowledge resulting from their work are reasons why librarians have supported Wiki Ed's work. Librarians at higher education institutions graciously host teaching with Wikipedia workshops on their campuses, recommend our program to faculty, and, when they teach courses, integrate Wikipedia assignments into those courses. And they offer to host Wikipedia Visiting Scholars through Wiki Ed's second program.

WIKIPEDIA VISITING SCHOLARS

While our class-based program is the flagship work of Wiki Ed, our second program is deeply integrated into libraries. In the Visiting Scholars program,[14] a campus library provides a log-in to an experienced Wikipedia editor. The log-in enables this experienced Wikipedian to get access to sources that are otherwise behind a paywall. Some university libraries offer access to special collections. In return for access to these sources, the Visiting Scholar improves or creates Wikipedia articles on broad topic areas that are of interest to the host institution. The Visiting Scholars program originated within The Wikipedia Library program from the Wikimedia Foundation, but the U.S. and Canada Visiting Scholars were spun off to Wiki Ed in 2015.

The Visiting Scholars program is much smaller than our class-based program, partly because developing relationships between an institution and a scholar takes much more staff time to facilitate. For some colleges and universities, providing a university log-in for library resources to someone who is unaffiliated with the campus is a bureaucratic process full of red tape. And pairing an experienced Wikipedian who needs access to sources with an institution that has a particular topic area of focus can be a challenge; the narrower the focus, the harder it is to find an appropriate candidate. Nevertheless, the small but effective Visiting Scholars program has added a significant amount of content in several key focus areas.

The Wikipedia editor Gary Greenbaum, who is a Visiting Scholar at George Mason University, focuses on U.S. history as part of his position. He's already written five "featured articles" thanks to his access to sources through his Visiting Scholars position. Featured articles are those that have met Wikipedia's highest article quality standard, and endure a rigorous peer review process before receiving the designation.

The Wikipedia editor Barbara Page, who is a Visiting Scholar at the University of Pittsburgh, focuses on health as part of her position. Thanks to her training as a nurse and her access to sources through Pittsburgh's library, she's improved countless articles on women's health issues, general health topics, and related articles like that on rape.

These important topics require a deep knowledge of Wikipedia, as well as access to legitimate sources. By pairing an experienced Wikipedian with the resources of a university library, the Visiting Scholars program is able to increase the quality of information available in important subject areas. The nine Visiting Scholars that Wiki Ed has facilitated have added more than 450,000 words to Wikipedia, for articles that have been viewed nearly 100 million times. The university libraries play a crucial role in giving access to sources so articles on important topics can be improved on Wikipedia.

LOOKING AHEAD

As we enter the fourteenth term of formally supporting student editors as they contribute content to Wikipedia in spring 2017, we see the importance of our program even more. The role of fake news and propaganda in recent public discourse has made two elements of our program more important now than ever before: teaching students how to be media-literate citizens through the source evaluation processes that go into writing Wikipedia articles, and providing well-cited, neutral information on academic topic areas that are relevant to the everyday lives of people around the world.

The Wiki Education Foundation is looking to expand our program, especially in areas like public policy, sociology, law, and history that are important to enable people to be informed citizens. We've already added more than 29 million words to the English Wikipedia; with more instructors, more student editors, and more Visiting Scholars, we can continue adding important content. And we see the value in teaching those media literacy skills to more students. While more than 28,000 students have already gained crucial skills through our program, we can provide these skills to even more students.

Although librarians have been integrated into our program since its beginnings, we think there is more potential to collaborate. As the librarian profession shifts more into digital spaces, as librarians are more frequently tasked with teaching students media literacy skills, and as higher education not only embraces but prioritizes Wikipedia, we envision more and more collaborations emerging. We look forward to working with librarians to continue to foster the collaboration between Wikipedia and education.

NOTES

1. Frank Schulenburg and Klaus Wannemacher, "Wikipedia in Academic Studies—Corrupting or 'Dramatically Improving' the Quality of Teaching and Learning?" in *Looking Toward the Future of Technology Enhanced Education: Ubiquitous Learning and the Digital Native*, ed. Peter Ebner and Mandy Schiefner (Hershey, PA, 2009), IGI Global, 295–310.

2. "Geobiology," Wikipedia, https://en.wikipedia.org/w/index.php?title=Geobiology&oldid=679396847.

3. "How Geobiology came to Wikipedia – Wiki Education," https://wikiedu.org/blog/2016/07/05/the-roundup-how-geobiology-came-to-wikipedia/.

4. "Geobiology," Wikipedia, https://en.wikipedia.org/wiki/Geobiology.

5. Adrianne Wadewitz, Anne Ellen Geller, and Jon Beasley-Murray, "Wiki-hacking: Opening up the academy with Wikipedia," Wikipedia, 2010, https://en.wikipedia.org/wiki/User:Wadewitz/TeachingEssay.

6. Amy Roth, "Student Contributions to Wikipedia," Wikimedia Outreach, 2011, https://outreach.wikimedia.org/wiki/Student_Contributions_to_Wikipedia.

7. United States and Canada student article quality research results, Wikipedia, Spring 2012, https://en.wikipedia.org/wiki/Wikipedia:Ambassadors/Research/Article_quality/Results.

8. Amy Roth, Rochelle Davis, and Brian Carver, "Assigning Wikipedia editing: Triangulation toward understanding university student engagement," *First Monday* 18, no. 6 (June 3, 2013), http://firstmonday.org/ojs/index.php/fm/article/view/4340/3687.

9. Wiki Education Dashboard. WikiEdu.

10. We have active partnerships with the American Chemical Society, American Society of Plant Biologists, American Sociological Association, Association for Psychological Science, Association for Women in Mathematics, Linguistic Society of America, Midwest Political Science Association, National Women's Studies Association, and Society for Marine Mammalogy.

11. When students edit Wikipedia, academic content thrives. WikiEdu.

12. Sam Wineburg, Sarah McGrew, Joel Breakstone, and Teresa Ortega, "Evaluating Information: The Cornerstone of Civic Online Reasoning," Stanford Digital Repository, 2016, http://purl.stanford.edu/fv751yt5934.

13. "Student Learning Outcomes using Wikipedia-based assignments, *Research Report*, Wikimedia Commons," Fall 2016, https://commons.wikimedia.org/wiki/File:Student _Learning_Outcomes_using_Wikipedia-based_Assignments_Fall_2016_Research _Report.pdf.

14. "Sponsor a Wikipedia Visiting Scholar," WikiEdu, https://wikiedu.org/visitingscholars/ sponsor/.

Wikipedia and New Service Models

An Exploration

LILY TODORINOVA AND YU-HUNG LIN

F ew resources are as popular and controversial among educators as Wikipedia. While there has been a shift toward acceptance of the online encyclopedia for certain classroom purposes, it continues to be difficult to find consensus as to what, if any, role Wikipedia should play in information literacy (IL) sessions and, more generally, on its future role in the library and information science (LIS) profession. This chapter will consider one case study of an academic library's attempt to envision a role of Wikipedia in its organization. This pilot involved two parts: a study of undergraduate students' use of the online encyclopedia as a gateway for academic research, and a case study of a project involving academic librarians in the creation of a new Wikipedia article as part of the Rutgers University Libraries' (RUL) participation in the Wikipedia Visiting Scholars program (see Wikimedia Foundation, 2015). During our work with Wikipedia, we asked the following questions:

1. Do students use and value Wikipedia as a gateway to academic research?
2. Do students and novice researchers need IL assistance when evaluating sources in Wikipedia?

3. Can librarians benefit from engaging with Wikipedia editing practices in the crowd-sourced writing environment?

As the sixth most popular website on the Internet, Wikipedia's ubiquity ranks alongside Google, Facebook, and Amazon and ahead of Twitter and LinkedIn (Alexa Company, 2015). Wikipedia is the primary place where students encounter scholarly content on the open web, before consulting their library's website or even Google Scholar. Routing these users to the library's page from Wikipedia can, at least in theory, take place through the hyperlinked bibliographies and citations in Wikipedia (figure 8.1).

The question is whether students use these links to access content cited by the Wikipedia article. Related to this is an even more fundamental question of whether or not the importance of citations and bibliographies in academic research is sufficiently addressed in IL sessions and the curriculum. External sources are the fundamental basis of Wikipedia's platform, and how students and researchers interact with them can have important implications for user education.

We will first share data and findings from a student usability study of Wikipedia, which revealed students' perceptions of the resource's usefulness, authority, and reliability as a starting point for academic research. At the center of the study was the question of the viability of the online encyclopedia as a gateway to academic information. At a time when libraries are heavily investing in their approaches to discovery and working with companies such as OCLC, EBSCO, ProQuest, and others, it seems worth examining how discovery also happens on the open web. Wikipedia's popularity would suggest that students overwhelmingly prefer it as a starting point for academic research, compared to the library's home page. If libraries can bring users to their holdings from the open web, thereby increasing the discoverability of research collections, this would also enable students who do rely on the open web as their method of doing background research to reconnect to the institutional holdings and expertise of their libraries—essentially a "win-win" situation.

We will also share the outcomes of our participation in a 2014 pilot program conceptualized by the Wikipedia Library Project. RUL, along with a handful of other institutions, was invited by its contacts in OCLC to participate in the Wikipedia Visiting Scholars program. The program supports Wikipedia's goal of improving its content by engaging with universities and their collections. Working with academic libraries can increase the quality of Wikipedia entries by allowing seasoned Wikipedia editors to have access to institutionally licensed

FIGURE 8.1

References on Wikipedia entry

References [edit]

1. ^ The Editorial Board (March 29, 2017). "Republicans Attack Internet Privacy"🔗. *New York Times*. Retrieved March 29, 2017.
2. ^ Wheeler, Tom (March 29, 2017). "How the Republicans Sold Your Privacy to Internet Providers"🔗. *New York Times*. Retrieved March 29, 2017.
3. ^ E. E. David; R. M. Fano (1965). "Some Thoughts About the Social Implications of Accessible Computing. Proceedings 1965 Fall Joint Computer Conference"🔗. Retrieved 2012-06-07.
4. ^ "Steve Rambam – Privacy Is Dead – Get Over It at The Next HOPE, July 16-18, 2010 in New York City"🔗. youtube.com. Retrieved February 2015.
5. ^ Pogue, David (January 2011). "Don't Worry about Who's watching"🔗. *Scientific American*. **304** (1): 32. doi:10.1038/scientificamerican0111-32
6. ^ "The Value of Privacy by Bruce Schneier"🔗. Schneier.com. Retrieved 2015-02-09.
7. ^ Bruce Schneier (May 18, 2006). "The Eternal Value of Privacy by Bruce Schneier"🔗. Wired.com. Retrieved 2016-07-19.
8. ^ Kang, Jerry (1998-01-01). "Information Privacy in Cyberspace Transactions". *Stanford Law Review*. **50** (4): 1193–1294. JSTOR 1229286🔗. doi:10.2307/1229286🔗.
9. ^ "Preventing Identity Theft and Other Cyber Crimes"🔗. onguardonline.gov.

materials. This fulfills the encyclopedia's mission of providing the best and most accurate information. RUL's participation in the Wikipedia Visiting Scholars program, along with the results of the student study, informed how RUL plans to engage with Wikipedia in the future. The data collected provides insights into the use of Wikipedia as a vehicle for IL instruction, as well as how librarians can be more involved in the emerging modes of scholarship in the crowd-sourced information environment of the twenty-first century.

LIMITATIONS

It should be stressed that the student study we will describe here was explorative, based on a small sample of undergraduates in one public research university, and was only meant to represent their attitudes toward Wikipedia. Future research would benefit from including a greater number of participants, as well as a variety of researchers, novice and advanced. Additionally, since this was a controlled web survey, real-time observations and ethnographic methods would add more valuable data to the discussion.

STUDENT STUDY: USE OF SOURCES IN WIKIPEDIA

Our student study involved two phases. In phase one, a small sample of undergraduate students from introductory English writing courses answered a series of multiple-choice, open-ended, and task-based questions regarding their attitudes toward source evaluation. Participants answered a pre- and post-questionnaire assessing their knowledge and attitudes regarding the selection of accurate and reliable information on the Internet. They were next given a hypothetical scenario, similar to an assignment that is part of the curriculum of their writing course. They were asked to explore information sources for the purposes of inclusion in a research paper, starting with a Wikipedia page. The students were prompted to consider the bibliography of the Wikipedia page and examine its usefulness for further research. The students ranked the likelihood of following up and locating citations they found in Wikipedia using the library catalog and databases.

One of the main takeaways from this first phase of the study is that students found ease of access to be the most important consideration when selecting sources to include in their paper, and they ranked this above other considerations, such as, for example, whether or not the source is published in a scientific journal, or found in a library database (figure 8.2). Students also overwhelmingly did not consider the quality of the bibliography of a source to be an indication of the overall quality of that source. This suggests that there is both a need for libraries to integrate their resources and services in the open web, in order to optimize the seamless nature and ease of that environment, as well as a pedagogical need to stress the role of bibliographies in source evaluation. It is possible that if this issue is addressed, more students would use Wikipedia as a gateway to the library's resources. In the study, when given a hypothetical scenario where students were asked if they would ever consider following up citations that they find in the Reference section of a Wikipedia article, in order to obtain further information, only 5 of the 30 students in this sample indicated their willingness to do so.

Students also exhibited uncertainty regarding the fundamental structure and format of bibliographies, as well as an inability to evaluate these external citations. They preferred sources they recognized, such as the *New York Times*.

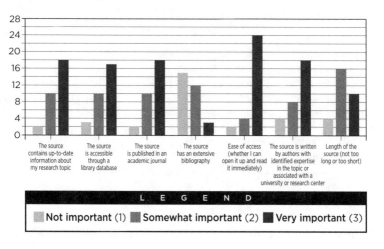

FIGURE 8.2

Criteria for selecting sources

Most importantly, students mistakenly thought that the first couple of citations in the article were the *most* relevant ones, suggesting that they did not know that these sources merely appeared first in the body of the article.

This initial phase of the study prompted a larger investigation into IL interventions that can show users the importance of the sources cited in a Wikipedia page. In a follow-up study with a larger sample of the same population, 60 English Writing students, half of the participants were presented with a rubric in order to help them evaluate the quality of the Wikipedia article and its external citations (figure 8.3). The rubric used is an adapted and shortened version of a popular educational tool created by TurnItIn (TurnItIn, 2015). The students who had the rubric rated the authority of Wikipedia to be higher than the students who had no guide for evaluating the source. Moreover, students who used a rubric in Wikipedia to evaluate sources seemed better able to articulate why a source is useful (or not). This finding, curiously, suggests that having an evaluation tool within Wikipedia may help students navigate the difficulty of determining what makes a source "good."

FIGURE 8.3

Source credibility rubric

Highly Regarded	Credible	Discreditable
A highly regarded article that has been reviewed for accuracy, is well-referenced with sources, and is written by individuals with expertise in the field. It reflects a broad range of points of view and shows no identifiable bias.	A credible article that offers reputable information, is referenced with sources, and is edited for accuracy. It reflects no identifiable bias toward a particular point of view.	A discreditable article that provides no sources for the information it provides. It reflects a bias toward a particular point of view.

Students also elaborated about their general perceptions of Wikipedia in their open-ended responses:

- I would first find some background information about the topic in order to have a broad understanding. Then I would do minor research. Next, I would look for credible sources from the library's databases. My last resort would be books.
- Wikipedia is my favorite starting point. I like to get an overview before proceeding to anything else. Sometimes references are a good direction to go in. Then the library's resources. Google is my last resort . . .
- We usually need credible sources to cite in papers; thus, I would use Wikipedia to gain general knowledge of the subject and then use academic articles from the Rutgers Databases for more reliable information. It is more convenient to use online databases for academic articles than to actually find books at the library.
- Last thing I would do would be to use the reference section because it is the last section of the article that not many people (including me) read or even take their time to look over.
- I usually go on Wikipedia first to get an overview of the topic and try to find more specific details that I can research and look up on. I then go to the library database to find articles. I usually use Wikipedia as a guide as to what to research and as a background. I rarely look for books in the library unless a book is needed as a source and I do not usually look at the reference section of Wikipedia.

Regarding the quality of sources cited in Wikipedia, respondents displayed a concern about their overall reliability:

- I was taught not to use Wikipedia as a reliable source, so searching through Wikipedia to find a related article would not be likely.
- I am not sure how reliable and credible the links from the references on Wikipedia are.
- While there are many citations available in Wikipedia, at times some sources [links] are dead or quotes are buried within dense texts. I would feel more comfortable searching for sources myself to double-check Wikipedia.
- Many of the sites that Wikipedia [has] may very well be credible, but they just look messy and cluttered and it makes me not want to get more information from them. I barely ever scroll down far enough to see the reference notes because the articles are usually very long and provide necessary information. If I go to Wikipedia, I would prefer to go there for a summary, but not for very detailed and specific information.

DO STUDENTS USE AND VALUE WIKIPEDIA AS A GATEWAY FOR ACADEMIC RESEARCH?

Overall, students' attitude toward and understanding of Wikipedia is complicated and even contradictory, according to these experiments. It should be noted that while the participants in the study were relatively novice researchers, the results of the pre- and post-tests indicated that they had a fairly advanced understanding of issues related to the authority of academic sources. One hundred percent of the pre-test responses indicated that students preferred academic journal articles to newspaper sources, when asked which they would pick to include in an academic paper (though, as mentioned, in the controlled assignment, they mostly relied on recognizable popular news sources). Ninety percent said that academic sources are more likely to have the best research on a given topic. The data seems to indicate that students in the sample found Wikipedia to be generally a good starting point for exploratory research. The open-ended responses suggest that students often start with Wikipedia and then move on to other sources, which sometimes include the library databases. This indicates that even novice researchers can recognize that Wikipedia is best used as a gateway to academic research, rather than as an end point.

However, later in the survey, students also showed that they were unsure of the credibility of Wikipedia and had been warned by faculty not to use it at all. This indicates the same ambiguity, also noted in a study by Sormunen and Lehtio (2011), which showed that, while students use Wikipedia, they are unlikely to admit it or document it as a background source to their instructors and professors. Furthermore, while students indicated in their responses that they may sometimes use Wikipedia as a stepping-stone to library databases, they also indicated that they are just as likely to go to Google or another search engine and, moreover, they are very unlikely to consult the library catalog. This suggests an inconclusive link between Wikipedia and the library resources, which could be strengthened. One recommendation from this finding is for information literacy sessions to incorporate "correct" scenarios of using Wikipedia for exploratory research, by showing students how they can locate materials cited in Wikipedia in the library databases and catalog.

DO STUDENTS NEED ADDITIONAL IL ASSISTANCE WHEN EVALUATING SOURCES IN WIKIPEDIA?

The results of these experiments suggests that in the area of information literacy, there are many possibilities for librarians to embrace new ways of teaching in relation to Wikipedia. The fact that students indicated that ease of access is very important to their selections of academic sources confirms prior research, including a 2013 study by Mizrachi and Bates, which showed that students consistently arrange their information-gathering, both physical and digital, in ways that maximize accessibility and visibility (p. 1603). Authority and credibility were ranked below accessibility and availability, which seems to confirm the hypotheses that students require more assistance when evaluating sources on the open web. This could also be addressed in a typical IL session. Moreover, the fact that students considered "extensive bibliographies" to be unimportant is also problematic, since it may indicate that they need assistance in understanding the value of bibliographies to academic research generally.

One of the major findings of this study is that students can benefit from using a structured rubric within Wikipedia to examine the quality of the citations provided. In fact, using the rubric caused students to second-guess their choices and engage in more nuanced thinking about the credibility of their sources. It is interesting that a small percentage of respondents even admitted that the external citations they chose in Wikipedia were not credible at all. The data, overall, indicates that applying IL rubrics to Wikipedia entries can be of benefit to students (figure 8.4). By embracing the new 2016 *Association of College & Research Libraries (ACRL) Framework* and the use of rubrics in the classroom, librarians can really make a difference in how students perceive and use Wikipedia, as well as how critical they are of information on the open web generally. The framework stresses information as process and authority as construction, which are exactly paralleled in Wikipedia's environment (see Association of College & Research Libraries, 2016). The use of rubrics, in fact, strengthens the case in favor of Wikipedia as a useful and generally accurate source, which positions librarians and Wikipedia editors closer together than they may have otherwise assumed.

FIGURE 8.4

Benefit of the rubric

Q31: Is using an evaluation scale to determine the authority/quality of a source beneficial to your ability to select sources?

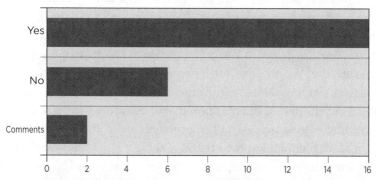

#	Answer	%	Count
1	Yes	66.67%	16
2	No	25.00%	6
3	Comments	8.33%	2
	Total	**100%**	**24**

Comments
I'm not sure, we never learned how to evaluate sources.
I feel like that is an important skill to learn.
It will allow people to review the information themselves to make an informed decision.

CASE STUDY OF LIBRARIANS WRITING IN WIKIPEDIA

As described in the introduction, the study of students' use of Wikipedia was inspired by RUL's participation in the Wikipedia Visiting Scholars program. The results of the study are meant to inform whether librarians wish to incorporate Wikipedia into their work as IL instructors and in efforts to promote the use and discoverability of library sources on the open web. Since the results confirmed the fact that students continue to rely heavily on Wikipedia and, moreover, are challenged by it, in terms of being able to critically evaluate it, librarians at this institution decided to move forward with the Visiting Scholars program.

To participate in this project, we formed a team of seven academic librarians specializing in the subject fields of jazz study, health science, Asian studies, scholarly communication, and information literacy. The goal of the project was to increase the visibility of library content on the open web by creating a Wikipedia entry that highlights a distinguished area of research for the university. In addition, librarians wanted to see if it is useful to incorporate Wikipedia further into library services. Since librarians had limited Wikipedia editing experience, two experienced Wikipedia editors ("Wikipedians") were recruited through the Wikipedia Visiting Scholar program to provide assistance. These individuals worked remotely with librarians to familiarize them with Wikipedia's editorial rules and etiquette. The Wikipedians also created a project sandbox (i.e., a space in which to write article drafts) in Wikipedia and shared useful editorial guidelines and templates. The Wikipedians hosted two basic training sessions, during which librarians were given additional editing tips and shortcuts. This support enabled two of the librarians (one of whom is an author of this article) in the team to begin the writing and editing process. When problems arose, the Wikipedians were available for consultation. For their part, the subject librarians hosted database training sessions to help the Wikipedians efficiently access the libraries' licensed and unique collection. In a period of three months, this collaboration resulted in the creation of a new Wikipedia article entry on a health sciences topic.

The successful recruitment of the two Wikipedians through the Wikipedia Visiting Scholar program was critical. Their involvement was helpful on several fronts. The training sessions and editorial support they provided enabled the librarians to begin and complete the project within a short period of time. When the librarians felt uncomfortable using Wikipedia's wikitext markup code for citations, the Wikipedians showed the librarians how to enable the "Visual Editor" feature that allowed the librarians to easily edit and, critically, to create citations without having to memorize wikitext. The Wikipedians' assistance enabled librarians to quickly learn how to create and edit Wikipedia content. Supported by authoritative, verifiable reference sources and peer-reviewed by a subject expert with established credentials, the published article contributes considerable informational value and quality to the site and reflects a close collaboration between the Wikipedians and the librarians.

CAN LIBRARIANS BENEFIT FROM ENGAGING WITH WIKIPEDIA EDITING PRACTICES IN THE CROWD-SOURCED WRITING ENVIRONMENT? YES! BUT IT'S COMPLICATED . . .

Through the experience of writing a Wikipedia article, the authors learned that all Wikipedia content must adhere to a set of editorial guidelines, conventions, and etiquette. In addition, because the researchers were keen on learning how the new article would be received by other editors, they closely monitored the "Talk" tab—a forum for editors to discuss and communicate how to improve an article—and the "View History" tab—a page that lists all revisions made to a page, as well as the reviewers' information and date and time information—and they regularly tracked the article's traffic statistics. From monitoring the article's status, the researchers learned how the crowd reviewing process works in Wikipedia. Another important lesson learned is that what makes Wikipedia unique is that it involves crowds, not discipline experts. Barnhisel and Rapchak (2014) noted that Wikipedia may never be objectively reliable for that very reason—its content is not overseen by credentialed experts (Barnhisel and Rapchak 2014, 156). Rather, reliability can hinge on popularity and the assumption of collective wisdom: the more popular a Wikipedia page is, the more frequently it will be viewed, vetted, and corrected for errors by Wikipedia users. Librarians are not always comfortable with this idea of crowd wisdom, but it is important for the future of the LIS profession that we continue to challenge ourselves and engage in dialogue with the Wikipedia community.

The case study seems to indicate that librarians can benefit from engaging in Wikipedia editing practices by learning about the wiki platform and contributing scholarly materials to enhance the overall accuracy of the encyclopedia, which is one of the goals of the Visiting Scholar program. As we have also shown by our discussion of the student study, there is ample opportunity for librarians to then pass that knowledge on to students and engage in creative and effective IL instruction through Wikipedia. However, there is more to be done in drafting the future of the relationship between Wikipedia and the academic library, and RUL is still looking for concrete ways to go beyond this pilot. Engaging students in meaningful ways with Wikipedia takes time and expertise, and librarians need the support of Wikipedia editors to become more confident in both technical matters and the culture and philosophy of being a Wikipedia contributor. Internally, librarians have to also rethink their own roles in the organization and, with their administrators, find ways to structure Wikipedia work within their busy daily activities.

Meanwhile, the "low hanging fruit" of collaboration with Wikipedia continues to involve areas where many libraries are already working, such as integrating Wikipedia into one-shot and semester-long courses and continuing to engage students and faculty in editing Wikipedia. At RUL, librarians are already teaching several first-year seminars about Wikipedia, and the researchers have obtained a grant to execute a follow-up study which involves the use of Wikipedia by academic faculty, whose voice also has to be included in the conversation. We hope that, in the near future, we will be able to actively involve all of our communities—students, faculty, librarians, and administrators—in productive discussions about the many ways Wikipedia intersects with our work as librarians.

CONCLUSION

This study involved two parts: a survey of undergraduate students' use of Wikipedia and a case study of one academic library's involvement in the Wikipedia Visiting Scholars program, resulting in a librarian-authored Wikipedia article. The two methods were intended to inform each other and the future of library services involving Wikipedia. Both types of involvement with the online encyclopedia can potentially lead librarians in new directions and define new service models—both in terms of hiring new library professionals and structuring academic library work. From the student survey, the researchers discovered that students consider Wikipedia to be a reasonably reliable gateway to information. It remains inconclusive, however, whether or not Wikipedia directly links to a library's holdings. The results also show that students need additional information literacy assistance, as in the form of a rubric, in order to critically evaluate source material in Wikipedia. Finally, the experience of two academic librarians writing in Wikipedia, as part of the Wikipedia Visiting Scholars program, shows potential for the future of the library's involvement with the online encyclopedia. As a result of this pilot, RUL librarians are energized to continue studying the role of Wikipedia in the research practices of both students and faculty and to maintain a collaborative relationship with Wikipedia editors.

REFERENCES

Alexa Company. 2015. "The Top 500 Sites on the Web." www.alexa.com/topsites.

Association of College & Research Libraries. 2016. *Framework for Information Literacy for Higher Education.* www.ala.org/acrl/standards/ilframework.

Barnhisel, Greg, and Marcia Rapchak. 2014. "Wikipedia and the Wisdom of Crowds: A Student Project." *Communications in Information Literacy* 8, no. 1: 145–59.

Mizrachi, D., and M. J. Bates. 2013. "Undergraduates' Personal Academic Information Management and the Consideration of Time and Task-Urgency." *Journal of the American Society for Information Science and Technology* 64, no. 8: 1590–1607.

Sormunen, Eero, and Leeni Lehtio. 2011. "Authoring Wikipedia Articles as an Information Literacy Assignment: Copy-Pasting or Expressing New Understanding in One's Own Words?" *Information Research: An International Electronic Journal* 16, no. 4. www.info rmationr.net/ir/16-4/paper503.html.

TurnItIn. 2015. "The Source Educational Evaluation Rubric (SEER)." http://go.turnitin.com/ seer-rubric.

Wikipedia. 2015. "Wikipedia: The Wikipedia Library/Wikipedia Visiting Scholars." https:// en.wikipedia.org/w/index.php?title=Wikipedia:The_Wikipedia_Library/Wikipedia _Visiting_Scholars&oldid=661851131.

Edit-a-Thons and Beyond

SARA SNYDER

T he first time I heard the phrase "Wikipedia edit-a-thon" was in 2011. I remember it clearly because it seemed so crazy to me at the time. Volunteers assembling to edit a crowd-sourced encyclopedia together, *for hours?* Had I died and gone to nerd heaven?

The Smithsonian's Archives of American Art, where I worked back then, was hosting our first-ever Wikipedian in Residence, Sarah Stierch. Stierch suggested that we hold a daylong "Backstage Pass and Edit-a-Thon" event, inviting members of the Wikimedia community behind the scenes for a tour of our achives' closed stacks. This would be followed by an afternoon of article creation and enhancement focused on the notable artists represented in the archives' collections. I was intrigued and excited by the prospect of engaging a completely new audience with our materials, especially the online finding aids and digitized collections that were at the center of my own work there.

"Figure out how many people we can accommodate," I remember Stierch telling me, "because there is definitely going to be a waiting list!"

Since 2011, I've organized and attended dozens of Wikipedia edit-a-thons, most of them connected to libraries, archives, and museums in the Washington, DC region. I've seen huge turnouts and intimate gatherings, watched successes and struggles, forged friendships with repeat attendees, and given "first edit" tutorials to hundreds of would-be Wikipedians. Along the way, I stopped thinking of myself as an outside interloper from the GLAM (Galleries, Libraries, Archives, and Museums) space, and embraced my identity as a member of the Wikipedia community—a vibrant, global, multilingual network of passionate open-knowledge advocates. Wikipedia edit-a-thons have transformed the way I think about outreach. They make the digital labor of writing and editing an online encyclopedia into a rich, interactive experience that is filled with real-world faces, names, personalities, and memories.

So how does one host a successful edit-a-thon? What is the secret? The key is to take the core structure of the event, and then tweak it to suit your goals. In software engineering, there is the concept of a "design pattern," which refers to a repeatable solution—a flexible yet tried-and-true method for achieving a certain outcome. In this chapter, I'll discuss the edit-a-thon (or sometimes, "editathon") as a "pattern": one proven, reliable way to plan a successful Wikipedia-focused event. I'll also talk about tips and resources for maximizing the impact of your edit-a-thon by focusing on your objectives. Rather than a rigid formula, I hope you'll come to see how the edit-a-thon is just one template which can be customized to meet the goals and constraints of your library or organization.

I also hope that by gaining some awareness of the history of edit-a-thons, and how they became popular in the library world, you will feel inspired and empowered to reshape them, and even generate entirely new types of Wikipedia events in libraries, using your own creativity and professional savvy. For while it is the best-known type of event at present, and has achieved a certain level of "brand recognition," the Wikipedia edit-a-thon format can and should be treated with flexibility. I'll finish the chapter by arguing that we information professionals would be well-served to think beyond the type of edit-a-thons currently being held and explore or invent new types of events that help foster collaboration not only with the Wikimedia community, but also among and between GLAMs ourselves. GLAM/Wikimedia partnerships can and should be relationships of mutual benefit where compatible educational missions are thoughtfully aligned, and there is still a lot of great work for us to do together to make that mutuality a reality.

A HISTORY OF WIKIPEDIA EDIT-A-THONS, AND THE GLAM-WIKI CONNECTION

Like any good student of history, I now exhort you to understand the present moment we inhabit by casting your eyes on the past! Not the distant past, but, then again, in Internet years, the inception of Wikipedia is practically ancient history. The encyclopedia was founded in 2001, with rapid growth in popularity and the rise of a self-organized contributor community defining its first decade of existence. After these years of rapid growth, maturing internal organizational and communications structures meant that the Wikimedia community was finally able to start looking outward. In 2006 there began an organized global series of "Wikipedia Academies"; these were public outreach events, usually lasting one or two days, that were designed to coach academics and other subject matter experts in how to contribute to Wikipedia. These events were often hosted by academic or scholarly organizations such as universities or nonprofits, and all but one of these "academies" took place outside of North America.

Outreach and partnership efforts with cultural entities such as GLAMs, in particular, reached a critical point around 2008–2009. Numerous GLAM professionals had been attempting to participate in Wikipedia for years, but with mixed success. Many saw their first edits reverted, and felt frustrated that the Wikipedia community didn't welcome or appreciate their authority or professional expertise. On the Wikimedian side, a number of community members perceived their relationship to cultural institutions as a mission focused on "content liberation": acquiring high-resolution imagery of artifacts and objects—by any means necessary—to be uploaded for use by Wiki projects. This was more about hacking and scraping websites for images than it was about talking to and engaging with the GLAMs in question. This approach and ethos began to shift with a series of extraordinary collaborations. In 2008, a partnership between Wikimedia Deutschland and the German Federal Archives, Das Bundesarchiv, resulted in the donation of over 100,000 archival images to Wikimedia Commons. In addition, in 2008 the "Wikipedia Loves Art" photographic scavenger hunt was held across numerous art museums around the world, including North America; and the first museum "backstage pass" tour for Wikipedians was held in Sydney's Powerhouse Museum in 2009.[1]

The rapid progress in GLAM-Wiki relationships that followed was due, in no small part, to the intensive and pioneering outreach efforts of an Australian Wikimedian named Liam Wyatt. In 2010 Wyatt spent five weeks as an unpaid volunteer at the British Museum, serving as the world's first ever Wikipedian in Residence. He took care to draw attention to the shared educational mission and values that GLAM staff and Wikipedians are likely to possess, emphasizing commonalities over differences between the two groups of volunteers and professionals. The unprecedented role of an in-house Wikipedian at a national museum led to mainstream media coverage in the *New York Times* and elsewhere, provoking widespread interest and excitement within the Wikimedia community, and catching the attention of other GLAM institutions.[2] The following year, 2011, marked a remarkable turning point in the United States in particular, when outreach and education efforts led to the spread of Wikipedians in Residence to North American organizations like the National Archives and Records Administration and, as I mentioned in my introduction, the Smithsonian Institution's Archives of American Art.

The year 2011 also witnessed the coinage and first use of the term "Wikipedia edit-a-thon" to describe a public event. The portmanteau of "edit" and "marathon" is attributed to the British Wikimedians Mike Peel and Thomas Dalton, who helped to organize the January 2011 "Backstage Pass and edit-a-thon" at the British Library.[3] "Backstage pass" events had been happening for several years, but the addition of a "marathon" of dedicated editing time—and a fun, catchy name for it—were notable innovations. Later that same year, October also saw the establishment of the first annual coordinated "Wikipedia Loves Libraries" events, which "brought Wikipedians and librarians together for knowledge-sharing and edit-a-thon events across the U.S. and Canada" (although the term "edit-a-thon" appears on the "Wikipedia Loves Libraries" page description now, it was not added there until a later edit, made in 2013).

Edit-a-thons in libraries, archives, and museums continued to spread during 2011–2013, including events that were frequently organized around a special theme, collection, or exhibition. The release of the Wikimedia Foundation's first ever comprehensive editor survey in spring 2011 revealed the incredible fact that over 90 percent of active Wikipedia editors were male: a striking gender gap. Gender gap awareness gave rise to events intended to help address that lack, such as edit-a-thons dedicated to creating or expanding biographies of notable women artists or scientists. In 2014 the organizers of the Art+Feminism initiative launched their project, and they brought Wikipedia edit-a-thons into the mainstream consciousness, thanks to their leaders' exceptional energy and communications savvy. The concept of edit-a-thons as a means of addressing bias or imbalance in the encyclopedia became a major feature of the public's awareness of the Wikimedia community.

The face of the edit-a-thon has evolved and shifted dramatically in the few short years since its inception in 2011. Notably, the impetus for these early partnerships and events came from within the Wikimedia volunteer community, and it focused on *established* Wikipedians leveraging the knowledge and collections in the repositories for the benefit of the encyclopedia project. What was, perhaps, not fully anticipated back then was just how powerful the concept of the edit-a-thon would turn out to be as a tool for recruiting members of the public as *new* editors and advocates, even those who had never considered contributing to Wikimedia projects before. As a case in point, the first Backstage Pass and Edit-a-thon that I helped organize, in 2011, was open and advertised to established Wikipedians only, via invitations on their user talk pages. There were no instructional presentations about editing at the event; we didn't need them. Instead, experienced Wikipedians showed up and got right down to work, amidst the hovering observations of our Smithsonian staff and interns. And just as Sarah Stierch had predicted, there was indeed a waiting list to attend. At the time, the term "Wikipedia edit-a-thon" was novel, something which few people had heard of, as evidenced by the tenor of the press coverage that the event received in the *Chronicle of Philanthropy*. What a contrast to the current style of edit-a-thon, where editing tutorials for new contributors tend to play a central role.

Today, the term "edit-a-thon" has itself become commonplace in the U.S. GLAM sector, with librarians, archivists, and museum professionals showing a common familiarity with the concept. Many of us have attended or helped organize such events ourselves. What follows are some practical, hands-on recommendations for holding a successful Wikipedia event or meet-up.

A GLAM INSIDER'S PROCESS FOR PLANNING WIKIPEDIA EDIT-A-THONS

Step 1: Setting a Goal for Your Event: Why Do You Want to Hold an Edit-a-Thon?

The early edit-a-thon events, which were often organized by established members of the Wikimedia community or Wikipedians in Residence, were focused on improving the quality of the encyclopedia around a very specific focus area (the Hoxne hoard, American artists in the 1913 Armory Show, etc.) by incorporating GLAM knowledge and digital assets. Success for these events was measured in article number and quality. The Art+Feminism events have the goal of filling gender-related content gaps in Wikipedia by increasing the number of female contributors. Success for them could be measured by the numbers of new women editors participating. What organizational goals could a Wikipedia event (or series of events) help *your* library to meet? Talk these goals over with your colleagues or leaders; agree on them, and write them down. It seems like an obvious step, but we often neglect to clarify our goals for an event or initiative, which makes it hard to understand and evaluate whether they were successful afterward, or to make plans on where to change our approach for the next time.

A commitment to improving the online encyclopedia is *always* a goal, an unwavering principle of the Wikimedia community, that we all must agree to in order to proceed. But why shouldn't there be other, complementary goals that spring from within the library itself, and are connected to your library's specific mission and strategic goals? I have never seen a library mission statement that runs counter to the mission of Wikimedia projects. On the contrary, they tend to be remarkably well-aligned, often speaking in nearly interchangeable terms about freedom, access, education, and online reach. Therefore, event planners should think hard about their own mission and goals. For example, is there a specific strength in your library's collections that should be made easier to discover by using those assets to improve Wikipedia? Is information literacy, or educating students or patrons on how to evaluate sources, a strategic goal? Does your repository focus on a specific region or history? Is addressing gender, geographic, or linguistic gaps in the current Wikipedia important to your library? Remember that there are almost 300 different language Wikipedias out there, so this is not a project that is limited to English; engaging native speakers of other languages to edit or translate Wikipedia in their own language may be appealing. Do you have initiatives related to educating patrons on a particular subject area, and can Wikipedia be a complementary tool for that existing effort? Perhaps your goal even includes education and training on how Wikipedia works for your own library staff or faculty? In sum: is the primary impact you are hoping to achieve one that changes the shape of the *encyclopedia,* or one that has an educational impact on *people* such as patrons, students, or staff? Depending on what is most important to you, you may come up with a different set of strategies.

In my view, the most successful edit-a-thons are not just about producing the greatest number of citations, new articles, backlinks, and image uploads. The fact is, a significant impact on the encyclopedia itself will take time and dedication from repeat contributors, not just sporadic interjections by newbies. As wonderful and fulfilling as those first edits might be in terms of meeting educational or information literacy goals, they might only gain you a handful of quality paragraphs on Wikipedia.org. And while the Wikimedia community might be tempted to try and measure success by the number of new recruits that are converted into committed contributors and editors, I'm not sure this is the only measure of success either. Edit-a-thons can be about an unquantifiable opening of minds, and learning about where Wikipedia—and, crucially, the verifiable, factual sources it cites—fit into the modern information ecosystem. Edits happen, certainly, but the best events could just as reasonably be called "learn-a-thons."

Step 2: Strategizing on Audiences, Presenters, and Sources

Now that your goal(s) and focus for the edit-a-thon are defined and written down, the decisions about your location, schedule, and agenda can flow consequently from this focus. Who are you hoping will attend, to best meet these goals? Let's imagine, for example, that your library has a strong regional focus, bolstered by special collections; that your staff has expertise on reliable sources about the geographic area; and that you have a mission to help the public learn about local history. Your goal might therefore be to improve coverage related to your region on Wikipedia. To meet this goal, your ideal audience might include as many experienced Wikipedians as possible, plus a good helping of tech-savvy history enthusiasts or students—good researchers and writers who are likely to really make an impact on content. The more digitally savvy the participants, I find, the more work they are quickly able to accomplish on the encyclopedia itself. You might also want to conceive of the work as a series of events, since one edit-a-thon might not be long enough to make the impact on your to-do list.

Or if, by contrast, your goal is focused more on cultivating a community or audience around information literacy, you might not choose to restrict yourselves to a topic or theme at all. You might instead sponsor a "Wikipedia club" or a meet-up series, where patrons can edit as a community on topics that they personally find to be of interest. Presentations can be short, or more community-driven. You could work through a curriculum of Wikipedia skills or tutorials together, earning badges or prizes along the way. In either case, knowing the demographics of your ideal, target attendees will help you make choices about the subsequent logistics.

Attracting and Tracking RSVPs

Once the right audiences are identified, reaching them takes creativity and planning. At least a month of lead time is recommended, so that you have time to contact the relevant groups. Think about your ideal attendees, and what e-mail lists or social media, meet-up, community, civic, and campus groups they might belong to. Depending on the preferences and generational characteristics of your target audience, you can put a listing in a print paper or use an online platform like Meetup.com or Eventbrite.com. If you have a small budget for paid social media promotion, a targeted Facebook ad or event listing, for example, can bring good results for a modest cost.

It is traditional for Wikipedia events to keep an attendee list on the wiki-based meet-up page itself, but this can be a tricky place to track initial RSVPs, since new editors may not understand how to add their name to the list. As an organizer, I always prefer to collect RSVPs that include e-mail addresses, so that I can reach out to attendees with reminders before the event (time and location reminders, instructions, reminders to bring a laptop with them and any other needed supplies). Think about how you might collect this information while also respecting users' privacy.

Presentations and Tutorials

Since most edit-a-thons will attract at least a few new editors, and often more than a few, there is likely a need for at least a short "how to edit" tutorial. The person who leads this tutorial should have some familiarity with how Wikipedia works, and be ready to answer questions about it, both during and after the presentation. There are lots of example presentations out there, from the free, downloadable slide decks that Art+Feminism has put together, to presentations given by other members of the community (see an example of a new editor tutorial I posted recently to Slideshare.net, http://bit.ly/2qNM15i). I like to aim for presentations of twenty minutes or less, but since there is quite a bit of information for new people to absorb, and the community's norms and best practices are very important to ultimately being successful on Wikipedia, it pays to be comprehensive on matters like the "Five Pillars of Wikipedia," how to avoid conflicts of interest, and understanding the basic navigation of the editing menus.

Depending on the goals you've identified, and whether a specific theme is involved, an additional content-focused presentation or a tour could share knowledge and spark curiosity about the topic—if interesting, and logistically feasible. Just as important is identifying a focused, not too overwhelming to-do list, accumulating relevant resources (both print and digital) for research and citation within the encyclopedia.

Step 3: Logistics—Where, When, How

You've identified goals, audiences, presenters, and sources. The intellectual heavy lifting of "why" and "who" has been done. Now what about extension cords? Scheduling the right room? Coffee and cookies?

Powered Up

A colleague or staff member who is familiar with the logistics of hosting events is a great asset here. A variety of skills are needed to pull together a successful edit-a-thon, from digital resources knowledge, to marketing/outreach skill, to being good at calculating how many cups of coffee 25 people might consume over the course of 5 hours. The coffee mention here isn't gratuitous; it is actually really important. Would you run a marathon without water and fuel for your body? Of course not. Similarly, no one can run a successful edit-a-thon without power for people (caffeine, calories) and power for machines (power strips, extension cords, and super Wi-Fi).

If you don't have a budget for refreshments, look into Wikimedia Foundation grants, or inquire into whether there is a local Wikipedia user group or chapter in your region that might be able to help by applying for Wikimedia Foundation funding on your behalf. Or visit local bakeries or restaurants, and see if someone might be willing to sponsor your event by an in-kind donation of food or drink. If you are unable to provide any refreshments at all, or the meeting room you've chosen doesn't permit it, please do let your attendees know that they might want to include water or other snacks to bring with them, to stay hydrated and keep their energy up during the event. In addition, you should understand that the more you give them to eat and drink, the *longer* they will stick around to work on helping you achieve your goals.

Registering Accounts

I highly recommend asking potential new attendees to register a Wikipedia account and make a few experimental edits before the event begins (give them very specific instructions, and ask them to submit their user names to you in advance, so that you can track if they've done it). The reasons for this are twofold. First, there is a limit on the number of new Wikipedia accounts that can be created on the same IP address range in a day. To overcome this limitation, you either need a full Wikipedia administrator, or someone with account creator rights, who can override the automatic block. Second, there are editing restrictions on new accounts. Until an account is 4 days old and has 10 edits, it is limited in a number of ways, including new article creation. It is important to be aware of the IP limit, and plan for the potential issues.

Optimal Schedules

Based on your desired audience, the time and day will be really important. A Saturday event will help you reach people who work during the weekdays. However, you may be competing with the outdoors and people's scheduled weekend plans or family obligations. Friday afternoons are often a good compromise, since students and other people may have flexible schedules that allow them to come at that time. However, this could change, depending on your location and the patterns and schedules of your target audience.

Table 9.1 is an example of a schedule for a full-day edit-a-thon focused on women artists at my current place of work, the Smithsonian American Art Museum (SAAM). This is not meant to be an "ideal" model, but is just one example of how you can think about organizing the day.

You may find that a full day's event is beyond what you can commit to. But for substantial editing to take place, you really do need at least a couple of hours. I personally like the pace of a four-hour afternoon event; so long as presentations are kept to a minimum, it is long enough to get into an editing groove. I've run edit-a-thons as short as sixty minutes, but in those cases, the participants were experienced Wikipedians who were able to hit the ground running. In a 60 or 90-minute event with new editors, you'll spend a lot of time just doing your "How to" presentation and teaching them the mechanics, leaving very little time for research or writing.

TABLE 9.1

Sample edit-a-thon schedule

Time	Activity	Location
10:00 a.m.	• Check-in at the museum entrance • Coffee, introductions, and computer set-up in the event space	SAAM entrance, 8th ST NW & G ST NW, Washington, D.C.
10:15 - 11:00 a.m.	• Behind-the-scenes tour focused on women artists in SAAM's collection	SAAM 2nd floor, permanent collection galleries
11:00 a.m.	• Round-robin attendee introductions • Presentation: Introduction to Editing Wikipedia, with Sara Snyder • Begin editing!	MacMillan Education Center, SAAM
1:00 p.m.	• Lunch arrives (sandwiches courtesy of the Wikimedia DC chapter) • Continue editing!	MacMillan Education Center, SAAM
5:00 p.m.	• Event ends	

Providing Resources

If your edit-a-thon is focused on a theme, a bit of research legwork in identifying quality sources is a benefit and time-saver that we can offer attendees. I like to bring a mix of print books into every edit-a-thon, to help engage the attendees and remind them that the online encyclopedia actually really values and favors print sources as citations in Wikipedia articles. In addition, I recommend pulling together some links to online sources, and including them alongside the topic in your to-do list.

For example, the extract below was one entry on a "to-do" list from a March 2013 Women in the Arts edit-a-thon at the Archives of American Art. The article was a red link, meaning that the page had not yet been created; any underlined text represents hyperlinks to authoritative online sources.

Rosalind Bengelsdorf Browne—American painter, *works in the Smithsonian American Art Museum, biography on the Luce Foundation Center website, Rosalind Bengelsdorf Browne Papers in Archives of American Art*

Because the research on Rosalind Bengelsdorf Browne had already been started, and high-quality sources suggested, it was easy for the edit-a-thon participant—a fairly inexperienced editor—to create and publish a new article that day. It's still there.

THINKING BEYOND THE EDIT-A-THON

Type the query WP:Editathon (yes, with the colon) into Wikipedia's search box, or even Google, for that matter, and you'll pull up a page called "How to run an editathon." This is a Wikimedia community-focused perspective on how edit-a-thons can and should be organized. There is a lot of advice on this page, and much of it is good, but—like a lot of Wikipedia instruction pages, and possibly this chapter—it can also be a bit overwhelming.

I know I've just spent quite a few pages singing the praises of the edit-a-thon, but I also want to remind us all that there was a time, not so very long ago, when nobody had heard of Wikipedia edit-a-thons at all. This was a model for engagement that was invented and refined by a series of volunteers, regular people thinking creatively about how we all might interact with each other and with a massively networked online knowledge project. It is one design pattern, but it is not the only way.

These days, I think a lot about sustaining editorship, not just as an annual event during Women's History Month, but as an ongoing part of someone's day-to-day life, or even as part of their job. What if every time a cataloger or archivist updated an online record, or published a finding aid, they took a peep at Wikipedia to see if it could use a similar sprucing up? Do we really need an "a-thon" to meet institutional goals for better encyclopedic coverage of subject matter that we hold dear? Or could that content be created and sustained another way? I've been thinking of starting a series of virtual collaborations at my own museum, "On Fridays We Wiki," that would just be an hour or two of staff learning and contributing to American art-related Wikimedia projects. Other models might mean engaging more of the technical staff to participate in ambitious data projects like Wikidata, and see where small events might be able to make a big impact in that emerging space.

Or, if public engagement or education, rather than content, is the primary goal, then what if instead of planning big-deal events, we threw smaller, more frequent "Wikipedia parties"? Perhaps they would feel more like the meetings of a book club or lunchtime knitting circle than global, newsworthy initiatives like the Art+Feminism juggernaut. This idea has been promoted before, by the Wikimedia Foundation staffer Siko Bouterse among others (her 2013 blog post is called "Let's throw more Wikipedia editing parties"), and it is a notion worth revisiting within the context of a library or other GLAM institution. Could we host small-scale, informal Wikipedia editing office hours . . . or "wiki-hours"?

There is wisdom in the notion of starting small, and perhaps piggybacking on events or activities that your library is already committed to, and adding a Wikipedia learning component. OCLC's Merrilee Proffitt and the OCLC Wiki-pedian in Residence Monika Sengul-Jones are sources of numerous good ideas on this topic. For example, they've suggested that author-focused events such as talks and book signings could benefit from a topically related Wikipedia editing or citation-adding component, either before or after the event. Another idea is a combination of local history architecture walks and Wikipedia editing. For example, the attendees might first read over a set of Wikipedia articles about the local area, then be led on the history/architecture walk, where they observe and learn about the local built environment. Upon returning, participants could improve the articles based on what they learned and using some preselected library sources.

These are a handful of ideas, but they are far from the only ones. Above all, I encourage us as a profession to feel free to remix the edit-a-thon model, or invent something entirely new. The next popular Wikimedia event portmanteau is out there, just waiting for *you*, Wikibrarians, to coin it!

NOTES

1. Seb Chan, "Working with Wikipedia—Backstage Pass at the Powerhouse Museum," *Fresh + New(er)*, April 2, 2009, www.freshandnew.org/2009/04/working-with-wikipedia -backstage-pass-at-the-powerhouse-museum.

2. Noam Cohen, "Venerable British Museum Enlists in the Wikipedia Revolution," *New York Times*, June 4, 2010, www.nytimes.com/2010/06/05/arts/design/05wiki.html.

3. Published sources relating to the origins of the term "edit-a-thon" are scarce, but Mike Peel mentions his role on his website, www.mikepeel.net/wikimedia/, and the story was confirmed to me by Liam Wyatt and other community members in an exchange over Twitter; see https://twitter.com/sosarasays/status/858020485421989889.

Embracing Wikipedia
at the New York Public Library
A Personal View

BOB KOSOVSKY

t seems laughable that in a world with so much media and commercial saturation, people would be drawn to writing encyclopedia articles. Yet this attraction is exactly what has made Wikipedia not just a hobby but a passion among thousands of people the world over.

It is easy to argue that editing Wikipedia could raise your library's profile and drive more traffic to your physical library. But working with Wikipedia in a deeper way allows you to achieve engagement and to reach deeper levels of connection between your library, your library patrons, and your community—all using Wikipedia as a source of that connection.

It is my firm belief that libraries and library staff should embrace Wikipedia. I'd like to tell how we at the New York Public Library (NYPL) have embraced Wikimedia projects by setting forth a variety of levels of engagement.

TYING UNIQUE CONTENT TO THE WORLD'S LARGEST ENCYCLOPEDIA

At the lowest level of engagement, a number of our staff have added external links to our archival collections when the subject of a Wikipedia article is a person or organization for which NYPL holds papers or records. This is a practice that is done by many libraries and archives, and our practice probably looks similar to many others. Our workflow for newly processed archival collections includes encouraging the processing archivist to add a link to the collection and its finding aid in the relevant Wikipedia article. For the thousands of legacy collections or those that have been processed and made available before we adopted these practices, staff in the relevant division of our library can create links to those collections. This allows Wikipedia readers to learn about the wealth of archival collections related to a subject of interest.

In this respect, NYPL's Wikipedia engagement is diffuse. Thus far there is not a large enough community of confident Wikipedia editors among the staff to organize a coordinated Wikipedia effort. Interested staff have the freedom to take it upon themselves to edit as they see fit and as time allows. While this may seem somewhat chaotic, in truth it allows greater freedom, since individuals can edit to the maximum of their abilities and not have to worry about adhering to institution-wide guidelines.

Most editors will leave your library's links to archival materials alone, recognizing them as important resources for researching the topic at hand. Wikipedia editors are watchful for "external link spam" because "adding external links to an article or user page for the purpose of promoting a website or a product is not allowed, and is considered to be spam." In some ways, adding links to archival collection descriptions can look, to a protective editor, like link spam, and there have been times when the links we have added have been removed by other editors. While to a librarian or archivist, a link to an archival resource is an obvious good, to others it may appear to be just an attempt at promotion. And indeed, because of its open nature and the huge amount of web traffic it receives, Wikipedia is a tempting target for those who simply want to promote their product or website. Because this happens with great frequency, a less-experienced editor may mistake a link to a finding aid as link spam. In such cases, the librarian editor who inserted the link must contact the editor who wants it removed and explain why it is not an attempt at promotion, but rather provides important information that helps to amplify the article topic. However, there is an important lesson here for eager new editors: you should not be using Wikipedia as a means of "promotion" and you should consider your purpose in editing Wikipedia. Is your sole purpose to promote use of your collections? If your sole activity in editing Wikipedia is to add links to your collections, you may well be accused of link spam. When adding your links, think of such editing as your initial step in engaging your library with Wikipedia. Perhaps you can add links to other related archival collections held at other institutions, or perhaps you can take some time to improve the article in some other small way. These small steps will not only increase your own confidence with editing, but will also contribute bit by bit to improving Wikipedia.

CREATING NEW ARTICLES: LEVERAGING STAFF EXPERTISE ALONGSIDE COLLECTIONS

In addition to adding links to archival collections for existing Wikipedia articles, those who process archival collections are encouraged to create new articles on the creator or subjects contained in the processed archival collection. Creating new articles represents a level of deeper engagement with Wikipedia. As with adding links, NYPL staff have the freedom to create articles relevant to our artifacts and collections.

New articles that are not well developed can attract negative attention from watchful editors. I highly recommend writing a new article as much as possible in one's personal sandbox. In this way one can exert as much control over it before it is moved to the mainspace of the encyclopedia.[1] When I create an article, I want to do as much as I can before opening it up to others. Although there may be a sense of "instant gratification" with Wikipedia since one's edits are immediately apparent, I recommend taking one's time. For substantive articles, I normally give myself three to five weeks so I have time to make sure I have the best sources, proofread the article, and anticipate criticisms. Once I'm satisfied with what I've done, I copy the article from my sandbox and create the new article. But even though I started the article, once that article is moved from my sandbox to the mainspace, I relinquish my control over it, knowing that others will shape it as they see fit. Wikipedia editors frown on "article ownership"—the idea that one editor has sole control over an article's content. I like to conceive of the articles I've created as collaborations. By watching others edit the article, I also learn about Wikipedia style preferences and expectations, all of which can make me a better editor.

The subjects of archival collections are not the only source for new articles. If potential articles meet the criteria for notability, the topics available for article creation by librarians are limited only to the creator's knowledge and creativity. Candidates for articles could be notable archival collections, notable manuscripts, unique items, and unique collections. Although public libraries may not have archival collections, many have curated books and ephemera devoted to local people, places, or other topics that are of local or regional importance. These are excellent resources with which to enhance Wikipedia. If a library administrator has had a particularly prominent career, he or she might meet the notability requirements and merit a separate article. Benefactors and donors might merit an article (or, if they are not notable enough for a separate article, they could be mentioned within a larger article on the library). Here new editors should be mindful of the guidelines around conflicts of interest.

The creation of new articles on more specialized or obscure topics also has its challenges. While relatively few people might have the knowledge needed to review, for example, an article on a unique Baroque music manuscript, the danger can exist that another editor or administrator might question such an article on the grounds that it is too localized. Therein lies a challenge. While library staff can create an article, the standards and customs of Wikipedia mandate that articles should be integrated into the encyclopedia. This means that an article should not be an orphan (as they are called on Wikipedia) but should be integrated into the encyclopedia, where links exist to and from terms and topics found in the newly created article. Conversely, one who wants to see an important topic integrated within the encyclopedia should think of appropriate articles where the person or topic will be mentioned and will enhance those existing articles.

I have created a number of articles on significant seventeenth-century music manuscripts held by the New York Public Library. The notability of these manuscripts was not in question: each had generated scholarly interest over the years and some had even been issued in facsimile. These scholarly articles greatly helped the creation of Wikipedia articles on the manuscripts.

One of my better efforts is the article on Drexel 4257, a seventeenth-century English music manuscript.[2] Not only are there articles written about this artifact, but a musicologist (who later became an important librarian) wrote his doctoral dissertation on this manuscript. The dissertation served as an invaluable source of content for the Wikipedia article, which was enhanced by the author's ample bibliography.

The article on Drexel 4302 presented an interesting case.[3] Though the manuscript itself presents a fascinating study, controversy surrounds its copyist. For over a century it was thought to have been copied by a seventeenth-century English recusant, Francis Tregian the Younger. Recent paper studies have shown that the accepted attribution rests on very dubious grounds. Despite these new findings, existing older literature repeats the notion that Tregian was the copyist. To do justice to an article on this manuscript, I had to greatly enhance the biography of Tregian who, aside from his doubtful attribution (which had been transmitted and enhanced over the course of a century), showed almost no connection to the musical world of his time. Thus, readers of the article on Drexel 4302 will be referred to the Tregian article and get a lesson not just in the life of a seventeenth-century recusant, but will also learn about paper studies and the danger of amplifying theories based on meagre evidence.

I know these articles on Baroque music manuscripts have been influential, as indicated not only by Wikipedia's page views, but because other institutions have contacted us in the Music Division of NYPL, wanting copies of the manuscript, saying they saw it described on Wikipedia. In one case a British library told us they hoped to create similarly detailed Wikipedia articles for some of their important music manuscripts.

My experience with Lynne Carter serves as an admonition. In general, the more obscure a subject, the more challenging it will be to establish its notability and integrate the subject within Wikipedia. Carter's main claim to notability is that he was the first drag performer to have an entire solo event at Carnegie Hall. It required dialogue with other editors to convince them of the notability of a female impersonator. While Carter's notability was eventually accepted, it was more difficult preventing the article from being an orphan. It was particularly challenging to find other Wikipedia articles to link to the Lynne Carter article, since in the 1960s and 1970s drag performance was not nearly as well-known and accepted as it is today, hence documentation in reputable sources was more difficult to find. I found that one of his mentors was Josephine Baker, who coached him in French and provided him with some of her gowns. It was therefore reasonable to introduce a link to Carter in the Baker article. Carter had appeared in a variety of local New York venues. Sometimes articles on venues in Wikipedia contain an abbreviated list of people who performed there, so a link to the performer is appropriate. I was able to link to Carter from some of the articles devoted to the venues where he had appeared. The lesson here for orphan articles is to seek ways to link from the people and places mentioned in the article to the article.

A "Social Encyclopedia"

Most people who look up information on Wikipedia probably don't see beyond the article or articles which they are seeking. Many users don't realize that each

Wikipedia article has a "talk" page where editors can offer feedback and discuss the article through criticism and conversation. When one engages in discussions on the talk pages, not only does one learn how to improve articles, but one also begins to recognize the social nature of Wikipedia.

I've long posited that Wikipedia is a social encyclopedia. To maximize one's contributions, one should engage with other editors. I consider these interactions to be just as important as editing the encyclopedia. It is through engagement with other editors that one can become fluent with Wikipedia's guidelines, learn how to improve articles, sharpen one's editing skills, and improve one's overall critical abilities.

When I began editing Wikipedia, one of my writing characteristics that fell afoul of editors was my penchant for describing a point of view. I described people as "acclaimed" or "world famous," using these clichés for subjects with which I was familiar from readings within the subject field. This did not sit well with editors, who asked me to cite sources each time I used one of these superlatives. I often could not locate exactly how I knew someone to be "world famous." By watching editors remodel my sentences, I learned how to find "the neutral voice" that is one of Wikipedia's fundamental pillars.

Editors on Wikipedia are no different from people in real life, and there are times when discussions with other editors can be contentious. Some may cling to certain beliefs, and it can be hard to get them to consider alternative points of view. This is even more challenging when multiple editors hold fast to a point of view with which you disagree. My initial reaction to those disagreeing with me on Wikipedia was to get angry, and to declare that it was not worth the effort to engage with faceless people who disagreed with me. Even though I would silence myself in frustration, I kept watching how other editors related to each other. I gradually recognized that the contention was not personal. Though I have encountered a few editors who might be called "stubborn," I find that most editors will respond to an appropriate choice of words and the reasoned presentation of evidence. It is through changing my approach that I can get other editors to consider what I have to offer.

Most editors want the best for the encyclopedia. Watching editors engage in give-and-take in order to achieve consensus can be amazingly instructive. Being able to convince others of a point of view by presenting convincing evidence is an important and valuable skill.

Deeper Engagement: WikiProjects

Once one has discovered and communicated using article talk pages, one can approach the next level of social engagement on Wikipedia: WikiProjects. As defined by Wikipedia, a WikiProject is "the organization of a group of participants in a wiki established in order to achieve specific editing goals, or to achieve goals relating to a specific field of knowledge." There are hundreds of WikiProjects, many devoted to particular subject areas. There are also many WikiProjects devoted to the mechanics of the encyclopedia, identifying articles in need of maintenance (there are numerous groups devoted to correcting formatting, for instance).

WikiProjects generally identify a collection of articles as being of interest to the project. Typically, a WikiProject will have hundreds or even thousands of articles under its watch. It's often the case that an article will have been identified by more than one WikiProject; for example, the article on the New York Public Library has been identified as being important to WikiProject Libraries, WikiProject New York City, WikiProject New York, and WikiProject Architecture. One function played by WikiProjects is assessing articles for quality, using the well-established guidelines for assessment. (Although many thousands of articles have not yet been assessed, quality assessment provides one indication to readers about the extent to which they can rely on any given article.)

WikiProjects can serve as forums for discussions of how to improve not just individual articles, but all the articles for which the particular WikiProject has assumed watch. Observing discussions on WikiProject talk pages is a way one can glimpse a small portion of the Wikipedia community in action. It is through these projects that editors can correspond with each other, and discuss and reach consensus on issues. This is a path by which one can feel the pulse of some of the participants and communities that comprise Wikipedia. By joining a WikiProject, a user can participate in one of these vibrant communities.

Wikipedia communities—such as WikiProject participants—are in continual discussions that result in incremental but continuous revision of the encyclopedia. This is one characteristic of Wikipedia which strongly differentiates it from traditional encyclopedias. Unlike a print encyclopedia whose text is fixed until the following edition or printing, Wikipedia is constantly in a state of flux due to the thousands of people who are continually editing it. It is not unlike an ant or bee colony, an organic community that is constantly maintaining and improving itself.

Connecting and Creating Community

The library that really wishes to engage with Wikipedia can find ways to not just edit the encyclopedia, but engage with its community. One manner of engagement is through edit-a-thons, events in which experienced editors can engage and train novices in editing. Edit-a-thons can be run in a variety of ways. Most often there is a brief introduction where a speaker introduces the topic or theme of the edit-a-thon. Once the introduction has concluded, novices can ask for the assistance of experienced editors and learn how to edit. Most edit-a-thons publicize a topic or theme. Topics have included the creation and enhancement of articles dealing with the institution hosting the edit-a-thon, special topics for which the library is known, the neighborhood in which the edit-a-thon is taking place, or subject areas like science, musical theater, film, art, and many others. Lately many edit-a-thons have chosen to concentrate on creating and improving articles devoted to notable women in all walks of life.

Having a topic or theme for an edit-a-thon provides motivation for the community to attend. For its first edit-a-thon, the New York Public Library chose to focus on musical theater. Fans of musical theater tend to be extremely knowledgeable and intensely passionate. The excitement generated by the thirty attendees, many of whom had never been to the New York Public Library for the Performing Arts, led to the event being covered in the press.

Over the years the formula for edit-a-thons has generally remained the same, but with various improvements. Many hosting institutions offer food and refreshments. Some have guest speakers whose appearance can promote attendance and inspire the attendees. Others can offer tours of their facilities. As with all marketing, it takes some skill to determine the most advantageous times to hold edit-a-thons. Black History Month (February) and Women's History Month (March) have proved to be good thematic matches for edit-a-thons, but editing events can also coincide with birthdays, holidays, and any number of occasions, limited only by the creativity of the library staff.

Even without experienced editors on hand to help manage an edit-a-thon, a library can still provide a welcoming atmosphere for Wikipedia activities.

Edit-a-thons need not be only social; they can also be transformed into an informational event. In planning events of mutual interest, Wikipedians and librarians can invite speakers who will discuss issues of significance to Wikipedia and the Wikipedia movement. The range of topics can include those specific to the encyclopedia, as well as issues that have societal relevance such as open access, neutrality in speech and writing, conflict of interest, free culture, net neutrality, systemic bias, the gender gap in various occupations, and many others. Library staff will recognize that all these issues also affect the library world.

In summary, engagement with Wikipedia presents opportunities for a library. As witnessed at the New York Public Library, Wikipedians have a long-term passion for the encyclopedia. The library can serve as the focal point for this community's enthusiastic engagement with Wikipedia. Ranging from simple editing, to providing a space for editing activities, to offering education and discussion of current issues, the library, by incorporating Wikipedia in its programming, can strengthen and serve its community in new ways that not only help the encyclopedia but make for a more informed citizenry.

NOTES

1. In addition to his or her own talk page, each Wikipedia editor has a "sandbox" that can function as a space to write article drafts and experiment with Wikipedia markup and display. Though experienced editors can find these sandboxes, they are mostly invisible to ordinary readers. The "mainspace" refers to the public portion of the encyclopedia.

2. "Drexel 4257," Wikipedia, https://en.wikipedia.org/wiki/Drexel_4257.

3. "Drexel 4302," Wikipedia, https://en.wikipedia.org/wiki/Drexel_4302.

Wikidata and Libraries

Facilitating Open Knowledge

MAIRELYS LEMUS-ROJAS AND LYDIA PINTSCHER

ibraries and archives are increasingly embracing the value of contributing information to open knowledge projects. Users come to Wikipedia—one of the best-known open knowledge projects—to learn about a specific topic or for quick fact-checking. Even more serious researchers use it as a starting point for finding links to external resources related to their topic of interest. Wikipedia is just one of the many projects under the umbrella of the Wikimedia Foundation, a nonprofit charitable organization. Wikidata, for its part, is a sister project to Wikipedia. It stores structured data that is then fed back to the other Wiki projects, including Wikipedia, thus providing users with the most up-to-date information.

This chapter focuses on Wikidata and its potential uses for libraries. We hope to inspire information professionals (librarians, archivists, library practitioners) to take the next step and start a conversation with their institutions and colleagues to free their data by contributing it to an open knowledge base like Wikidata.

WHAT IS WIKIDATA?

Wikidata is the newest project of the Wikimedia Foundation and was launched on October 29, 2012 (Wikidata, 2017). It is a free knowledge base that can be read and edited by both humans and machines. Wikidata runs on an instance of MediaWiki, the software used to run all Wikimedia projects, which means that its content can be collaboratively added, modified, or deleted ("Wikidata:Glossary," 2017).

Wikidata was conceived as a means of addressing the need for a centralized repository to store structured and linked data. Having a central repository allows information to be updated in one place; all other Wikimedia projects that have decided to connect to Wikidata are updated automatically. Currently, there are about 285 active language Wikipedias (such as the English Wikipedia, Spanish Wikipedia, German Wikipedia, and so on), which are all individual encyclopedias ("List of Wikipedias," 2017). Before Wikidata was created, there was no easy way to update data across the different language Wikipedias. Changes made by editors to the structured data of one Wikipedia needed to be manually made in all other Wikipedias, which proved cumbersome. Now editors are able to make these changes in Wikidata, allowing all Wikimedia projects to use that structured data. For instance, Wikipedias can make use of Wikidata's data to maintain their infoboxes[1] with the most up-to-date information. Another advantage of using Wikidata's data to power infoboxes is that information will be displayed consistently across all language Wikipedias. An example of an article in the English Wikipedia that makes use of Wikidata's structured data to populate its infobox is the article for the South Pole Telescope. In its infobox, there is a pencil-like icon displaying next to some of the entries. When a user hovers over this icon, it shows a message suggesting that if changes need to be made, they should be made in Wikidata (see figure 11.1). Once the icon is clicked, the Wikidata item opens up for the user to edit. Changes made in Wikidata would then be reflected not only in the English Wikipedia for this article, but also in any other language Wikipedia that is connected to the knowledge base.

Wikipedias that do not make use of Wikidata's structured data are missing the opportunity to access and display the most recent data available for a specific subject. For instance, by looking at the South Pole Telescope article in the Spanish Wikipedia (see figure 11.2), we can begin to see noticeable differences in terms of content compared to its English counterpart, since the Spanish version does not yet harness the power of Wikidata. Being able to access consistently structured and linked data in Wikidata provides humans and machines with the ability to traverse information and programmatically retrieve relevant pieces of information that often contain links to other data sources (Bartov, 2017).

Screenshot of the South Pole Telescope infobox in the English Wikipedia

Image of the South Pole Telescope in the Spanish Wikipedia

WIKIDATA DATA MODEL

Wikidata contains a collection of entities, which are "the basic elements of the knowledge base" and which can be either properties or items ("Wikibase/Data-Model/Primer," 2017). All properties and items have their individual namespaces and their own Wikidata page with their respective label, description, and aliases in different languages. The label is the actual name that aids in identifying an entity. The meaning of the label can be clarified further in the description field. For instance, if we search for "Havana" in Wikidata we get multiple items matching our search: entries for the capital city in Cuba, cities in Mason County, Illinois and Gadsden County, Florida, and an entry for a romantic movie, among others. Because of the information entered in the description, we are able to quickly disambiguate these entries that have the same label ("Wikidata:Glossary," 2017). In the same way that we can have multiple items with the same label, we can also have more than one item with the same description, since descriptions do not necessarily have to be unique. However, there cannot be more than one item with the same combination of label and description. Items in Wikidata are the equivalent of a Wikipedia article in that they contain data about a single concept. It is also useful to list under aliases all alternative names by which an entity is known. This is helpful in cases where a search is made for a name that is not the one assigned to the label. For instance, the item Q65, with the label "Los Angeles," has the following aliases: L.A., LA, Pink City, The town of Our Lady the Queen of the Angels of the Little Portion, and Los Angeles, California. Having this additional information added to entities facilitates their discoverability.

All properties and items are assigned unique identifiers, which are formed using the letter P for properties and Q for items, followed by a sequential number. For instance, building on the previous example of Havana, the capital city of Cuba, we have Q1563 as the unique identifier for its item, while property P1082 is used to record its population. Due to the multilingual nature of Wikidata, having a unique identifier is needed to differentiate entries, since names are not unique and can change over time. Having a canonical identifier assigned to an item means that regardless of whether there are multiple items with the same name or whether the name changes, the integrity and uniqueness of the item will remain intact.

Properties are similar to cataloging/metadata fields in that they are used to better record metadata values. The Wikidata community has the ability to propose properties, which are documented on the property proposal page ("Wikidata:Property proposal," 2017). Proposals receive open discussion and debate within the Wikidata community. After discussion, the community votes. If the majority agrees to include the property, it is added to the knowledge base. Once included, it can be used with any item in Wikidata.

Items can contain statements to describe a concept in more detail. There can be multiple statements for both items and properties. The main part of a statement is a property-value pair. Statements can also contain qualifiers and references. For instance, as seen in figure 11.3, the English writer Douglas Adams has the property *educated at* (P69), and its value is *St John's College* (Q691283). We can then enrich statements with the use of qualifiers. Qualifiers also contain a property -value pair and are used to refine metadata values ("Wikibase/DataModel/ Primer," 2017). Looking again at figure 11.3, we can tell the period of time when Douglas Adams attended college (*start time: 1971, end time: 1974*) as well as his academic major (*English literature*) and academic degree (*Bachelor of Arts*). Each statement can be supported by a reference to indicate where a particular claim was made, when the source was published and retrieved, its language, URL, and so on. A reference can include anything from websites and scientific papers to datasets.

FIGURE 11.3

Data Model in Wikidata

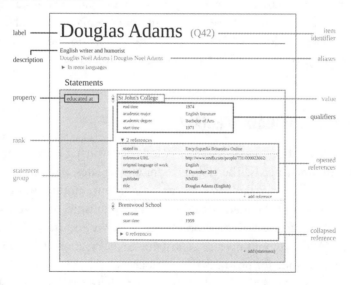

By Charlie Kritschmar, via Wikimedia Commons.

USE OF EXTERNAL IDENTIFIERS

Wikidata also allows for the integration of external identifiers. These identifiers, which were created and reside in outside sources, are reconciled in Wikidata. There are currently 1,746 external identifiers in Wikidata, some of which are familiar to the library community because information professionals have direct involvement in facilitating the creation of their corresponding authority/archival records. These identifiers include the Virtual International Authority File (VIAF ID: P214), the Library of Congress Control Number (LC/NACO Authority File ID: P244), and the recently added Social Networks and Archival Context ID (P3430). Adding these external identifiers to Wikidata items provides links that point to another set of data residing elsewhere, which aids in establishing connections and providing additional information about the items.

CONTRIBUTORS AND CONTRIBUTIONS

Wikidata's content is represented in almost 300 languages. The Wikidata community plays an important role in the contribution of data to the knowledge base, as reflected in table 11.1. Wikidata has more than 2.8 million registered contributors, of which only about 18,000 are active contributors (an active contributor is one who has had some activity in the last 30 days). The Wikidata community is also involved in the creation and use of tools and bots to make actionable edits to Wikidata. The statistics in table 11.1 reflect the dedication and commitment of the community to making Wikidata a successful project.

WHAT MAKES WIKIDATA SPECIAL?

As a free collaborative knowledge base, Wikidata is evolving with its community members and their needs. The global community creates, edits, and maintains the structured data in Wikidata. One can access, copy, modify, and/or distribute all the content of Wikidata because its data is published under the Creative Commons Public Domain Dedication 1.0, which allows free use ("Wikidata:Data access," 2017). The community also contributes to the creation of documentation that serves as a guide for prospective contributors.

Wikidata was conceived as a central place where data created by people from different cultures and languages can coexist. It is designed to deal with

TABLE 11.1	

Wikidata statistics

Registered contributors	~2.8 million
Active contributors	~18,000
Languages represented	over 300
Items	over 26 million
Labels	over 140 million
Aliases	over 14 million
Descriptions	over 210 million
Properties	3,475
Statements	~158 million
Page edits	~512 million

the complexity of the world that we live in. This means that it accommodates multiple, even conflicting, data points about a topic, which eliminates the need for contributors to be in agreement with the contributed information. These contributions can then be qualified with additional information to specify, for example, where a certain belief is held. All of these qualifying statements can be supplemented with references. The references, in turn, provide users with information that indicates where the data is coming from—a valuable feature for deciding which data point to employ for their use case.

Wikidata also recognizes that those who do not speak or read English have access to limited information online compared to those who are fluent in English. Wikidata provides all of its data in hundreds of languages, all in a single site. This means that its editors work on the same data regardless of their language expertise, which benefits those who speak and read less well-represented languages. This also facilitates making changes to a smaller Wikipedia (which usually has a smaller community of contributors) more quickly and effectively, and ensures that information is accurate across all Wikipedias connected to Wikidata. Although Wikidata has not been in existence for long, it has already shown tremendous potential for storing high-quality and reliable information. This is due, in part, to the multilingual nature of the knowledge base and the fact that information is stored in one central location for everyone to access, enhance, and validate. Being transparent about sources of information and providing reliable data are important because this demonstrates the viability of the knowledge base.

WIKIDATA AND LIBRARIES

Why Should Libraries Get Involved with Wikidata?

Anyone can contribute to Wikidata, but why is it important for information professionals to use their expertise to contribute to a project like Wikidata? In the library community we collect, describe, organize, preserve, and provide access to physical and digital materials. Information professionals have long created and contributed authority records to help disambiguate personal, corporate, and jurisdictional names by providing a standardized form for them. For example, in the United States, authority file contributions are made through the Name Authority Cooperative (NACO) program, which allows institutions to either contribute directly to the Library of Congress Name Authority File (LCNAF) or to contribute through a NACO Funnel. As part of this work, the library community has had the opportunity to participate in the development and implementation of standards and rules used in the creation of authority files, which has led to a deep appreciation and understanding of the value of creating structured metadata.

A partnership between library institutions and Wikidata seems appropriate given that we have a common interest in documenting and preserving our heritage and history, and providing access to knowledge. The library community can make a significant impact on improving the reliability and augmenting the size of Wikidata's knowledge base, as well as enhancing the quality of the data already contributed to it. Additionally, information professionals have the experience and necessary skills to join efforts in exploring how to model concepts like the FRBR (Functional Requirements for Bibliographic Records) for all types of bibliographic materials in Wikidata. For instance, both communities could collaborate in finding a solution to better represent expressions (translations) and manifestations (editions) of the works in the knowledge base. There is a critical need to address this issue in order to more accurately model resources in Wikidata, and the library community has the expertise to make a substantial and much-needed contribution in this area.

Despite the fact that many libraries are able to make use of and take advantage of systems like OCLC Connexion—a client that allows users to create bibliographic and authority records—there are still many institutions that are unable to do so. Even in instances where they are able to contribute bibliographic records, not all of them are NACO participants, which means that they are not able to create authority records. As an alternative, those institutions could make use of Wikidata's data to extract relevant information to be imported into their databases. Similarly, they could use Wikidata as a solution for creating authority records for underrepresented creators and organizations. It would be useful for the library community to actively participate in the development and documentation of the Wikidata knowledge base because there is much potential for future use and information integration.

Library Implementation: Use Cases

Libraries are starting to invest time and resources in continuing to build a comprehensive Wikidata knowledge base. An example of an institution that has taken a leading role in contributing to Wikidata is the National Library of Wales, which had the vision to bring a Wikidata specialist on board in 2016 as its first Wikidata Visiting Scholar ("Our Wikidata Visiting Scholar," 2016). The Visiting Scholar has been working with metadata from the Welsh Landscape Collection as part of the Linking Landscapes project. The idea behind this project is to provide a presence in Wikidata for all the prints in the collection and to explore opportunities for future work with the structured data ("Life and Times," 2016). Another institution that has been actively contributing to Wikidata is the Department of Digital Preservation at the Yale University Library. They hired a CLIR (Council on Library and Information Resources) postdoctoral fellow in data curation to focus on digital preservation for software curation. As part of this project, they are building a "digital preservation model in Wikidata" to be able to describe the software available in their library's collection. For instance, they have been adding statements for items related to digital preservation, and they have been proposing properties to be able to describe file formats, hardware, emulated environments, and so on (Thornton and Cochrane, 2016). These two examples demonstrate that there is interest in our community to not only contribute data to the knowledge base, but also to participate in the development of models to be able to more accurately describe and represent artifacts and materials in Wikidata.

How to Access and Retrieve Wikidata's Data

All the data stored in Wikidata can be easily accessed using the Wikidata application programming interface (API). Another way to access the data is by querying
it. Wikidata offers the Wikidata Query Service (https://query.wikidata.org/),
which is powered by SPARQL, an RDF query language for triplestores. Using
the SPARQL end point, users are able to query using a combination of triples to
obtain everything that Wikidata knows about a subject ("Wikidata:Data access,"
2017). The SPARQL end point is currently receiving over 7 million requests
per day. The Wikidata Query Service offers a list of examples that can be used
and modified as needed. For instance, one of the examples allow users to run a
complex query in order to find out which American universities were founded
before the states where they are located were created (see figure 11.4). This query
asks Wikidata to retrieve only ten results, but the limit can be adjusted as needed.

The resulting data provides the names of the universities, the dates when
they were founded, the names of the states, and the dates when the states were
created (see figure 11.5). These are the kinds of questions that we can ask Wikidata and expect to get results. The resulting data can be downloaded in various
formats, including XML, JSON, TSV, and CSV. The completeness and accuracy
of the results depend on the data that is stored in Wikidata, which is why it is so
imperative to contribute to that knowledge base.

FIGURE 11.4

SPARQL query from the Wikidata Query Service

```
1    #American universities founded before the states they reside in were created
2    #added before 2016-10
3      SELECT ?uLabel ?founded ?stateLabel ?stateStart
4    WHERE
5    {
6          ?u wdt:P31/wdt:P279* wd:Q3918 .
7          ?u wdt:P131+ ?state .
8          ?state wdt:P31 wd:Q35657 .
9          ?state wdt:P571 ?stateStart .
10         ?u wdt:P571 ?founded .
11         FILTER (?founded < ?stateStart) .
12         SERVICE wikibase:label {
13             bd:serviceParam wikibase:language "en" .
14         }
15    }
16    LIMIT 10
```

FIGURE 11.5

Query results from the Wikidata Query Service

uLabel	founded	stateLabel	stateStart
University of Utah	Jan 1, 1850	Utah	Jan 4, 1896
University of Hawaii	Jan 1, 1907	Hawaii	Aug 21, 1959
University of Minnesota	Jan 1, 1851	Minnesota	May 11, 1858
Brigham Young University	Jan 1, 1875	Utah	Jan 4, 1896
University of Denver	Jan 1, 1864	Colorado	Aug 1, 1876
Transylvania University	Jan 1, 1780	Kentucky	Jun 1, 1792
Utah State University	Jan 1, 1888	Utah	Jan 4, 1896
New Mexico Institute of Mining and Technology	Jan 1, 1889	New Mexico	Jan 6, 1912
Carroll University	Jan 1, 1846	Wisconsin	May 29, 1848
University of Delaware	Jan 1, 1743	Delaware	Dec 7, 1787

How Can Information Professionals Contribute to Wikidata?

The first step toward contributing to Wikidata is to set up an account. Users who have an account from other Wikimedia projects can use it to contribute data to Wikidata. In cases where an account needs to be created, a pseudonym can be used as a user name if that is the user's preference. However, users should not include information that describes their institution because accounts are meant to be personal. Being registered with Wikidata ensures that edits are made under the user's account. Otherwise, edits are recorded under the user's IP address, and that information is made publicly available. When contributing to Wikidata as part of one's job, it is recommended to add a conflict-of-interest statement to one's user page to indicate any institutional affiliation. New users will benefit from consulting Wikidata's interactive tutorials in order to become familiar with the knowledge base ("Wikidata:Tours," 2017). An important aspect of contributing data to Wikidata is to determine the "notability" of a subject. One of the criteria that Wikidata requires for entries to be considered notable is to have one sitelink from any other Wikimedia project, such as Wikipedia, Wikivoyage, Wikisource, Wikibooks, and so on added to the items ("Wikidata:Notability," 2017).

A Wikidata entry features all information pertaining to a specific entity, a history page, and a discussion page for communicating about issues related to the entry. On the history page, users are able to see when an edit was made (specific date and time), the user name of the user who made the edit, and the size (in bytes) of the contribution. Because changes are always recorded, they can be reverted to a previous version, if needed.

Information professionals can make a significant impact in shaping Wikidata. One way in which they can contribute to Wikidata is by adding references to statements. There has been a strong interest in bridging the citation gap in Wikipedia as part of the #1lib1ref global campaign. Since the campaign first launched in 2016, libraries around the world have recognized the importance of backing up statements in Wikipedia with reliable sources and have actively participated in this effort, as shown in the Wikipedia social search page.[2] With the support of library institutions, a similar campaign could be devised to address citation gaps in Wikidata. Of equal importance is to get involved with initiatives like WikiCite, which is aiming to build a repository of sources from all applicable Wiki projects in order to store them in Wikidata.

Another area in which informational professionals can help is by making sure their archival collections are represented in the Wikidata knowledge base. Once that is done, it would also be useful to have those collections attributed to the institution that holds them. For instance, Wikidata has property P485 labeled as *archives at,* which is used to indicate the name of the institution that holds an archival collection. Until 2014, this property (P485) was one of the least used in Wikidata, with only 133 uses (Vrandečić and Krötzsch, 2014). However, as of June 2017, it had already been used 5,063 times, showing a steady increase in usage. ("Property talk:P485," 2017). Inputting values in this field would allow for a more accurate representation of institutional archival holdings, and libraries and archives are well-positioned to continue carrying out this task. It could be accomplished by either contributing data via manual editing (one item at a time) or through the use of tools or bots (to make repetitive tasks without human intervention). Wikidata editors can submit bot requests if there are none already available for the specific task they want to accomplish. A justification for the need to create a bot should be shared to provide the community with all of the necessary information needed to make an informed decision ("Wikidata:Bot requests," 2017).

Information professionals can find many ways to build Wikidata, including adding value to the development, implementation, and improvement of Wikidata properties, creating new items, adding references to existing items, contributing to the creation of data models, verifying the accuracy and completeness of existing data, and adding identifiers. Adding identifiers to items, some of which have been directly or indirectly created by library institutions, helps to validate and enrich the data, and facilitates connections with external sources. When libraries contribute data to the Wikidata knowledge base, they are building opportunities to ask more complex questions through the Wikidata Query Service about their collections—questions that would not otherwise be possible using a local integrated library system.

BEYOND WIKIDATA

There are many tools, projects, and applications that have been built using Wikidata's data. They have been created by the Wikidata community and are aimed at achieving very specific goals. Some are intended to aid users in reviewing and contributing data to the Wikidata knowledge base, while others aim to provide new meaning to the data. Histropedia is one example of how the data can be used and presented in a more meaningful way. It aims to be a "new type of website" where a combination of data from Wikidata and Wikipedia is used to generate timelines. These timelines allow users to visualize history in dynamic ways, and can be used by institutions for educational purposes (Histropedia, 2014).

Another example of a tool that was built to display Wikidata's data is Reasonator. It acts as a "discovery interface" that brings together all the data available in Wikidata related to an item and includes images, audio, and maps. It can also display a timeline based on available data (Reasonator, n.d.). In contributing data to Wikidata we would not only enrich the knowledge base, but would potentially facilitate the discovery of library collections through the use of this tool and many other tools powered by Wikidata.

Another project to highlight is Inventaire. As its name suggests, it maintains an inventory of all its users' books. Inventaire draws from Wikidata and uses the Wikipedia links present in Wikidata items to build authors' biographies, which are displayed in a nicely formatted presentation. The code and data of this web application are open source. Inventaire allows users to keep an inventory of their favorite books, connect with the community, and check what materials are available to give, lend, or sell (Inventaire, n.d.). Users are able to specify their location in order to see the availability of materials in their geographical surroundings. Once they find materials in the area where they reside, these can be picked up in person or sometimes dropped in a box that the lender and borrower have agreed upon. This level of interaction adds a social component because users are able to meet others with similar interests. This prototype is yet another great example of what can be achieved by accessing and using open knowledge data.

A final open-source application to showcase is Scholia. Scholia is hosted on the Wikimedia Tool Labs page, and its code can be found on GitHub. This application takes advantage of the richness of the data in Wikidata to effectively create and display profiles of notable scholars. The data is presented in what the application identifies as *aspects,* which can be an "author, work, organization, venue, series, publisher, sponsor and topic" (Nielsen, Mietchen, and Willighagen, 2017). Scholia has the potential to be used by library institutions because library practitioners could create profiles for notable faculty by contributing relevant personal and publication information on them to Wikidata. Scholia can then be used to search for an aspect, at which point the application queries Wikidata and displays all relevant information (Scholia, n.d.). Exploring the potential of giving new meaning to Wikidata's data through these web applications and tools might be useful in helping the library community to get a better sense of what can be achieved when using data from the knowledge base.

CONCLUSION

We encourage library institutions to embrace Wikidata as they have begun to embrace Wikipedia, and to consider the benefits that a partnership would provide for both communities. Information professionals have the necessary skill set to undertake the task of contributing library and archival data to the Wikidata knowledge base. Establishing a connection between library institutions and their collections in Wikidata is just a small but crucial step in preparing the ground-work that would facilitate discovery and the potential for experimentation in current and future projects.

NOTES

1. Infoboxes are templates that contain structured metadata about the subject being described. An infobox usually displays on the right-hand side of a Wikipedia article for languages that read from left to right.

2. The Wikidata social search page (http://tools.wmflabs.org/hashtags/search/11ib1ref) allows users to search for hashtags present in Wikipedia edit summaries and displays specific information about the contributions.

REFERENCES

Bartov, A. February 9, 2017. "A Gentle Introduction to Wikidata for Absolute Beginners (including Non-Technics!)" (video file). https://en.wikipedia.org/wiki/File:A_Gentle _Introduction_to_Wikidata_for_Absolute_Beginners_(including_non-techies!).webm.

Histropedia. 2014. http://histropedia.com.

Inventaire. N.d. https://inventaire.io.

"Life and Times of Mr. Herbert Ellerby: Linking Llandudno, Lancashire, and Moggill, Australia." June 23, 2016. The National Library of Wales blog. https://www.llgc.org.uk/ blog/?p=11702.

"List of Wikipedias." 2017. Wikipedia. https://meta.wikimedia.org/wiki/List_of_Wikipedias.

Nielsen, F. Å., D. Mietchen, and E. Willighagen. 2017. "Scholia and Scientometrics with Wikidata." Cornell University Library. Joint Proceedings of the 1st International Workshop on Scientometrics and 1st International Workshop on Enabling Decentralised Scholarly Communication.

"Our Wikidata Visiting Scholar." December 4. 2016. https://www.llgc.org.uk/blog/?p=11246.

"Property talk:P485." 2017. https://www.wikidata.org/wiki/Property_talk:P485.

Reasonator. N.d. https://tools.wmflabs.org/reasonator/?.

Scholia. N.d. https://tools.wmflabs.org/scholia.

Thornton, K., and E. Cochrane. October 1 2016. "Wikidata as a Digital Preservation Knowledge base." http://openpreservation.org/blog/2016/09/30/wikidata-as-a-digital-preservation -knowledgebase.

Vrandečić, D., and M. Krötzsch. 2014. "Wikidata: A Free Collaborative Knowledgebase." *Communications of the ACM* 57, no. 10: 78–85. http://dx.doi.org/10.1145/2629489.

"Wikibase/DataModel/Primer." 2017. Wikidata. https://www.mediawiki.org/wiki/Wikibase/ DataModel/Primer.

"Wikidata." 2017. Wikidata. https://www.wikidata.org/wiki/Q2013.

"Wikidata:Bot requests." 2017. Wikidata. https://www.wikidata.org/wiki/Wikidata:Bot_ requests.

"Wikidata:Data access." 2017. Wikidata. https://www.wikidata.org/wiki/Wikidata:Data
    _access.

"Wikidata:Glossary." 2017. Wikidata. https://www.wikidata.org/wiki/Wikidata:Glossary.

"Wikidata:Notability." 2017. Wikidata. https://www.wikidata.org/wiki/Wikidata:Notability.

"Wikidata:Property proposal." 2017. Wikidata. https://www.wikidata.org/wiki/
    Wikidata:Property_proposal.

"Wikidata:Tours." 2017. Wikidata. https://www.wikidata.org/wiki/Wikidata:Tours.

Wikipedia and Wikidata Help Search Engines Understand Your Organization

Using Semantic Web Identity to Improve Recognition and Drive Traffic

KENNING ARLITSCH AND JUSTIN SHANKS

Semantic Web Identity (SWI) is the condition in which search engines formally recognize entities and their relationships. Entities can be people, places, organizations, landmarks, or other "things," but in this chapter, entities will be defined as academic organizations: libraries, but also other academic units such as universities, colleges, departments, centers, and institutes. An entity can be said to have achieved SWI if a formal display known as a Knowledge Graph Card (KC)[1] appears for it in search engine results pages (SERP). The KC offers information about the entity directly in the search engine window, including such elements as address, phone number, hours of operation, description, link to the website, user reviews, and so on. More importantly, the KC is an indicator that the search engine has achieved a machine-based comprehension of the existence and nature of the entity. With this understanding, the search engine can be more precise in its referrals and can hand off information about the entity to other semantic technologies. Far from being an end in itself, the display of an accurate and robust KC should simply be considered a positive indicator of SWI. Unfortunately, most academic organizations have not achieved SWI at this time.

A search engine displays a KC when it has gathered enough verifiable facts about an entity. Search engines gather some facts organically while indexing website documents. But verifiable facts are more likely to be harvested from proprietary knowledge bases such as Google My Business, and from knowledge bases on the Linked Open Data (LOD) cloud, such as Wikipedia and Wikidata. Academic organizations have the best chance of controlling their SWI by proactively creating and curating records in these knowledge bases.

This chapter will (1) explain the significance of SWI, (2) describe a new library service developed at Montana State University that helps campus organizations implement SWI, and (3) demonstrate how SWI was successfully achieved in three case studies.

WHY IS SWI IMPORTANT?

The achievement of Semantic Web Identity implies that a search engine understands certain things about an entity, such as the nature of the enterprise, its relationships, and its location. "Understanding," in this case, implies a machine-based comprehension of facts, which search engines can use to provide more accurate search results and help surface otherwise undiscovered relationships that may lead users to organizations they would not have thought relevant to their queries. This comprehension also helps search engines transfer that information to semantic technologies, such as mapping applications and intelligent personal assistants. A type of database known as a knowledge graph is used by search engines to "define, structure, and link hundreds of millions of entities . . . to improve the answers of their artificial personal assistants" (Bernstein, Hendler, and Noy, 2016). Apple's Siri, Amazon's Alexa, Microsoft's Cortana, and Google Now are examples of personal assistants that become more competent at providing accurate directions to an organization if they can tap into the verified information that search engines have assembled in their knowledge graphs.

Higher Education

Information-seeking behavior in higher education almost always begins (and often ends) with Internet search engines (Connaway and Dickey, 2010), but the effect of SWI in the discovery process is only gradually becoming understood.

In academia, SWI tends to be most robust at the top levels of the institution; searching for the name of a university will usually yield search engine results that include the presence of a robust KC. However, that comprehension quickly diminishes as the search moves deeper into the institution to the level of college, department, and research institute and center. KCs for those lower-level organizations are often missing altogether, display a paucity of information, or even show an organization that is different from the one searched.

A lack of search engine comprehension of organizations can logically be assumed to result in fewer referrals. If the search engine doesn't understand the academic organization, then it is less likely to send its users to the physical or digital location, particularly if the search engine has other options in its knowledge graph. The diminished level of referral may negatively affect the attraction of research funding, faculty talent, and students. For instance, funding agencies which seek evidence that a university is engaged in specific research may fail to find a credible connection if the relevant research institute hasn't addressed its SWI. Students seeking a match for their study interests may likewise not be referred if a particular university department hasn't addressed its SWI, leaving search engines to rely on potentially inaccurate information that other sources may supply (DePianto, 2016). These interrelated factors could even negatively affect university rankings and reputation if research funding doesn't find its way to the institution, if student enrollment declines, or if faculty can't be recruited because they are not attracted by the university's stated research interests.

SEO TO SWI

The Origins of Semantic Web Identity

Semantic Web Identity can trace its roots to the practice of search engine optimization (SEO), which developed in response to the competitive nature of commerce on the Web. SEO practices have proved necessary to ensure use and justify the investment in locally developed library digital repositories (Arlitsch and OBrien, 2013).

The search engine landscape was crowded in the late 1990s, but by the early twenty-first century Google had cemented its dominance and many search engines fell by the wayside ("Timeline of Web Search Engines," 2016; Wall, 2017). Google continues to control two-thirds of the "explicit core search engine market" in the

United States (comScore, Inc., 2016), and estimates range as high as 90 percent for Google's search engine market share in Europe (Meyer, 2015). Although Microsoft's Bing is a competitor and should not be discounted, Google's dominance is the driver behind most SEO and SWI efforts. SWI is an offshoot of SEO in that its aim is to optimize the way search engines interact with a digital presence, but SWI is specific to entities (people, places, things) in the environment of the Semantic Web.

Semantic Web

Producing search results in previous generations of the World Wide Web was limited to algorithms that weighed a series of "signals" against strings of text. The latest generation of the Web is known as the Semantic Web, and it is commonly understood as an entity-based environment in which machines interact with data records to better understand concepts, identities, and relationships.

Tim Berners-Lee and his colleagues formally introduced the concept of the Semantic Web in 2001 as an evolved version of the Web, where data and information could be processed automatically by computers that have access to structured collections of information (Berners-Lee, Hendler, and Lassila, 2001). These data records are stored in numerous knowledge bases that comprise a Linked Open Data (LOD) cloud intended "to enrich the Web with structured data" (Thalhammer and Rettinger, 2014). In this environment, search engine practices have evolved from the previous limitation of matching search queries to textual strings, to a new process in which queries are matched with verified facts about entities and their relationships. The Semantic Web promises greater accuracy of search results, often providing answers to search queries rather than a list of websites: "Search engines no longer only return documents—they now aim to return direct answers" (Vaish et al., 2014). The phrase "strings to things" has come to serve as a metaphor for the transition to the Semantic Web (Singhal, 2012).

Knowledge Graphs

Graph databases have existed for decades, but they have seen a resurgence in use as the Semantic Web has grown. The nodes, properties, and edges that characterize graph databases are more adept at organizing and quickly retrieving Semantic Web data (and data relationships) than the hierarchical system of tables in relational databases. Google's Knowledge Graph and Bing's Satori are examples of graph databases recently built by search engine companies. The graph databases are populated with facts about entities and their relationships, drawn from "the publication of interlinked datasets on the Web, in a form that enables people and computer programs to use these datasets for navigation, integration, and web-scale reasoning" (Bouquet, Stoermer, and Vignolo, 2012).

Search engines populate their knowledge graphs with entities that are defined and verified in knowledge bases that the search engines trust. Some of these knowledge bases are proprietary (ex., Google My Business), while others are publicly available on the LOD cloud.[2] Over 1,000 knowledge bases currently comprise the LOD cloud, and many of these contain information about entities from which search engines can learn (Schmachtenberg, Bizer, and Paulheim, 2014). The knowledge bases considered to be the most significant are represented near the center of the LOD cloud, and include DBpedia (Auer et al., 2007), Wikipedia (Lih, 2009), YAGO (Suchanek, Kasneci, and Weikum, 2007), the CIA World Fact Book (Central Intelligence Agency, 2015), and Wikidata (Erxleben et al., 2014). Freebase was once a significant source of information for Google's Knowledge Graph, but Google began shutting it down in 2014 (Butzbach, 2014) and facilitated a migration project that transferred Freebase data into Wikidata (Tanon et al., 2016).

Google has acknowledged that its Knowledge Graph draws information from some LOD knowledge bases (Singhal, 2012; Sullivan, 2012), but it is difficult to know exactly which sources Google and Bing tap for their respective knowledge graphs. For instance, while Google acknowledges that its Knowledge Graph uses "public sources such as Freebase, Wikipedia and the CIA World Factbook" (Singhal, 2012), there is no evidence from Google that it draws data directly from DBpedia, which seems odd since DBpedia publishes rich structured linked-data records extracted from Wikipedia entries. Google will only characterize its relationship to DBpedia as one of "transivity," meaning that it is indirect and established only insofar as it draws from sources that do have direct relationships with DBpedia (Mendes and Jakob, 2012). Microsoft also only hints at its use of LOD knowledge bases, such as this quote from its patent application for a process it developed for entity detection and disambiguation: "the entity-based search system recognizes particular content sources as authoritative sources for discovering entity information. For example, the system may identify

Wikipedia as having particularly strong and trustworthy entity information and may recognize various pages at that site as describing entities" (Li et al., 2013).

Knowledge Graph Cards as Indicators of SWI

Google's Knowledge Graph and Bing's Satori database are invisible to the public, but the Knowledge Graph Card (KC) is one visible manifestation that Google began to display in 2012 (Singhal, 2012) in its search results. Bing followed a short time later with its own version of the KC. Aside from providing quick and easy "answers" about an organization to users, the display of a KC serves as an indicator that the search engine has discovered sufficient verified facts about the organization to establish it as an entity in its knowledge graph. The authors characterize this condition as Semantic Web Identity (SWI). Conversely, when a KC fails to appear for an organization, or it displays few or inaccurate facts, the condition may be characterized as lacking SWI, or poor SWI, respectively.

KNOWLEDGE BASES THAT HELP ESTABLISH SWI

Google My Business

Google My Business (GMB) is a proprietary knowledge base owned by Google. Registering or "claiming" a business or organization with GMB helps promote that organization and facilitates interactions with customers (Shenoy and Prabhu, 2016). Registering with GMB also has the wide-ranging effect of integrating with multiple Google properties. Registering with GMB may be the single most effective step an organization can take to begin achieving SWI. Registration consists of a two-step "claim and verify" process that helps Google ensure the veracity of the claim and the location of the organization (Google, Inc., 2017).

Wikipedia

Wikipedia is most useful to the Google Knowledge Graph as a source of descriptive text that is used to populate the "Description" element in the KC. Google appears to use the first sentence of the Wikipedia article verbatim for the description in the KC, so academic organizations would do well to craft that sentence very carefully. While Wikipedia does not explicitly forbid editors from writing about organizations or companies with which they are affiliated, it does publish community-generated guidelines and behavioral norms. Editors are encouraged to identify any conflicts of interest. Provided that an editor is able to maintain a neutral point of view, utilizes reliable and published sources, and demonstrates transparency about connections with subjects, it is possible for an organizational employee to write and edit Wikipedia content pertaining to that same organization.[3] Indeed, the iterative processes of researching, writing, and editing can provide opportunities for critical self-reflection which encourage editors and organizations to think thoughtfully about organizational history and strategic goals. Nevertheless, editing an article about one's own organization is an activity that should be approached with caution.

Wikidata

Wikidata is a sister project to Wikipedia (both are administered by the Wikimedia Foundation) and is fast becoming a significant source of structured data records. Launched in October 2012, it uses a crowd-sourcing model to create and edit structured data records while reconciling data from various Wikipedia language versions. It currently contains over 27 million items and has over 2.9 million registered contributors, of which more than 17,000 are active (Wikimedia Foundation, Inc., 2016), and the data are exposed in machine-readable formats such as JSON, XML and RDF (Vrandečić and Krötzsch, 2014). Wikidata administrators acknowledge its role in helping to populate Google's Knowledge Graph, but they are quick to point out that it does not replace Freebase. "Whereas Freebase was the open core of the Knowledge Graph, this is not true for Wikidata. Wikidata is one source of the Knowledge Graph among many, but does not have the same standing as Freebase had" (Wikidata, 2015). Some consultants maintain that Wikidata does influence KC results, but stress that there are no guarantees (Edward, 2015).

SWI ENVIRONMENTAL SCAN

The 125 member organizations[4] of the Association of Research Libraries (ARL) were studied in 2015–2016 to determine the condition of their SWIs and to determine whether there was a correlation of SWI with the existence of records in certain knowledge bases (Arlitsch, 2017; Arlitsch, 2016). In addition to searching Google to determine whether a KC was visible for each organization, searches were conducted for the presence of records for the organizations in five knowledge bases: Google My Business, Google+, Wikipedia, DBpedia, and Wikidata.

Results

Data collected for this study demonstrate that there is room for significant improvement in the current state of SWIs among ARL libraries, as measured by the presence or lack of accurate KC, and most libraries have not created or maintained records for their organizations in Semantic Web knowledge bases.

The study results bring into focus the semantic difference between the concept of an entity and the name by which that entity must be located in a search engine. The names of ARL member libraries became an unexpected but important part of this study. ARL libraries voluntarily submit a primary (official) name to the ARL for inclusion in the ARL membership directory.[5] But 94 of the 125 member libraries also use alternate names,[6] and they use each of these names inconsistently and usually don't explain the relationship of the names to search engines.

Google searches for only the primary names of library organizations yielded accurate KCs just 46 percent of the time, while searches for only alternate names showed accurate KCs 79 percent of the time. Combined, only 60 percent of the 219 primary *and* alternate names of the libraries displayed an accurate KC during Google searches. Clearly, there is a discrepancy in the primary names that ARL libraries provide for lists like the ARL membership directory and how they represent themselves in other forums on the Web.

The analysis becomes much more interesting with the introduction of data that recorded the "same as" relationship when two KCs displayed for a given ARL member library. It can be stated that 82 percent of the ARL library organizations displayed an accurate KC when the results of primary *or* alternate names were taken into consideration. If the search engine understands that an organization has two different names, then a single KC will be displayed, regardless of whether the primary or the alternate name is being searched. However, the data show that only 37 percent of ARL libraries enjoy this "same as" status. When accurate KCs display for both the primary and alternate name of a member library, the two KCs are usually not the same. In addition, the two different KCs often display different facts about the same organization.

Approximately 11 percent of KCs that displayed during searches were for the wrong organization. In most cases, this inaccuracy was recorded because a KC displayed for a branch library on campus rather than the main library or the library umbrella organization that was being searched. For example, one would expect the name "Boston College Libraries" to be the umbrella name for all the libraries at Boston College, but using that search term in Google resulted in the display of a KC for the "Babst Art Library." Similarly, a search for "Yale University Library" displayed a KC for Yale's "Divinity School Library."

The data also show a low presence of records in Semantic Web knowledge bases, which correlate to the lack of KCs (see table 12.1).

TABLE 12.1

Number and percentage of records that exist in knowledge bases for primary and alternate names of ARL Libraries

Knowledge Base	Primary (% of 125)	Alternate (% of 94)	Total (% of 219)
Google My Business	28 (22%)	40 (43%)	68 (31%)
Google+ (unverified)	25 (20%)	17 (18%)	42 (19%)
Google+ (verified)	22 (18%)	19 (20%)	41 (19%)
Wikipedia (w/o infobox)	10 (8%)	16 (17%)	26 (12%)
Wikipedia (w/infobox)	30 (24%)	26 (28%)	56 (26%)
DBpedia	30 (24%)	39 (41%)	69 (32%)
Wikidata	26 (21%)	37 (39%)	63 (29%)

SWI AS A SERVICE

Surveys conducted by our research team as early as 2012 identified shortcomings in the Montana State University Library's representation on the Semantic Web, as well as numerous other organizations on campus. In August 2015, we launched a new library-based service that establishes robust SWI from the top of the institution (colleges and departments) down to centers, institutes, and laboratories. The goal of the SWI service is to overcome ambiguity, incomplete description, and partial understanding of academic entities.

Methods developed during our research not only hold great promise for improving the SWIs of academic entities, but also blaze an exciting new path of service-oriented research for academic libraries and librarians. In addition to describing the development and implementation of these new services, this section addresses the reasons why academic libraries are ideally situated and academic librarians are uniquely qualified to engage in this "new knowledge work."

Goals of an SWI Service

1. *Disambiguation*—Accurate and authoritative content in LOD sources reduces ambiguity. For example, Montana State University hopes that an open web query for "MSU College of Business" will provide search results featuring information about the Jake Jabs College of Business and Entrepreneurship (JJCBE). However, this query is beset by ambiguity. Query language is incomplete,[7] the "MSU" abbreviation is used by various institutions,[8] a colloquial name is used, and "College of Business" is a commonly used name. SWI service improves machine comprehension by translating the query "MSU College of Business" from a string of terms into a specific thing in a particular place with unique relationships with other entities.

2. *Curation*—Creating and curating content allows machines to ingest information about an entity, including its name, location, type, function, characteristics, and its relationship to other entities. While many LOD sources are aided by community contributions, monitoring the content over time ensures accuracy and minimizes staleness.

3. *Search Results*—Robust, reliable, and contextual search results are a strong proxy indicator that an entity is well described within LOD sources and has achieved some degree of SWI. When entities are understood within contextual relationships, search results and machine-generated recommendations can be contextual and adaptive.

4. *Reputation*—SWI service also intends to credibly enhance the reputation of an academic entity. Increased discoverability and confirmed information about the organization increase credibility and trust, creating a virtuous cycle of increasing reputation.

Demonstrating Value

Demonstrating the value associated with an SWI service can be tailored to the specific interests of stakeholders. To maintain partner involvement and to clearly demonstrate the value of SWI service, the MSU Library provides bimonthly analytics briefs (i.e., a jargon-free slide deck that includes quantitative data, screenshots, and proposed next steps). Additionally, library staff routinely meet with stakeholders, share updates with the university administration, present at conferences, publish research articles, and so on. While the modes, methods, and frequency of communication will vary as needed, there are two primary metrics that provide universal applicability for demonstrating the value of SWI service: visibility and reputation.

Visibility Measured via Web Analytics

Comprehensive web analytics data are used to demonstrate the efficacy and impact of the SWI service. The MSU Library collects and analyzes data from Google Analytics, Google Search Console, and Google My Business Insights.

Google Analytics—Widely used in academic libraries and various other industries, Google Analytics[9] is a powerful web analytics platform that tracks and reports numerous website traffic variables. The platform collects copious amounts of data, including anonymized user demographics, geolocation, route to website, behaviors within website, and so on.

Google Search Console (GSC)—Data gathered from GSC indicate how Google search engine crawlers interact with the website, which in turn affects how the website appears in search results. Understanding what search engines know (or don't know) about the website, and what problems they encounter while crawling, enables the optimization of website performance in search results. GSC provides information about *search appearance*—the presence and functionality of structured data, reports errors, and suggests HTML improvements; and information about *search traffic*—search terms, clicks, impressions, click-through rate (CTR), position; Google search engine indexing, site-mapping, and so on. It is important to note that GSC only provides a sliding ninety-day window from which data can be accessed.

Google My Business Insights (GMB)—GMB Insights[10] provides data about how users find the entity[11] on the Web and actions users take with provided information. After an entity has been claimed and verified, GMB Insights provides information about *how* (i.e., searching directly for entity name or searching for category, product, or service) and *where* (i.e., search or maps) users search for the entity. Additionally, GMB Insights indicates actions that users take on the GMB listing (i.e., visiting the website, requesting driving directions, making a phone call, viewing photos).

The consistent review of analytics data provides various quantitative measures of change in the visibility of an entity. Moreover, thoughtful consideration and comparison of analytics data over time and among entities provides a data-rich guide for engaging in curation activities to further refine techniques and content.

PROCESS

The MSU Library has developed a systematic and iterative process for collaborating with academic units to create and curate content required by LOD sources. The process developed at the MSU Library focuses on building partner relationships (*Outreach*), identifying any existing components of SWI (*Baseline*), populating (*Creation*) and maintaining (*Curation*) trusted LOD sources, and monitoring changes in entity visibility and reputation (*Analysis*). As depicted in figure 12.1, data gathered during *Analysis* is likely to lead to the creation of additional content or guide the curation of existing content.

To date, the MSU Library has used this process to establish successful partnerships with twenty-two academic entities across campus (see table 12.2). After successfully enhancing the SWI of the MSU Library, our research team conducted a pilot with our first on-campus partner, the Center for Biofilm Engineering[12] (CBE). Lessons learned from the CBE pilot led to further refinements of the SWI service process.

Outreach

Outreach is a critical first step in building a successful partnership and must continue throughout the duration of partnership. Maintaining open communication and providing partners with frequent updates help to maintain partner involvement and clearly demonstrates the value of SWI service.

FIGURE 12.1

Iterative process of establishing and curating Semantic Web Identity as developed by Montana State University Library

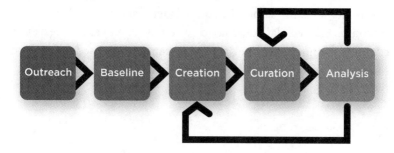

TABLE 12.2

List of Montana State University entities currently participating in MSU Library's Semantic Web Identity service

Pilots	Wave 1 Fall 2015	Wave 2 Spring 2016	Wave 3 Summer 2016	Wave 4 Fall 2016	Wave 5 Spring 2017
MSU Library	Campus Planning, Design and Construction	College of Agriculture	Office of Admissions	College of Arts and Architecture	Gallatin College
Center for Biofilm Engineering	Honors College	College of Education, Health and Human Development	Office of International Programs	School of Architecture	College of Nursing
	Jake Jabs College of Business and Entrepreneurship	College of Engineering	College of Letters and Science	School of Art	Western Transportation Institute
	Office of the Provost	MSU Extension		School of Film and Photography	
		Graduate School		School of Music	
		Food and Health Lab			

Baseline

Before engaging in efforts to enhance the SWI of an academic entity, it is important to document what search engines and LOD sources already know, don't know, or think they know about the entity. Documenting SWI baseline is most easily accomplished via data download (when available) and screenshots (the most common method). Baseline data and screenshots are used routinely during analysis, and data should be well-described, organized, and preserved.

Creation

When machines better understand an entity, search engines are more likely to present relevant and actionable information to a search user. SWI service focuses on creating verifiable content in three trusted LOD sources.

Google My Business

Creating a GMB listing is arguably the single most important step an academic organization can take to establish robust SWI. Since GMB is a proprietary database owned by Google, the creation of a GMB property includes the wide-ranging effect of integrating with multiple Google platforms. For example, claiming and verifying a GMB property generates a verified Google+ profile.

Two paths can lead to the creation of a GMB listing: claiming an existing property or creating a new property. *Claim*—Begin by conducting an open web search for the entity. If search results display an organic KC, then clicking the "Own this business?" link will initiate the process of claiming the entity. *Create*—If search results do not display a KC, then it is necessary to navigate to GMB, search for the entity, and follow the steps for creating a new GMB listing.

Verification of a new GMB listing is required for information to appear in other Google platforms. When claiming or creating an entity within GMB, a user is required to provide a physical address. GMB then mails a postcard containing a unique verification code to the entity's physical address. Entering the entity address and requesting a verification postcard is relatively straightforward. GMB expects most postcards to arrive within five days.

Academic addresses pose problems for the timely delivery of GMB verification postcards. Academic addresses might be expressed as a room number and building name, and a single academic building likely contains multiple entities.

Campus mail systems regularly utilize campus-specific post office boxes featuring a distinct postal code. Many campus mailing addresses operate independent from the physical street address of an entity. For these reasons, postcard delivery may require more than the five days expected by GMB.

When postcard delivery becomes significantly delayed, GMB is willing to provide alternate methods for verifying the authenticity of a listing. Having requested, but not received postcards for some entities, the MSU Library has been able to verify GMB listings via phone conversations, e-mailed photographs of the entity, and Google Hangouts (i.e., live-streaming video). Certain entities may be eligible for phone, e-mail, or instant[13] verification. GMB Help[14] can clarify verification processes or request alternative verification methods.

Wikipedia

Creating an encyclopedic Wikipedia entry is an important component in establishing a robust SWI for an academic entity, but it may also be the most time-consuming component of the creation phase of SWI service, since it involves the iterative process of researching, writing, and editing. However, creating a stub entry may be enough to get experts in the community to help research, write, and polish the article, thereby leveraging the power of crowd-sourcing.

At its most collaborative, creating Wikipedia content involves equal investments by the library and the academic partner. Equitable distribution of the workload tends to enable more efficient creation of encyclopedic content. Conversely, in a more centralized model, the library is predominantly responsible for the bulk of researching, writing, editing, and publishing activities, with only limited input from the academic partner.

No matter what the degree of collaboration, it is the responsibility of the library (as the SWI service provider) to expertly guide the research, writing, editing, and publication of encyclopedic Wikipedia content. Representatives from the academic entity are most familiar with that entity and are therefore well-positioned to identify source materials and provide tacit knowledge. However, creating encyclopedic content for Wikipedia differs in tone, purpose, and process from the marketing and promotional content traditionally produced by academic entities. Wikipedia should not be used as a soapbox or means of promotion. Articles that do not maintain a neutral point of view or lack reliable sources are likely to be revised or deleted by the community of editors. Offering SWI service requires the library to provide expertise regarding Wikipedia's purpose, formatting, organization, and other norms. In short, the academic entity provides content knowledge and the library offers process and context expertise.

The researching and writing process tends to work most smoothly when the library uses its Wikipedia expertise to develop a richly descriptive template for the academic partner. With preliminary headings and suggested references, the template provides a framework to initiate the collaborative research and writing process. Research regarding Wikipedia best practices suggests that any entries about academic entities (see figure 12.2) should, at a minimum, include an infobox,[15] lead (i.e., abstract), and table of contents. Additional encyclopedic information (e.g., historical background, location and institutional affiliation, description of academic programs, distinguished faculty, notable alumni, and nonacademic partnerships) should be appropriately situated among various sections of the entry.

The degree of collaboration will influence the assignment of specific responsibilities during the creation of Wikipedia content. The SWI service recipient (i.e., academic partner) and SWI service provider (i.e., library) will collaboratively conduct research and cowrite a draft. Thereafter, the library will provide editorial feedback based upon its expert knowledge of Wikipedia principles and SWI best practices. Editorial feedback will result in revisions, additions, and redactions. As indicated in figure 12.3, the creation of Wikipedia content is inherently iterative and is necessarily connected with subsequent and ongoing efforts to curate content.

Those unfamiliar with writing or editing content for Wikipedia are encouraged to familiarize themselves with the encyclopedia's fundamental principles.[16] Reviewing how-to guides, such as "Wikipedia:Your first article,"[17] is an easy method for increasing your Wikipedia fluency. In general, all Wikipedia content must adhere to three core principles:

Neutral Point of View—the fair, proportionate, and non-biased representation of significant views that have been published on a topic
Verifiability—readers can confirm that information is drawn from reliable, published sources
No Original Research—articles should not present new analysis, and content must be attributable to reliable, published sources

In addition to reviewing Wikipedia documentation, it is tremendously helpful to connect with the institution's Wikipedia Visiting Scholar[18] (if available) and/or

Wikipedia entry for Jake Jabs College of Business and Entrepreneurship

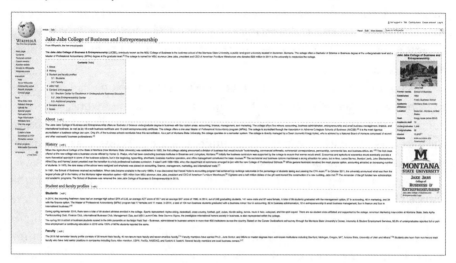

When creating a Wikipedia entry, it is important to abide by Wikipedia standards and select appropriate templates. As shown in the Wikipedia entry for "Jake Jabs College of Business and Entrepreneurship,"* important features include "Lead," "Table of Contents," and "Infobox" with important (and oft-used by LOD applications) structured statements and image/logo from Wikimedia Commons. This March 2017 screen-shot displays a portion of the entry, but does not display all information.
*en.wikipedia.org/wiki/Jake_Jabs_College_of_Business_and_Entrepreneurship

Iterative Process of creating and curating Wikipedia content to enhance Semantic Web Identity of academic entities

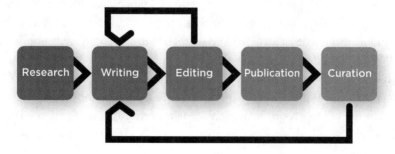

contact veteran Wikipedians for insight. These individuals will be able to provide expert feedback about the scope, tone, and references for intended entries as well as guidance regarding Wikipedia norms. Also, be sure to investigate how the parent institution is represented within Wikipedia. Contact university communications if there is no Wikipedia entry for the institution or if the existing entry is insufficient. If available, be sure to utilize the existing Wikipedia template and/or category.

As a final note, it is important to acknowledge that Wikipedia is an ongoing, open, and collaborative project. Its content is editable by anyone, and those contributing to the project should surrender the notion of control and embrace the idea of collaboration with the community of editors. While it is undeniably important to create the best possible (i.e., neutral, verifiable, authoritative, notable, descriptive, etc.) entry, it is equally critical to recognize that upon publication the entry will require recurring maintenance (see the "Curation" section below). There is much that can be written about an academic entity, but resisting the compulsion to write as much as possible about it is not only in the best interest of time and personnel resources, but also follows Wikipedia best practices. Wikipedia entries should contain enough information to demonstrate encyclopedic depth, but they should avoid unnecessary detail that results in an information deluge.

Wikidata

After the successful publication of an encyclopedic Wikipedia entry, attention is next turned to the free and open knowledge base, Wikidata. A connected Wikidata record will be created either by machine or a Wikimedia community member at some point after the publication of a Wikipedia entry.

It is tempting to follow a laissez-faire approach to record creation and allow a Wikidata record to simply appear. However, there are two discernable benefits associated with proactively creating a Wikidata record immediately after the successful publication of a Wikipedia entry. First, the proactive approach to Wikidata establishes a structured data record immediately after publication of a Wikipedia entry, providing a second source of verified information for search engine knowledge graphs. Second, the laissez-faire approach most often results in skeletal Wikidata records which contain only the most basic information. Although these records can eventually be enriched, it is more expedient to immediately create a highly descriptive and well-sourced Wikidata record via SWI service.

Wikidata record for Jake Jabs College of Business and Entrepreneurship

As depicted in this record for "Jake Jabs College of Business and Entrepreneurship,"* Wikidata records are most often associated with Wikipedia entries (but can also exist without a corresponding Wikipedia entry), present a short textual description, contain alternative names, and display structured data statements about an academic entity. This March 2017 screenshot shows a partial Wikidata record, but does not display all "Statements," "Identifiers," or "References" for the entity.
*www.wikidata.org/wiki/Q23303133

Creating a new Wikidata record requires three primary components: label, description, and aliases. This information provides the foundation for structured data and appears in a table atop every Wikidata record (see figure 12.4):

Label—the most common name by which the entity will be known; only one label is allowed per record; it is recommended (but not required) that the Wikidata label be identical to the connected Wikipedia entry title

Description—non-biased information that briefly describes and disambiguates a label

Aliases—alternative names for the entity; an entity can have as many aliases for an item as necessary; this is a crucial field for establishing "same as" relationships for alternate names as discussed in the "SWI Environmental Scan" section earlier in this chapter.

In addition to the three primary components, a robust Wikidata record consists of various statements expressed as property-value pairs. Each property is populated with predefined fields. A singular property can be paired with multiple values. Statements can be further enriched with additional details (i.e., qualifiers) and supported by references. When creating a Wikidata record for an academic entity, some of the more common statements include "instance of," "location," "parent organization," "official website," and "Commons Category," as well as various "Identifiers."[19]

Curation

Populating trusted LOD sources with accurate, authoritative, and consistent information is a significant step toward the establishment of a robust SWI for an academic entity. An academic entity's SWI can only be as accurate, authoritative, consistent, and useful as the information upon which it is built. Given the ever-evolving nature of information, it is necessary to attentively and recurrently curate LOD sources to ensure the ongoing accuracy of information.

The curation of LOD sources can be grouped into two categories:

Respond—It is necessary for an SWI service team to either confirm or correct changes suggested by other users within Google My Business, Wikipedia, or Wikidata. To assist with responsive curation, each of the three LOD sources mentioned above provides various notification methods. The GMB dashboard provides an "Account Summary" that indicates the status of listings as well as a "To-do" list that identifies problem areas or suggested changes for all listings. Both Wikipedia and Wikidata allows users to add pages to their "Watchlist," which tracks recent changes made to watched pages. Wikipedia and Wikidata users can opt in to receive e-mail notifications when any watched page is changed.

Update—Academic entities morph, merge, and otherwise evolve. An academic entity's SWI can only be as robust as the underlying information. As new information becomes available about an academic entity and its relationships, it is important for the SWI service to update the appropriate LOD sources. Although the library can carefully watch for updates, changes, or news from academic partners, it is more effective to receive updates directly from SWI service recipients. An academic entity is in the best position to know about any changes pertinent to its description and/or relationships.

It is possible for the library and academic partner to share some curation responsibilities. An academic partner may have resources to curate its GMB listing—for example, updating special hours or adding new photos. The library is best suited to maintain structured data in Wikidata. The specifics of the collaboration curation agreement will vary with each partnership. SWI service tends to operate most efficiently and generate the greatest impact when leveraging the combined strengths of a fully collaborative partnership.

When developing the SWI service model, the MSU Library made the strategic decision to locate its SWI activities with its Department of Resource Description and Metadata Services (RDMS). There is no doubt that our SWI service leverages the skills, knowledge, and personnel from other areas of the organization. However, as information curators, database managers, and controlled vocabulary experts, RDMS possesses expertise that ideally aligns with the description and curation of information, which in turn aid in the discovery of entities.

CASE STUDIES

The following case studies demonstrate how MSU's SWI service helped achieve SWI for three academic entities. The first case study addresses the internal application of SWI service to the MSU Library. The subsequent case studies examine the Jake Jabs College of Business and Entrepreneurship (JJCBE) and the Honors College, which were two of the earliest adopters among SWI service recipients (see table 12.1 for a full list of academic partners at MSU). JJCBE and the Honors College at MSU differ in their academic disciplines, organizational history, and student bodies, but both entities saw the strategic benefits associated with SWI service.

◙ Montana State University Library

About the MSU Library

The Montana State University Library serves the students, faculty, and surrounding community of Montana State University, a land-grant research university whose flagship campus is located in Bozeman, Montana.

Baseline

In November 2012, a Google search for "Montana State University Library" revealed a surprising entry in Google's Knowledge Graph display. Instead of displaying the flagship library of the Montana State University system, located in Bozeman, the search results page included a Knowledge Card for a branch campus academic library located on another MSU campus in Billings, Montana (see figure 12.5). In early 2013, several MSU Library staff and faculty initiated the first formal steps that would eventually lead to a dramatically improved SWI for the MSU Library and eventually give rise to our SWI service model.

From the perspective of the Google search engine, the MSU Library in Bozeman simply was a text string and did not exist as a "thing" (entity). With the exception of Freebase, no records existed for the organization in knowledge bases (table 12.3). The information being ingested by the Knowledge Graph led Google to incorrectly conclude that the MSU library was a building in Billings, Montana.

Process

The process to establish SWI at the MSU Library began in early 2013. The actions to establish an authoritative and visible SWI are summarized in table 12.4.

Current Conditions

Populating trusted LOD sources with authoritative information about the MSU Library has resulted in a search results page (figure 12.6) that is markedly improved from the November 2012 screenshot (figure 12.5).

In addition to the improved website and social media content found in the left-hand column, the right-hand column of the search results page now presents a very robust KC for the MSU Library. Based upon information added to the knowledge bases, the search engine is able to determine that the query "montana

FIGURE 12.5

November 2012 screenshot of Google search results page for "Montana State University Library"

TABLE 12.3

Summary of SWI Conditions—Montana State University Library, January 2013

Google Knowledge Graph Card	Displayed incorrect organization and incorrect location
Google My Business	Neither claimed nor verified
Google+	Two profiles existed. Neither profile verified.
Wikipedia	No entry
DBpedia	No record
Wikidata	No record*
Freebase	A record for Renne Library (the alternate name for the MSU Library) was created on March 10, 2012 by someone unknown to the MSU Library. There was no evidence of a record for Montana State University Library.

*Launched in October 2012, Wikidata was initially very limited in its scope (Vrandečić and Krötzsch 2014). Given the timing and initial aim of Wikidata, there is little reason to expect that Wikidata would contain a record for MSU Library in January 2013.

TABLE 12.4

Summary of SWI Actions and Results—Montana State University Library

Google My Business	Business claimed and the record improved by August 2014.
Google+	Officially verified in August 2014. Duplicate Google+ profile successfully deleted.
Wikipedia	Research and writing began in the spring of 2013 under the guidance of experienced Wikipedia editors. The article was published on September 5, 2013.
DBpedia	Record appeared in April 2014 data release.
Wikidata	Record generated from Wikipedia by a bot on November 29, 2013.
Freebase*	A new Freebase record was auto generated on September 10, 2013, five days after the publication of the Wikipedia article. The record was titled *Montana State University Library* and was generated by a bot called "wikirecon_bot." MSU Library faculty added a "same as" declaration to the *Renne Library* Freebase record that linked it to the *Montana State University Library* Freebase record.
Google Knowledge Graph Card	An accurate KC began to appear for the MSU Library in September 2013, and gradually evolved to become much more robust as other knowledge bases were populated.

*Freebase was acquired by Google in 2010. In 2014 Google announced that it would cease building Freebase in favor of Wikidata (Butzbach, 2014). Therefore, MSU Library is the only instance of SWI service that incorporates Freebase. All subsequent partnerships have removed Freebase from the SWI service process. Migration of Freebase records to Wikidata was completed in 2016 (Tanon, Vrandečić, Schaffert, Steiner, & Pintscher, 2016). Freebase is now available in "read-only" mode at https://developers.google .com/freebase/.

state university library" refers to the academic entity located within the building known as Renne Library on the campus of Montana State University. Within the KC, search users are presented information about the MSU Library, including its physical location, contact information, type of entity, a short description (ingested from Wikipedia), map location, verified social media profiles, and so on. The information presented within the KC is actionable (e.g., visit website, get directions, call phone number), indicates a high degree of interoperability (pulling data from GMB, Wikipedia, Wikidata, social media, etc.), and seeks to answer likely questions (e.g., How do I contact MSU Library? Is MSU Library currently busy? What do other users think about MSU Library?). The creation of

FIGURE 12.6

March 2017 screenshot of Google search results page for "montana state university library"

authoritative content within trusted LOD sources facilitated machine learning, which in turn presents more robust, authoritative, and useful information to human search users. In short, the query "montana state university library" has evolved from a search of a string of words to a search for a thing in a specific place with particular relationships to other things.

Jake Jabs College of Business and Entrepreneurship

About the College

Previously known as the MSU College of Business, the Jake Jabs College of Business and Entrepreneurship (JJCBE) is the business school of Montana State University.

Baseline

Prior to SWI service, JJCBE was understood by search engines as a string of search terms, but not as an entity. Due to this lack of understanding, an open web search for "montana state university college of business" returned sparse, ambiguous, and loosely related results. As displayed in figure 12.7, the Google search results page features discrete bits of data functioning within stand-alone systems that do not readily communicate. There is some useful information, including a nicely site-mapped entry for JJCBE. However, search users are presented with unauthoritative information, which leads to ambiguity and uncertainty. After the initial result, the search user is left to wonder about the relevance of information about "Jabs Hall" or "Montana State University: College of Nursing." These results are influenced by absent and incomplete knowledge base records, as summarized in table 12.5.

Process

The process to establish an SWI for JJCBE began in August 2015. JJCBE was the first academic partner to receive SWI service based upon the iterative process explained earlier (figure 12.1). The actions taken to establish an authoritative and visible SWI are summarized in table 12.6.

Current Conditions

As displayed in figure 12.8, the post-SWI service search results page looks considerably different than the pre-SWI service screenshot (figure 12.7). The initial result item (a site-mapped website entry) is retained, but is now complemented by other authoritative, robust, and actionable information. The left-hand column contains links to contextually associated websites, popular news articles, and Wikipedia content.

The right-hand column of the search results page now presents a robust KC for JJCBE, including its physical location, contact information, type of entity, a short description (ingested from Wikipedia), map location, and verified social media profiles. The information presented within the KC is actionable (e.g., visit website, get directions, call phone number) and indicates a high degree of interoperability (pulling data from GMB, Wikipedia, Wikidata, etc.). In the event that the search user mistyped the query or was looking for another entity but could not quite recall the name, the JJCBE KC also presents some related entities that might be of interest.

Summary of SWI Conditions—Jake Jabs College of Business and Entrepreneurship, August 2015

Google Knowledge Graph Card	None
Google My Business	None
Google+	None
Wikipedia	No entry
Wikidata	No record
DBpedia	No record
Freebase	No record

FIGURE 12.7

August 2015 screenshot of Google search results page for "montana state university college of business"

TABLE 12.6

Summary of SWI Actions and Results – Jake Jabs College of Business and Entrepreneurship

Google My Business	Business claimed in late August 2015. Due to delays in receiving GMB postcard, the listing was not verified until November 2015. After two failed attempts to receive a verification postcard, an alternate verification method was arranged via Google My Business Help. JJCBE GMB listing was verified through a combination of phone calls and e-mailed photos of the entity's physical location.
Google+	Officially verified in September 2015.
Wikipedia	Research and writing began in August 2015 under the guidance of MSU Library's SWI Researcher and with assistance from MSU Library's Wikipedia Visiting Scholar. A staff member from JJCBE worked in close collaboration with MSU Library to research, write, and revise the initial content. The article was published on February 16, 2016.
DBpedia	Record appeared in April 2016 dataset release.
Wikidata	Record created by user:Danrok on March 20, 2016.
Google Knowledge Graph Card	An accurate KC began to appear for JJCBE in November 2015 (after the GMB listing was verified). The JJCBE KC gradually evolved to become much more robust as other LOD sources were populated with authoritative information.

FIGURE 12.8

March 2017 screenshot of Google search results page for "Montana State University College of Business"

Honors College at Montana State University

About the College

Originally established in 1964 as an honors program and elevated to college status in 2013, the Honors College at Montana State University now provides enriched academic opportunities for more than 1,300 MSU students annually.

Baseline

As displayed in figure 12.9, the Google search results page for the Honors College featured some useful information, yet much more information remained buried and unavailable to search users. Aside from clicking one of the provided links and then searching a different website for the desired bits of information, search users are presented with few options. These results are influenced by absent and incomplete records in knowledge bases trusted by the search engine, as summarized in table 12.7.

TABLE 12.7

Summary of SWI Conditions—Honors College at Montana State University, August 2015

Google Knowledge Graph Card	None
Google My Business	None
Google+	None
Wikipedia	No entry
Wikidata	No record
DBpedia	No record

FIGURE 12.9

August 2015 screenshot of Google search results page for "Montana
State University Honors College"

Process

The process to establish an SWI for the Honors College at MSU began in August
2015. The Honors College was among the first cohort of academic partners to
receive SWI service. The actions taken to establish an authoritative and visible
SWI are summarized in table 12.8.

Current Conditions

After application of the SWI service to the Honors College at MSU, an open web
search for "montana state university honors college" now provides search users
with a rich assortment of authoritative and actionable information.

TABLE 12.8

Summary of SWI Actions and Results – Honors College at Montana State University

Google My Business	Business claimed in September 2015. Due to delays in receiving the GMB postcard, the listing was not verified until November 2015. After two failed attempts to receive a verification postcard, an alternate verification method was arranged via Google My Business Help. The Honors College at MSU GMB listing was verified through a combination of phone calls and e-mailed photos of the entity's physical location.
Google+	Officially verified in October 2015.
Wikipedia	Research and writing began in August 2015 under the guidance of MSU Library's SWI Researcher. Due to time and personnel constraints, the Honors College at MSU could only provide editorial comments on the initial Wikipedia content. The article was published on July 11, 2016. Since publication of the Wikipedia article, staff and faculty from the Honors College at MSU have provided MSU Library with information updates to aid in curation of Wikipedia content.
DBpedia	The most recent DBpedia dataset release occurred in April 2016. This dataset release contains Wikipedia data dating from March/April 2016. Since the Honors College at MSU Wikipedia article was not published until July 2016, there is no record available in any existing DBpedia dataset releases.
Wikidata	Record created by user:Jdshanks (MSU Library's SWI Researcher) on July 19, 2016.
Google Knowledge Graph Card	An accurate KC began to appear for Honors College at MSU in November 2015 (within 24 hours of verifying the GMB listing). The Honors College at MSU KC gradually evolved to become much more robust as other LOD sources were populated with authoritative information.

As displayed in figure 12.10, the post-SWI service search results page looks considerably different than the pre-SWI service screenshot (figure 12.9). The initial result item (a site-mapped website entry) is retained, but is now complemented by other authoritative, robust, and actionable information. The left-hand column contains links to contextually associated websites, popular news articles, and Wikipedia content.

In addition to the website links found in the left-hand column, the right-hand column of the search results page now presents a robust KC for the Honors College at MSU, with similar information elements as the KCs for the MSU Library and the JJCBE.

March 2017 screenshot of Google search results page for "Montana State University Honors College"

Summary of Case Studies

In each of the three cases presented above, the iterative process outlined in figure 12.1 was applied. Each case resulted in clear improvements to the existing KC, or the creation of a new KC, with accurate information elements and interoperable features. Nearly twenty other organizations at Montana State University are now participating in the SWI service. Each instance has yielded similar results, clearly demonstrating that the approach of creating or improving data records in Google My Business, Wikipedia, and Wikidata works.

WHY IS THE LIBRARY BEST SUITED TO PROVIDE AN SWI SERVICE?

At first glance, components of the SWI service may appear to overlap with the aims and efforts of other divisions commonly operating within most contemporary universities. Some readers may wonder why a university's information technology (IT) office does not monitor DBpedia records or Wikidata records. Or perhaps they may wonder why a university's communications or marketing personnel are not engaging with Google+, Wikipedia, or GMB. Indeed, it is common for a university's communications and/or marketing personnel to manage a university-level Wikipedia entry, GMB listing, and/or Google+ profile. However, such efforts are focused at the top-level identity of an academic institution and tend to have little trickle-down benefit for colleges, departments, centers, institutes, or laboratories. Moreover, ensuring the visibility of all academic entities on campus requires the careful creation and consistent curation of LOD content. Working in isolation, IT or communications/marketing units are unlikely to have the resources or knowledge to successfully and consistently deploy SWI service for all academic entities across campus.

Given its role as a centralized, multidisciplinary information hub on college and university campuses, the academic library is well positioned to liaise and collaborate with other academic units in the course of implementing an SWI service. Moreover, with expertise as information scientists, data curators, and digital application developers, academic librarians are well-positioned to offer services that carefully populate and consistently curate structured data to ensure a robust, contextual, and authoritative SWI across their institution. Creating and curating structured metadata records is the business of libraries, even (or perhaps we should say especially) on the Semantic Web.

CONCLUSION

Semantic Web Identity is an exciting opportunity to develop new library services that are expected to become highly valued by the campus community. Driving more relevant user traffic to products and services is important to any organization trying to distinguish itself and increase its value proposition. Increased research funding, student enrollment, faculty recruitment, and institutional reputation and ranking are goals of great importance to higher education administrators. Libraries can provide technical solutions that address these strategic aims, and the SWI process established by the MSU Library has proven that libraries can be successful in this area.

Establishing SWI has boosted the visibility of MSU, its academic entities, and its scholarly products, and this visibility is expected to enhance MSU's reputation and positively influence student enrollment and grant funding. In addition to data collected from web analytics, the MSU Library is currently developing assessment methods to measure the influence of the SWI service on metrics of significance for our university partners. Combining web analytics with data collected by MSU partners (e.g., the Office of Admissions, Alumni Foundation, Office of Sponsored Programs, etc.) will demonstrate how the SWI service increases actionable events such as student applications, donations, and grant funding.

While solving the technical problems associated with this issue can be interesting, viewing SWI only from a technical standpoint misses the greater picture. The incredible advances in computational and network power have led to the "Internet of Things," where machines converse with each other's data records to surface robust and actionable information. These machine-based interactions are dependent on accurate and verified structured data records, which librarians have traditionally curated in library systems and can do so again on the Semantic Web in trusted LOD sources like Google My Business, Wikipedia, and Wikidata.

NOTES

1. A Knowledge Graph Card may also be known as a Knowledge Card, Knowledge Panel, or Information Panel.
2. Linking Open Data cloud diagram 2017, by Andrejs Abele, John P. McCrae, Paul Buitelaar, Anja Jentzsch, and Richard Cyganiak, http://lod-cloud.net/.
3. More information about conflict-of-interest editing in Wikipedia is available at https://en.wikipedia.org/wiki/Wikipedia:Conflict_of_interest.
4. The number of ARL member libraries declined to 124 in 2016, after the data collection had been completed.
5. ARL membership directory: www.arl.org/membership/list-of-arl-members.
6. Alternate names are other names by which libraries refer to themselves. Often these are building names rather than organization names.
7. Montana State University does not have an academic entity with the official or colloquial name "College of Business." Instead, accounting, finance, marketing, and other business courses and degree programs are housed within the academic entity known as the Jake Jabs College of Business and Entrepreneurship. Nevertheless, "College of Business" is common query language.
8. In addition to Montana State University, the MSU abbreviation is commonly used by Manonmaniam Sundaranar University, Michigan State University, Mississippi State University, Missouri State University, Moldova State University, Morgan State University, and Murray State University, among others.

9. Google Analytics: https://analytics.google.com.

10. Google My Business: https://business.google.com/manage.

11. Given its commerce focus, Google My Business refers to users as "customers" and entities as "business." While Google My Business Insights provide an array of useful and informative data, the application of such data for Semantic Web Identity services does require a certain degree of translation of variables.

12. Center for Biofilm Engineering Intranet, Montana State University: www.biofilm .montana.edu.

13. GMB provides instant verification if the entity's website has previously been verified with Google Search Console. Given that academic entities tend to operate as website sub-domains within a centralized structure of IT and web administration, this verification method is generally unavailable.

14. Google My Business Help Center, https://support.google.com/business.

15. There are various infobox templates that can be used when developing a Wikipedia entry. Research conducted by the SWI group at MSU Library suggests that "Template:Infobox academic division" is most appropriate for presenting structured data about academic entities. More information is available at https://en.wikipedia.org/wiki/ Template:Infobox_academic_division.

16. Wikipedia:Five pillars: https://en.wikipedia.org/wiki/Wikipedia:Five_pillars.

17. Available at https://en.wikipedia.org/wiki/Wikipedia:Your_first_article. "Wikipedia:Your first article" provides a thorough overview of Wikipedia concepts, guidelines, processes, and tools.

18. Wikipedia Visiting Scholars: https://en.wikipedia.org/wiki/Wikipedia:Visiting_Scholars.

19. Wikidata allows users to input statements that correspond to various types of external authority control. Wikidata automatically creates a separate section (titled "Identifiers") that groups all authority control statements. Some common external identifiers for academic entities include Facebook ID, Google+ ID, ISNI, Instagram username, Ringgold identifier, and Twitter username. A full list of Wikidata properties with data type "external identifier" is available at https://www.wikidata.org/wiki/Special:ListProperties/ external-id.

REFERENCES

Arlitsch, K. November 19, 2016. "Data Set Supporting the Dissertation 'Semantic Web Identity in Academic Organizations: Search Engine Entity Recognition and the Sources That Influence Knowledge Graph Cards in Search Results." Montana State University ScholarWorks. https://doi.org/10.15788/M2F590.

————— . January 11, 2017. "Semantic Web Identity of Academic Organizations—Search Engine Entity Recognition and the Sources That Influence Knowledge Graph Cards in Search results." Dissertation. Humboldt-Universität zu Berlin, Berlin, Germany. http://edoc.hu-berlin.de/docviews/abstract.php?lang=ger&id=43177.

Arlitsch, K., and P. S. OBrien. 2013. *Improving the Visibility and Use of Digital Repositories through SEO.* Chicago: American Library Association.

Auer, S., C. Bizer, G. Kobilarov, J. Lehmann, R. Cyganiak, and Z. Ives. 2007. "DBpedia: A Nucleus for a Web of Open Data." In *The Semantic Web,* vol. 4825, pp. 722–35. Berlin, Heidelberg: Springer Berlin Heidelberg. http://link.springer.com/10.1007/978-3-540-76298-0_52.

Berners-Lee, T., J. Hendler, and O. Lassila. 2001. "The Semantic Web." *Scientific American* 284, no. 5: 34–43. https://doi.org/10.1038/scientificamerican0501-34.

Bernstein, A., J. Hendler, and N. Noy. 2016. "A New Look at the Semantic Web." *Communications of the ACM* 59, no. 9: 35–37. https://doi.org/10.1145/2890489.

Bouquet, P., H. Stoermer, and M. Vignolo. 2012. "Web of Data and Web of Entities: Identity and Reference in Interlinked Data in the Semantic Web." *Philosophy & Technology* 25, no. 1: 5–26. https://doi.org/10.1007/s13347-010-0011-6.

Butzbach, A. December 9, 2014. "Freebase Is Shutting Down—What Does It Mean for the Knowledge Graph and SEO?" www.brafton.com/news/freebase-shutting-mean-knowledge-graph-seo/.

Central Intelligence Agency. 2015. *CIA World Factbook* (Government). https://www.cia.gov/library/publications/the-world-factbook/.

comScore, Inc. March 16, 2016. "comScore Releases February 2016 U.S. Desktop Search Engine Rankings" (Commercial). https://www.comscore.com/Insights/Rankings/comScore-Releases-February-2016-US-Desktop-Search-Engine-Rankings.

Connaway, L. S., and T. J. Dickey. 2010. *The Digital Information Seeker: Report of Findings from Selected OCLC, RIN, and JISC User Behavior Projects* (p. 61). Dublin, Ohio: OCLC Research. www.jisc.ac.uk/media/documents/publications/reports/2010/digitalinformationseekerreport.pdf.

DePianto, S. September 30, 2016. "Helping Prospective Students Make Decisions about Their Future." https://blog.google/topics/education/helping-prospective-students-make-decisions-about-their-future/.

Edward, T. May 1, 2015. "Leveraging Wikidata to Gain a Google Knowledge Graph Result." http://searchengineland.com/leveraging-wikidata-gain-google-knowledge-graph-result-219706.

Erxleben, F., M. Günther, M. Krötzsch, J. Mendez, and D. Vrandečić. 2014. "Introducing Wikidata to the Linked Data Web." In *The Semantic Web—ISWC 2014,* ed. P. Mika, T. Tudorache, A. Bernstein, C. Welty, C. Knoblock, D. Vrandečić, . . . and C. Goble, vol. 8796, pp. 50–65. Cham, Switz.: Springer International. http://link.springer.com/10.1007/ 978-3-319-11964-9_4.

Google, Inc. 2017. "Get Your Free Business Listing on Google" (Commercial). https://www .google.com/business/.

Li, K., Y. Li, Y. Zhou, Z. Lv, and Y. Cao. July, 2013. "Knowledge-Based Entity Detection and Disambiguation." https://www.google.com/patents/US20130173604.

Lih, A. 2009. *The Wikipedia Revolution: How a Bunch of Nobodies Created the World's Greatest Encyclopedia.* New York: Hyperion.

Mendes, P., and M. Jakob. August 24, 2012. "Who's New in Google Summer of Code 2012: Part 3." http://google-opensource.blogspot.co.uk/2012/08/whos-new-in-google-summer -of-code-2012_24.html.

Meyer, R. April 15, 2015. "Europeans Use Google Way, Way More Than Americans Do: Google's Huge Market Share Is Part of What Strengthens the EU's Antitrust Case." *The Atlantic.* www.theatlantic.com/technology/archive/2015/04/europeans-use-google-way -way-more-than-americans-do/390612/.

Schmachtenberg, M., C. Bizer, and H. Paulheim. August 30, 2014. "State of the LOD Cloud 2014." University of Mannheim. http://linkeddatacatalog.dws.informatik.uni-mannheim .de/state/.

Shenoy, A., and A. Prabhu. 2016. "Introducing the Google Tools Suite." In *Introducing SEO,* by A. Shenoy and A. Prabhu, 37–55. Berkeley, CA: Apress. https://doi.org/10.1007/978-1 -4842-1854-9_4.

Singhal, A. May 15, 2012. "Introducing the Knowledge Graph: Things, Not Strings" (Corporate). http://googleblog.blogspot.com/2012/05/introducing-knowledge-graph-things -not.html.

Suchanek, F. M., G. Kasneci, and G. Weikum. 2007. "Yago: A Core of Semantic Knowledge." In *Proceedings of the 16th International Conference on World Wide Web,* 697–706. Banff, Can.: ACM. https://doi.org/10.1145/1242572.1242667.

Sullivan, D. May 16, 2012. "Google Launches Knowledge Graph to Provide Answers, Not Just Links." http://searchengineland.com/google-launches-knowledge-graph-121585.

Tanon, T. P., D. Vrandečić, S. Schaffert, T. Steiner, and L. Pintscher. 2016. "From Freebase to Wikidata: The Great Migration." In *Proceedings of the 125th International Conference on World Wide Web,* 1419–28. Montreal: IW3C2. https://doi.org/10.1145/2872427.2874809.

Thalhammer, A., and A. Rettinger. 2014. "Browsing DBpedia Entities with Summaries." In *The Semantic Web: ESWC 2014 Satellite Events,* ed. V. Presutti, E. Blomqvist, R. Troncy, H. Sack, I. Papadakis, and A. Tordai, vol. 8798, pp. 511–15. Cham, Switz.: Springer International. http://link.springer.com/10.1007/978-3-319-11955-7_76.

"Timeline of Web Search Engines." September 14, 2016. Wikipedia. https://en.wikipedia.org/wiki/Timeline_of_web_search_engines.

Vaish, R., K. Wyngarden, J. Chen, B. Cheung, and M. S. Bernstein. 2014. "Twitch Crowdsourcing: Crowd Contributions in Short Bursts of Time." In *Proceedings of the SIGCHI Conference on Human Factors in Computing Systems,* 3645–54. Toronto, Can.: ACM. https://doi.org/10.1145/2556288.2556996.

Vrandečić, D., and M. Krötzsch. 2014. "Wikidata: A Free Collaborative Knowledgebase." *Communications of the ACM* 57, no. 10: 78–85. https://doi.org/10.1145/2629489.

Wall, A. 2017. "History of Search Engines: From 1945 to Google Today." www.searchenginehistory.com.

Wikidata. June 18, 2015. "By Adding to Wikidata, I Have a Free Ticket into Google's Knowledge Graph, Right?" https://www.wikidata.org/wiki/Help:FAQ/Freebase.

Wikimedia Foundation, Inc. October 9, 2016. "Wikidata:Statistics" (Nonprofit). https://www.wikidata.org/wiki/Wikidata:Statistics.

Bringing Archival Collections to Wikipedia with the Remixing Archival Metadata Project (RAMP) Editor

MAIRELYS LEMUS-ROJAS AND TIMOTHY A. THOMPSON

WIKIPEDIA AND ARCHIVES

Wikipedia has been in existence for sixteen years, but it was not until recently that GLAM (Galleries, Libraries, Archives, and Museums) institutions started to see it as a trusted source and one they were interested in contributing to. Libraries and archives, in particular, have been slowly embracing the idea of contributing to Wikipedia, often motivated by the prospect of increasing the visibility and impact of their distinctive collections, which have been carefully curated by librarians and archivists alike. Different approaches have been taken by libraries and archives when it comes to contributing to Wikipedia. Some institutions have focused on adding links to Wikipedia articles in order to point back to their unique archival collections, whereas others have concentrated on enhancing the content of existing articles. Another way in which librarians and archivists can work together to share our collections is to collaborate on projects to enrich and repurpose the metadata that has already been created to describe them.

The University of Miami Libraries took this approach and developed a tool to facilitate the creation of Wikipedia articles using relevant metadata from the libraries' finding aids (documents that describe the scope, content, and context of archival collections). In this chapter, we will introduce the RAMP (Remixing Archival Metadata Project) editor and share our experience working on a pilot project conducted to test its viability.

BACKGROUND

The RAMP editor (https://tools.wmflabs.org/ramp/) was developed to provide the cultural heritage community with the ability to reuse, remix, and republish curated metadata via the English Wikipedia. RAMP is a web-based editing tool that allows users to generate records for creators of archival collections and publish the content as Wikipedia pages. It is built around two metadata formats, Encoded Archival Description (EAD) and Encoded Archival Context–Corporate Bodies, Persons, and Families (EAC-CPF).

These formats have been developed to provide organized access to archival and special collections. Findings aids, typically encoded using the EAD XML schema, now in its third edition (Library of Congress, 2017), are hierarchically structured documents that reflect the arrangement and disposition of a collection within an archive. EAD-encoded finding aids can be complex or simple, depending on the time and resources available for metadata creation, but they usually contain a section of contextual information (the scope of the collection, the biography or history of its creator) and a list of the collection's contents, often divided into series that reflect the provenance and original or intellectual order of the material.

Compared to EAD, EAC-CPF is a newer standard, and it has been codified in a separate XML schema (Staatsbibliothek zu Berlin, n.d.). The importance of context in understanding and maintaining archival collections entails an emphasis on relationships, whether among collections or the individuals, families, and organizations responsible for creating their content. EAC-CPF was designed to serve as a kind of authority record for creators of archival collections, but its purpose extends beyond recording variant names, for example, and it provides a vehicle for recording the many collections that might contain works by a single creator (for instance, a literary author's papers might be held in multiple, geographically dispersed repositories), as well as relationships to other creators and content.

Building the RAMP tool was just a small step toward providing the cultural heritage community with a way to more easily repurpose and expose its archival metadata through a widely accessed platform, Wikipedia. For some, the notion of contributing to Wikipedia is challenging and even discouraging, and the idea that the global community rather than a formalized entity is curating and contributing to this body of knowledge is a concept that has not yet been fully embraced by information professionals. Wikipedia allows for many voices, and we should actively join the conversation rather than passively observing its evolution.

ORIGINAL TOOL DEVELOPMENT

The original development of the RAMP tool started in early 2013 and took approximately two months. This was an in-house project, and no external funding was used toward its development. RAMP is an open source tool, and its code is available on GitHub (https://github.com/UMiamiLibraries/RAMP) for the community to use and modify. This project presented an opportunity for cross-departmental collaboration at the University of Miami Libraries and brought together librarians, archivists, and programmers working toward a common goal.

The original version of RAMP was developed using the standard LAMP stack of Linux, Apache, MySQL, and PHP, with a JavaScript front end. Its architecture was based on a software design pattern known as Model-View-Controller (MVC). On the back end, the PHP programming language is used to model the basic structure of the tool and to interact directly with three main web services: the Virtual International Authority File (VIAF), WorldCat Identities, and Wikipedia.[1] Data from these services is processed using JavaScript, and then is returned to the user.

At the heart of the design are two data transformation routines executed by a suite of XSLT (Extensible Stylesheet Language Transformations) stylesheets. Raw data is ingested as EAD/XML, and biographical information and information about significant relationships are extracted from the EAD and converted into EAC-CPF/XML, which is then exposed for enhancement through data lookups or direct user editing. A second XSLT transformation converts the enhanced EAC-CPF from XML to wikitext for publication to Wikipedia. The wikitext can be edited, saved, and merged with existing Wikipedia pages within the tool.

A raw XML editing interface for EAC-CPF records is provided through integration with the code editing software Ace Editor (Ajax.org, 2017). Although not ideal from a user-interface perspective, this basic editing capability proved to be a lightweight solution for viewing the results of the data enhancement process. In the original RAMP design, a web form was also included to allow users to create new EAC-CPF records. Later, a decision was made not to continue supporting this feature because a robust EAC-CPF creation tool, the xEAC editor, was already available and under active development.[2]

RAMP PILOT PROJECT

To explore the potential of the RAMP tool, we conducted a pilot project in spring 2014. We were interested in finding out how long it would take to create a new Wikipedia article and whether this process was something that could be easily integrated into existing workflows without impinging on other responsibilities. We were also curious to find out whether our contributions to the encyclopedia would increase web traffic to the library's website.

Once we had established what we were interested in testing, we initiated a conversation with stakeholders from the University of Miami's Cuban Heritage Collection, who selected a set of collections to be used in the pilot project. These collections represented individuals and organizations active in Cuban theater circles, and the focus of their content was not well represented in the English Wikipedia. We started by reviewing a set of finding aids to identify potential candidates for inclusion in the encyclopedia. Our first criterion was to select those that had the most complete biographical notes.

Next, we considered the "notability" of each subject. Wikipedia guidelines require that subjects be notable in order to merit inclusion in the encyclopedia. The general notability guideline states that "if a topic has received significant coverage in reliable sources that are independent of the subject, it is presumed to be suitable for a stand-alone article or list" ("Wikipedia:Notability," 2017). Decisions about whether a subject is notable or not are often controversial and have been a sticking point in the past for librarians and archivists interested in contributing to Wikipedia (Tennant, 2013). To avoid potential conflict, we selected what we considered to be the most "notable" collections for the pilot project: a total of 18 out of the 32 available Cuban theater collections. These collections represented Cuban and Cuban American actors, playwrights, directors, costume designers, and theater companies.

Although we identified collections that had already been processed, we intended to continue the work beyond the pilot project. We devised a workflow that would function with new collections and would involve key players from various departments. Once a collection was processed and a finding aid was created, the archivist working with the collection would submit a work request via a web form. Librarians in Cataloging & Metadata Services would receive an e-mail with the details of the work request. At that point, a librarian would claim the task and start creating a collection-level record and related authority records in OCLC Connexion, which would later be pushed to our local integrated library system. Finally, the same librarian would begin working with the RAMP tool to create Wikipedia articles for selected subjects.

For the pilot project, because the finding aids had already been created, we followed a modified workflow. The finding aids had been written by many different staff members over the years, and we wanted to be certain they all reflected a neutral point of view.[3] In republishing biographical descriptions from finding aids, we tried to avoid "peacock terms" ("Wikipedia:Manual of Style/Words to watch," 2017) and removed language that described subjects in non-neutral terms such as a "versatile artist" or someone who had "devoted her life" to a pursuit. We received assistance from a staff writer in the library's Communications Department, who reviewed the finding aids and suggested edits. After she had finished revising them, we received an e-mail with the updated version of the text. We divided the finding aids between ourselves, but did not start working with them until we had become familiar with the culture and core principles of the Wikipedia editing community.

Once we started using the RAMP tool, we asked ourselves several questions when the results did not match what we expected to find. For instance, when we retrieved data from VIAF and received no results, this meant that no authority record had been created for a particular person or organization. The absence of an authority record reinforced the importance of providing a presence in Wikipedia for these underrepresented creators. It also allowed us to reflect on the value of creating and contributing authority records so that tools like RAMP could be used to share information in meaningful ways. Once we had completed the steps in the editing process and converted our EAC-CPF records into wikitext, we were ready to publish to Wikipedia. The tool provides the option to contribute information directly to a live Wikipedia page (in cases where data is used to enhance an existing article) or as a draft of a new article, created as a subpage under the Wikipedia editor's user page. Because seventeen of the articles were new to Wikipedia, we relied primarily on the draft article workflow, but we tested making live edits as well.

The backbone of a Wikipedia article is built on citations and links to external resources, which provide users with the necessary information to continue their research and validate the reliability of an article. We included links under the "External links" section (see figure 13.1) of each article, which referred readers back to the finding aid and any related digital collections. We also included a link to the library website and whenever available, we provided a link to the subject's respective page in the Cuban Theater Digital Archive (CTDA) website, a thematic database curated by University of Miami faculty member Lillian Manzor (Cuban Theater Digital Archive, 2011). We were careful to link to resources that we believed would be reliable and relevant to researchers.

RAMP assists editors in improving some of the key features of a Wikipedia article. For example, the tool can help supply basic data for the article's infobox,[4] such as birth and death dates when available (see figure 13.2). The biographical/historical section of the Wikipedia article is drawn from the biographical/historical note in the collection's finding aid. RAMP-created articles also include a "Works or Publications" section that contains data imported from WorldCat Identities during one of the processes run within the tool. RAMP adds a hidden category to each Wikipedia article that allows articles created using the tool to be tracked ("Category:Articles with information extracted by the RAMP editor," 2017).

We spent roughly twenty-five hours working on the pilot project. This total included time spent assessing the thirty-two theater collections and selecting which ones to include in Wikipedia, based on completeness and notability.

RIGHTS STATEMENT

During the planning stages of the pilot, we looked at Wikipedia's requirements for contributing data. Because we were copying text directly from the finding aids, it was necessary to indicate that the text we were repurposing had been appropriately licensed and could be copied verbatim. We added a rights statement to each of the finding aids we had selected, following Wikipedia guidelines ("Wikipedia: Reusing Wikipedia content," 2017). We added a Creative Commons Attribution-ShareAlike 3.0 license and a GNU Free Documentation license to

FIGURE 13.1

External links section of a Wikipedia article created using RAMP

FIGURE 13.2

Infobox of an article created using RAMP

Caridad Svich	
Born	July 30, 1963 (age 54)
	Philadelphia, Pennsylvania
Nationality	American
Education	University of North Carolina at Charlotte (BFA)
	University of California, San Diego (MFA)
Occupation	Playwright
Awards	2012 Obie Award for Lifetime Achievement

the finding aid pages, placing them in an "Other Note" field because there was no more specific field in the EAD schema to store this information. In the Wikipedia pages, we included a similar rights statement under the "Notes and References" section, with our citation of the finding aid document.

OUTCOMES

Bringing Diversity to Wikipedia

The need for greater diversity in Wikipedia, both in terms of content and the composition of the editing community, has been the target of much critical commentary. This focus has resulted in thematic edit-a-thons such as those organized by participants in the Art+Feminism collective (Art+Feminism, n.d.). Similarly, library and archival collections and the profession as a whole face their own issues with diversity. Important work is being done to critique and question the role of archives in perpetuating exclusionary norms that continue to privilege heterosexual white men. As Jarrett M. Drake (2016) states:

> I'm skeptical about archives in the United States. Even more specifically, I'm skeptical about archives in the United States that adhere to the standard tradition of archives in the Western world. I've spent hours and hours of my time this year and last reading, thinking, tweeting, and writing about the origins of my skepticism, while also reconciling what it means that I am so very much a part of the problem that I see in this work and trying to advocate for the abolition of the archaic, anti-black, transphobic, elitist and misogynistic aspects of archival administration.

Tools such as RAMP can be used to draw attention to both sides of this deficit of diversity and inclusion. Collections that showcase the work and accomplishments of women or minorities can and should be prioritized for "wikifying" in order to help fill important gaps and ensure that standards of notability do not simply reinforce existing patterns of oppression and inequality.

Measuring Web Traffic to Finding Aid Pages

In 2011 a project was carried out at Ball State University to update relevant Wikipedia articles with links to digital assets in the university's Hague Sheet Music Collection (Szajewski, 2013). Web traffic captured by Google Analytics was analyzed for the year preceding and following the addition of links, and it was found that in the subsequent year, page views of digital assets in the collection had increased by 610 percent (from 1,824 to 12,956), with Wikipedia accounting for nearly 76 percent of web traffic referrals.[5]

We undertook a similar analysis to measure the impact of adding backlinks from the Wikipedia pages we had created to their corresponding University of Miami finding aid pages. We produced a Google Analytics report for traffic to the finding aid website for the two-year period between April 2013 and April 2015. Incoming links from the University of Miami network domain were excluded from the report in order to minimize bias and eliminate traffic that had been incidentally generated by participants in the pilot project. This may have excluded legitimate traffic from other on-campus users, but we chose to limit our focus to external users for the purposes of this analysis. Two separate datasets were created: one for the finding aids used in the pilot project, and one for all other finding aid pages, used as a control group. Project pages were identified by matching the collection identifier (included in the finding aid URL) against the Google Analytics field that contained the relative URL path of the landing page for each browsing session.

Subsequently, the creation date of each Wikipedia page was added to the entries in the pilot project's Analytics dataset. This date was used to create a before-and-after marker so that the impact of linking from Wikipedia could be evaluated. All but one of the finding aid pages had received some traffic in the post-Wikipedia period, and total web browsing sessions had increased by 39 percent (from 505 to 701). A single browsing session can represent multiple page views, and there was an overall increase in page views of 36 percent (from 682 to 930). Before the pilot project, only one of the finding aids had been linked to from a Wikipedia page (with a total of 2 page views). After the pilot project, links from Wikipedia accounted for 21 percent of all page views for the pilot project's finding aid pages (192 out of 930).

The control dataset, which recorded web traffic to all finding aid pages except the ones included in the pilot project, also showed an increase over time, albeit a slightly smaller one. Total browsing sessions increased by 32 percent in the second period (from 10,861 to 14,331), and page views increased by 23 percent (from 28,856 to 35,449). In the period preceding the pilot project, Wikipedia accounted for about 2 percent of all page views in the control dataset (626 out of 28,856 total page views), and in the subsequent period, it again accounted for approximately 2 percent of page views (658 out of 35,449).

The pilot project data was inspected in greater detail using a one-way analysis of variance (ANOVA) procedure.[6] ANOVA results indicated that the difference between the mean value of page views for the two periods was not statistically significant at the 0.05 level ($p = 0.2347$). Although the frequency of page views had increased over time, the average number of page views had remained approximately the same: the mean number of page views in the pre-Wikipedia period was 1.35, versus 1.33 in the subsequent period (with a minimum significant difference of 0.107). Grouping the page views by month yielded some separation between the mean values for the two periods: the pre-Wikipedia mean number of page views per month was 38.85, and the post-Wikipedia mean was 50.07, but the difference was still not statistically significant at the 0.05 level ($p = 0.2869$, with a minimum significant difference of 21.246).

The impact of linking from Wikipedia was also examined using a difference-in-differences analysis of the control and pilot datasets.[7] To make the number of observations equal for both datasets, a random sample was taken from the control data for each time period (see table 13.1). The following regression model was tested:

Page views = $\beta_1 + \beta_2$Group + β_3Period + β_4(Group)(Period) + u_i

where Group represents the categorical variable for the control and pilot groups, and Period represents the categorical variable for the pre- and post-Wikipedia periods. A statistically significant value for the parameter β_4 would suggest that the addition of Wikipedia backlinks had led to an increase in web traffic to the finding aid pages.

Although the overall model was statistically significant (F = 29.33, p = < 0.0001), its practical significance was minimal. The adjusted R^2 value for the model was 0.0341, suggesting that only 3 percent of the variation in the number of page views could be attributed to changes in the independent variables, after adjusting for the number of independent variables. Values for the β_4 parameter indicated that there was no statistically significant evidence of a relationship between web traffic and the addition of backlinks (t = -0.41, p = 0.6824), holding the effects of the other independent variables constant. The only significant independent variable was the Group variable, which distinguished between control and pilot pages over both time periods. Results indicated that membership in the pilot

TABLE 13.1

Summary statistics for page views by cross-section and time period

	CONTROL GROUP			PILOT GROUP	
	Before (n = 505)	After (n = 701)		Before (n = 505)	After (n = 701)
Count	1445	2088		682	930
Mean	2.86	2.98		1.35	1.33
Std	4.63	6.56		0.77	1.04

group corresponded to a decrease in page views of 1.51089, holding the effects of the other variables constant.

Based on the Google Analytics data presented here, it can be concluded that the pages selected for the pilot project were already less likely to be viewed than other University of Miami finding aid pages. The numerically low average for pilot group page views over both periods suggests that the pilot pages were more likely to be of interest to specialized researchers than to the general public. The choice of subject matter for the pilot project (Cuban theater collections) was a factor that defined the scope of the project's prospective appeal, limiting it to a particular audience: namely, people who followed or studied theater generally and Hispanic American or Latin American theater specifically. In comparison, the Ball State project cited above involved adding backlinks to Wikipedia pages about well-known nineteenth- and twentieth-century popular songs such as "It's a Long, Long Way to Tipperary" (Szajewski, 2013). The subject matter selected in that case was one that already had the potential to appeal to a large audience of prospective users.

A comparison of the two projects (the University of Miami RAMP pilot and the Ball State project) highlights the tension between notability and visibility. The concept of notability seems beset by a catch-22: in order to be notable, a subject must first be visible, but in order to become visible, a subject must first be notable. Projects such as RAMP might be seen as a first step toward asserting notability through visibility. The process of actively constructing notability (rather than allowing it to limit the scope of our contributions) is part of a long-term effort to enrich the broader information ecosystem and, whenever possible, draw attention to traditionally marginalized and underrepresented content and content creators. The temptation to emphasize short-term goals such as boosting web traffic is one that should be resisted.

GOOGLE KNOWLEDGE GRAPH

More difficult to quantify, but easier to observe is the impact that having a Wikipedia page had on the web presence of the individuals and organizations that were the focus of the pilot project. Prior to the pilot project, information about creators of the collections we had selected was dispersed on the Web. The results of the project highlighted the fact that the creation of a Wikipedia page is really the creation of a knowledge hub that helps organize and aggregate related online information.

FIGURE 13.3

Google Knowledge Graph Card display for Caridad Svich
(captured June 1, 2017)

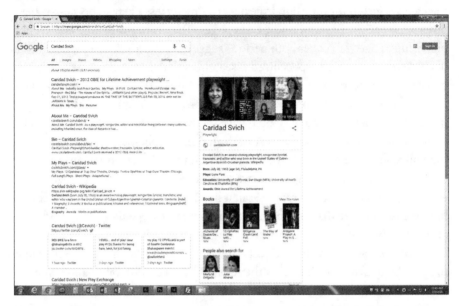

This effect is seen most notably in the example of Google's Knowledge Graph cards
(Google, 2017b). For instance, a Google search for "Caridad Svich," a playwright
who lacked a Wikipedia page before the project, now displays a prominent knowledge card: key biographical facts have been extracted from her Wikipedia article,
combined with photographs and relationships ("People also search for") aggregated
from the wider web (see figure 13.3). In effect, the creation of a Wikipedia page
entails the concomitant creation of a Google Knowledge Graph card.

LESSONS LEARNED

Despite our efforts to familiarize ourselves with and abide by Wikipedia community norms, there were still some lessons to be learned. In one instance, the
notability of one of our subjects was questioned by another Wikipedia editor
("Talk:Teatro Avante," 2017). The page that we had created was for Teatro Avante,
a theater organization located in the Little Havana neighborhood of Miami. The

editor argued that the article should be deleted because "the subject matter, a theater group, lacks notability. The article actually seems to be spam to support a software product called RAMP." We promptly responded, making the case that Teatro Avante was "a notable part of the cultural landscape of Miami's Little Havana neighborhood" and had been the recipient of funding from the National Endowment for the Arts. In addition, we clarified that RAMP was simply a tool designed to help librarians and archivists contribute to Wikipedia.[8] The issue was quickly resolved when a Wikipedia administrator declined the request to delete the article, accepting our argument for the subject's notability and agreeing that the content of the article was not promotional.

This minor dispute gave us a fresh perspective on the range of interactions we could expect to have with other editors. Cataloging and metadata librarians do not typically need to think about questions of notability in their daily work, nor do they interact with the community when creating descriptive metadata for library or archival resources. We could see here where the two communities (libraries and Wikipedia) diverged somewhat: one was more focused on following specific rules and using controlled vocabularies to describe and deliver information resources, whereas the other was more focused on determining whether a subject was notable enough to deserve a place in the expanding encyclopedia.

Some of our articles were tagged as orphans, which meant that no links had been added from already existing Wikipedia pages to these new articles. Often, the Wikipedia editor who tagged the articles as orphans also provided suggestions about the steps we could take to address the issue. We then worked to provide access from other Wikipedia pages back to our newly created ones. One perhaps obvious takeaway from the project was the realization that finding aid biographies have not been written with Wikipedia in mind. The project gave us the opportunity to reflect on ways to move beyond traditional archival standards and think about positioning our descriptive metadata in a way that could appeal to a wider audience of information consumers.

USABILITY TESTING

In order for other institutions to use RAMP, we knew that the installation process needed to be simplified, especially for small institutions with minimal IT support. In 2016 a round of usability testing was conducted to identify whether there were obstacles that would prevent the community from using and implementing the tool. Seven people (including library staff members, librarians, and archivists from various departments) agreed to participate. A Google form was created to track responses and suggestions from participants. The testing revealed that the user interface needed to be improved and that users needed an easy way to ingest and delete files. The need for an easier installation process was also confirmed. This information helped generate user stories that were employed as the basis for a subsequent two-week development sprint.

SECOND ITERATION OF THE RAMP TOOL

The primary issue addressed in the second round of development was the ability to install a local instance of RAMP without any assistance. Installation is now a three-click process and takes only a few minutes to complete. Another major improvement in the tool centered on the user interface. The previous version was text-heavy, and users would get lost when reading the instructions. This was addressed with a complete overhaul of the interface, which gave the tool a new look and feel. The process of logging into Wikipedia was also improved. Programmers ensured that all connections to Wikipedia were secure using the https protocol. We also explored using the OAuth standard to manage Wikipedia access ("OAuth," 2017), but decided not to pursue it because its implementation would have been too complex given the limited time frame of the sprint and the resources that were available for development. In the first iteration of RAMP, files needed to be ingested by creating a folder on the server side. Now users can ingest a single file directly into the database. The ability to delete files was also added, and JavaScript features were rewritten to conform to more modern single-page web application patterns, using a combination of JQuery and Underscore.js. Finally, maintenance event elements were added to the EAC/XML to record each action performed on a file.

CONCLUSION

In the library and archives communities we describe resources using standards and controlled vocabularies that in theory should facilitate the discovery and retrieval of information. Using these vocabularies ensures that resources are described in a consistent way, but it may also limit their findability because users are not always familiar with our terminology. We might be more successful in reaching a wider audience if we began to map our vocabularies and standards to the language of the wider web and disseminated even a portion of our information and content through a platform such as Wikipedia.

Our experience using the RAMP tool has convinced us that contributing to Wikipedia and engaging with the Wikipedia community is an important and even necessary activity, one that is directly relevant to our work as metadata librarians. The process of transforming and repurposing the rich contextual information often contained in finding aids forced us to think beyond traditional boundaries and reimagine the ways in which metadata about archival collections could be shared and presented. It also compelled us to grapple with fundamental questions about notability and visibility, questions that matter deeply to archivists as well. How do we decide what is worth archiving, describing, and preserving? How does the metadata we create reflect our professional values? As information professionals, the more we begin to do our work in public, on platforms such as Wikipedia, the more we will be challenged to see ourselves and our institutions as part of a shared, if contested, space of knowledge curation and circulation. We cannot expect to remain relevant as a profession unless we begin to think about how our metadata standards can be made to speak the language of the Web, which is increasingly the language of our users.

NOTES

1. VIAF (http://viaf.org/) and WorldCat Identities (http://worldcat.org/identities/) are both OCLC-hosted open data aggregating services. VIAF merges data from significant international name authority files and mints a single URI for unique identity clusters. WorldCat Identities aggregates data from across the WorldCat database to produce a single view of information related to personal, corporate, and subject-based identities, including works by, works about, associated names, and related authorities (OCLC Research, 2012).

2. xEAC (pronounced "zeek") is an open source EAC-CPF editor created by Ethan Gruber using the declarative programming language XForms. It provides both front-end and administrative interfaces, as well as integration with a range of web service APIs, including SNAC, DBPedia, VIAF, Getty AAT, Getty TGN, Geonames, the Pleiades Gazetteer of Ancient Places, and the LC Name Authority File for geographic places (Gruber, 2017).

3. The concept of neutrality is another foundational principle of Wikipedia. Wikipedia's neutral point of view guidelines state that "all encyclopedic content on Wikipedia must be

written from a neutral point of view (NPOV), which means representing fairly, proportionately, and, as far as possible, without editorial bias, all of the significant views that have been published by reliable sources on a topic" ("Wikipedia:Neutral point of view," 2017).

4. An infobox contains structured metadata pertaining to the subject being described in the Wikipedia article. It is usually displayed on the right-hand side of an article for languages that read from left to right.

5. According to Google's documentation, a pageview "is defined as a view of a page on your site that is being tracked by the Analytics tracking code. If a user clicks reload after reaching the page, this is counted as an additional pageview. If a user navigates to a different page and then returns to the original page, a second pageview is recorded as well" (Google, 2017a).

6. Statistical analyses were performed using the SAS 9.4 software package. Analysis of variance was applied using the GLM procedure. Levene's test for homogeneity of variance was not significant at the 0.05 level ($p = 0.2347$), indicating that the analysis of variance was an appropriate statistical method for the data.

7. Difference-in-differences is a quasi-experimental statistical method used to determine whether a particular treatment, intervention, or policy has had an impact over time. Binary variables are used to divide the data into two cross-sectional groups, treatment and control, and to differentiate between the before and after periods for each. Analysis of the interaction term (treatment and time period) indicates whether the intervention has had a statistically significant effect.

8. On Wikipedia, discussions about the content of an article typically take place on its corresponding "Talk" page, which provides a public forum in which different views can be expressed. This exchange did lead us to make changes to one of the templates we had been using in the project. Previously, we had included a small RAMP icon at the start of our finding aid citation under "Notes and References." We removed this icon to avoid the appearance of branding.

REFERENCES

Ajax.org. May 27, 2017. "Ace" (Github repository). https://github.com/ajaxorg/ace.

Art+Feminism. N.d. www.artandfeminism.org.

"Category:Articles with information extracted by the RAMP editor." 2017. Wikipedia. https://en.wikipedia.org/wiki/Category:Articles_with_information_extracted_by_the_RAMP_editor.

Cuban Theater Digital Archive. 2011. www.cubantheater.org.

Drake, J. M. October 22, 2016. "Liberatory Archives: Towards Belonging and Believing (Part 1)." In *On Archivy.* https://medium.com/on-archivy/liberatory-archives-towards-belonging -and-believing-part-1-d26aaeb0edd1.

Google. 2017a. "The Difference between AdWords Clicks, and Sessions, Users, Entrances, Pageviews, and Unique Pageviews in Analytics." In *Analytics Help: Acquisition Reports.* https://support.google.com/analytics/answer/1257084.

————. 2017b. "Suggest a Change to a Knowledge Graph Card." Google Search Help. https:// support.google.com/websearch/answer/6325583.

Gruber, E. January 13, 2017. "xEAC" (Github repository). https://github.com/ewg118/xEAC.

Library of Congress. March 9, 2017. *Encode Archival Description: Official Site.* https://www .loc.gov/ead/.

OAuth. 2017. Wikipedia. https://en.wikipedia.org/wiki/OAuth.

"OCLC Research." July 23, 2012. WorldCat Identities. www.oclc.org/research/themes/data -science/identities.html.

Staatsbibliothek zu Berlin. N.d. "Encoded Archival Context: Corporate Bodies, Persons, and Families." http://eac.staatsbibliothek-berlin.de/about.html.

Szajewski, M. 2013. "Using Wikipedia to Enhance the Visibility of Digitized Archival Assets." *D-Lib Magazine*, 19, no. 3/4. doi:10.1045/march2013-szajewski.

"Talk:Teatro Avante. 2017. Wikipedia. https://en.wikipedia.org/wiki/Talk:Teatro_Avante.

Tennant, R. October 24, 2013. "The Winter of Wikipedia's Discontent" (Blog post). *The Digital Shift.* www.thedigitalshift.com/2013/10/roy-tennant-digital-libraries/winter -wikipedias-discontent/.

"Wikipedia:Manual of Style/Words to watch." 2017. Wikipedia. https://en.wikipedia.org/wiki/ Wikipedia:Manual_of_Style/Words_to_watch.

"Wikipedia:Neutral point of view." 2017. Wikipedia. https://en.wikipedia.org/wiki/Wikipedia: Neutral_point_of_view.

"Wikipedia:Notability." 2017. Wikipedia. https://en.wikipedia.org/wiki/Wikipedia:Notability.

"Wikipedia:Reusing Wikipedia content." 2017. https://en.wikipedia.org/wiki/Wikipedia: Reusing_Wikipedia_content.

"I'm a Librarian on Wikipedia"

U.S. Public Librarianship with Wikipedia

MONIKA SENGUL-JONES

This chapter features stories of public librarians engaging with English Wikipedia to serve public librarianship in a digital age. Their experiences with Wikipedia are distinct and include editing, adding citations, information literacy, and partnership-building. What binds them together is their embrace of Wikipedia—and its dynamic community of editors—*because* of the content opportunities, technical features, and collaborative community it offers. These stories of public librarians demonstrate how to take a lead in bringing librarianship online by engaging with Wikipedia.

INTRODUCTION

This chapter tells the story of U.S. public library staff who have incorporated Wikipedia into their librarianship in order to better inform and serve a digitally connected public. Weaving together the voices of a dozen public librarians interviewed in March and April 2017 for the OCLC Wikipedia + Libraries:

Better Together project, the chapter highlights the specific reasons why they are engaging the online collaborative encyclopedia to better serve their vision of public librarianship in a digital age.[1]

There are many extraordinary articles in Wikipedia. The community has developed a robust consensus-based peer review process, and articles that have achieved "good" or "featured" status represent the best work in Wikipedia. But there's a lot of room to grow. Most articles have not achieved featured status. As of June 2017, there were 5,061 featured articles out of approximately 5,433,290 total articles on the English Wikipedia (about 0.1 percent). Moreover, more than 200,000 articles have no citations at all.[2] In addition to improving content, importantly, Wikipedia has room for—and needs—more content that is representative of the diversity of human cultures and knowledges. World geography, minority histories and cultures, and gender and women's histories are just a few areas that are ripe for contributions. In addition, the platform is more than the summation of its 5.4 million articles. Wikipedia is a community of editors who have created Internet-born tools in order to keep up the daily work of updating an online, open encyclopedia.

This chapter focuses on the experiences of public librarians who are already engaging with Wikipedia and why they find this to be a valuable practice. Their experiences encompass a range of participatory modes. Some have answered reference questions by editing Wikipedia articles. Librarians incorporate Wikipedia into information literacy and outreach programming. Librarians have organized outreach projects with local partner and minority advocacy groups in their communities for a new and important lens on diversity and equity online.

Ultimately, public librarians are in the vanguard of public librarianship on the Internet. In the sections of this chapter that follow, we will examine in greater detail the contextual precedents that prompted public librarians to take a lead in meeting the members of their communities on the open web with Wikipedia.

BACKGROUND

The insights from public librarians across the United States shared in this chapter were gathered as a part of the OCLC Wikipedia + Libraries: Better Together project from December 2016 through May 2018. OCLC Research was one of five winners of the Knight Foundation's 2016 News Challenge for libraries, which asked: How might libraries serve twenty-first-century information needs? The answer was an eighteen-month project designed to bring together public libraries and Wikipedia, based on the premise that the two have much in common—they both share a commitment to free and open access to information. Both benefit from collaboration—but formal collaborative projects have been limited. With a supplementary grant from the Wikimedia Foundation to bring on board a Wikipedian in Residence, the author of this chapter, the project's capstone activity was a free, online training program from September 13 to November 15, 2017. To design and deliver the curriculum of the online training program and best serve the enrollees, the project's first phase included qualititive research on what public libraries have already been doing with Wikipedia.

This chapter, as a result, shares stories from some of the interviews completed during the research. What was discovered is that public libraries which were early adopters of Wikipedia often are unconnected to other public library staff who are doing similar work with Wikipedia. Indeed, it is their relative isolation from each other that makes the similarities in these stories, and their reasons for engagement, quite striking. However, the interviews also surface social forces and organizational conventions that impede public library staff from engaging with or promoting Wikipedia to their patrons. This chapter thus offers a survey of what works and what doesn't work for public libraries. And it's a call to action: As Janos McGhie, a reference librarian at Saint Paul Public Library, surmises: "The mission of Wikipedia is the same as that of libraries: freely get information to people who need it. It behooves librarians to be a part of this project—and to help shape it."

ONLINE, WHERE THE PATRONS ARE

Let's hear more about how McGhie, a reference librarian, came to engage Wikipedia. When he explained why he started to edit, he started by sharing an uncomfortable experience he'd had at the reference desk in the Saint Paul Public Library a few years back. "Yet another patron had come up to me and said all the information is online these days," he said. The comment struck a nerve. McGhie admits he was taken aback: "Here I am in a room full of offline information—how can people assume all information is online?" But he decided to heed the comment as a call to action. This was an opportunity for McGhie to do something to meet patrons where they were at: online. "I had to do what little I could to move more offline information online," McGhie said. "That is where people assume it will be. Wikipedia was the most obvious venue for that. So I started contributing. And here I am."

McGhie's observation that librarians can serve patrons by editing Wikipedia has only become more pressing. The Saint Paul library—like libraries in other

U.S. metropolitan and suburban areas—has patrons who come into the library to access Wi-Fi. In fact, 97 percent of public libraries provide free Wi-Fi and this is a crucial public service, given the necessity of Internet access for jobs, reskilling, communication, entertainment, accessing governmental and social services, and more. In 2017, Wi-Fi hot spots that were offered as part of a pilot program in Saint Paul were the most popular resource for checkout. Rebecca Ryan, also a librarian in Saint Paul, told the *Star Tribune* in 2017 that patrons will sit on library steps with laptops before the doors open in order to access Wi-Fi.[3] These news reports, while about Saint Paul, illustrate a broader trend in user experiences that is crisscrossing the nation. Not only is there a high level of need among library patrons for free mobile access to information, but people use the Internet to begin their information inquiries. Indeed, more than 50 percent of the public went to a public library last year, and nearly 77 percent of the public has smartphones.[4] "A tiny fraction of the public wanders in and asks you [for reference help]," said McGhie. Given the popularity of Wikipedia, "it behooves librarians to be a part of this project—and to help shape it," McGhie said.

Of the digital media giants born online, Wikipedia is the only not-for-profit one in the top 100 platforms. The Wikipedia Foundation states that the organization is devoted to supporting a community and resource that is free, open, and accessible for Internet users to access "the sum of human knowledge." When public library staff learn to confidently edit and engage with others in the Wikipedia community, the results are positive for public libraries, which can easily understand the uniqueness of the editorial community, have made connections with other editors, and adeptly guide patrons' use of the online encyclopedia. Andrea Davis, of the San Francisco Public Library, acknowledged that learning to edit Wikipedia and meeting other editors meant the mystery of Wikipedia's production disappeared. "Wikipedia was no longer this thing that *they* do, *those* people. You do it. You have agency. Editing makes more sense to me as an information professional than critique alone. We need to look harder at where information is coming from and do our part to make the freely available sources of information on the Internet more reliable and verifiable."

EDITING TO EXPAND AND IMPROVE CONTENT ONLINE

In April 2017, a local history museum staff member from El Paso, Texas came to Susan Barnum for reference materials about Chihuahuita, a historic neighborhood in El Paso that runs along the Mexican border. Barnum was surprised that there was no Wikipedia article on this important area of the city, which, according to the National Trust for Historic Preservation, is an "endangered neighborhood."[5] Diving into her library's collection of secondary sources on El Paso, Barnum compiled a robust bibliography of two dozen books and articles—many of which were offline or behind paywalls—that could be used as a jumping-off point for research on Chihuahuita. Instead of simply sending the bibliography to the patron, Barnum drew on her five years of experience as a volunteer Wikipedia editor to use those references to write an encyclopedia article for Chihuahuita. Then she sent the patron that link:

- https://en.wikipedia.org/wiki/Chihuahuita

In other words, Barnum annotated the references and organized the work for a general audience, raising the profile online of Chihuahuita and the reference work she'd accomplished. Indeed, the article had nearly 400 page views in the two months after publication. "It would have taken me just as much time to compile all the references in a Word document," she said. "Writing the Wikipedia article makes this information available to everyone; it has longevity and visibility."

FIGURE 14.1

Sue Barnum took this photograph in April 2017 of houses in Chihuahuita, with the Mexican-American border fence in the background, to use in the article she wrote.

Credit: Susan Barnum (own work), CC BY-SA 4.0

Furthermore, on a drive in her city, Barnum took a photograph of the neighborhood in order to further expand the article and broaden the representation online of Chihuahuita, which runs along the border and is a historic place with ties to the Mexican Revolution and Pancho Villa.[6] The photograph, shown in figure 14.1, portrays a solitary street lamp casting a warm glow on to a residential side street that runs up against a two-story mesh fence: the Mexican-American border. Homes in Chihuahuita are nestled up to Mexico, said Barnum. Her article summarizes in detail the rich history of the borderland. Barnum was initially surprised at how little visibility the articles and books about this historic and dynamic neighborhood had online. But thanks to her efforts, there is now also a link from the "El Paso" Wikipedia article to the "Chihuahuita" article she started, and the article itself includes over 50 citations drawn from 11 sources, including JSTOR and Project MUSE. When a person searches for El Paso, or Chihuahuita, they'll be more likely to encounter these materials now, and thus as a librarian Barnum is bringing online visibility and dignity to an often-marginalized neighborhood in her city.

Barnum's work on Wikipedia is the outcome of years of engagement. She began as a Wikipedia editor after a staff training about five years ago, she said. Since that time she has become a vocal librarian on Wikipedia, an editor who identifies both as a Wikipedian and a librarian to other editors. She's earned community accolades and has worked to improve articles to gain the classification of a "good" or "featured article." Barnum said that she does this work because "it is important to contribute to a collective body of knowledge that is accessible," noting that many people who live in her city, and state, do not come into the library and use its resources. Instead, she can reach them online. Barnum has also organized Wikipedia editing events, but the turnout has been low. In order to serve her community, she said, "I am a librarian on Wikipedia."

Barnum's success with writing and sharing articles on Wikipedia is an outcome of the time she's spent learning the rules and guidelines of Wikipedia's editing community. Now she's able to answer reference questions by editing Wikipedia articles with relatively little additional work on her part, something that other library staff can also achieve once they've learned the Wikipedia community's norms. As a result, Barnum is able to facilitate online a deeper and wider level of access to the complex spectrum of knowledge that she oversees. This editorial work models how online engagement with Wikipedia is a space to champion a library's community and local resources, extending their reach beyond the library's physical space or opening hours.

Barnum's contributions are impressive: she's written or contributed to hundreds of articles, and her edit count totals are in the five figures. She advocates for bringing visibility to the rich cultural and social history of her community as well as to women's history globally. Barnum volunteers with two sub-communities within Wikipedia, the WikiWomen's Project and WikiProject Women in Red, both which are devoted to redressing the invisibility of women online. For the latter project, editors create articles in order to turn "red links" on Wikipedia into "blue links" (on Wikipedia a red hyperlink is a sign that there is no corresponding article). In 2014 fewer than 15 percent of the biographies on Wikipedia were about women. "I was shocked," said Barnum. She volunteered as a "Librarian in Residence" in the project to help guide other editors to reliable sources as they develop their research on women's history.[7] Barnum also edits articles using her position as a librarian to access buried references and paywalled articles. "If someone doesn't mine that out of the archives, these stories will remain in the dark and invisible. I've written articles about women whom you can't Google—there's nothing on them on the Web, but they have many offline references." Thanks to the efforts of Women in Red members, the percentage of biographies on Wikipedia that are about women has slowly increased to nearly 17 percent; this is still incomplete, but it is a move toward a more equitable representation of women's position in society worldwide.

Not every librarian who has engaged with Wikipedia has the same level of experience as Barnum. Others, however, have responded to the asymmetries in coverage and sought to elevate stories that matter to their local and diverse communities, taking the openness and vision of Wikipedia as a call to action. In the next sections, we will learn how public librarians have coordinated events, taught information literacy, and sought out ways to raise the visibility of their diverse local collections; these are efforts to offset biases on the Internet by learning and sharing information on how to edit Wikipedia.

ENGAGING WITH COMMUNITIES, STRENGTHENING DIVERSITY ON AND OFFLINE

Libraries in Brooklyn, New York, Dallas, Texas, and San Francisco have coordinated Wikipedia events with community partners in order to raise the profile of their diverse communities. The library staff members are often not experienced Wikipedia editors. The event coordination has become an opportunity to expose themselves and their colleagues to Wikipedia, to strengthen relationships with community allies, and to serve their public libraries' goals of community services.

Brooklyn, New York

In Brooklyn, this partnership has materialized as a series of ongoing "skill shares" about Wikipedia that focuses on the African American diaspora living in Brooklyn's neighborhoods (see figure 14.2). Alice Backer, a Wikipedian, a community activist and organizer, reached out to the Brooklyn Public Library to partner in 2015. Members of the Wikimedia New York chapter have also been involved in the organization of these events. "We've hosted at least a dozen different Wikipedia-related editing events, with refreshments and library laptops," said Melissa Marrone, one of the librarians who worked with Backer on coordinating the events. "They are open to the public, free, and focus on improving the representation of people of African descent online. This fits in with the goals of the public library, to be inclusive and support marginalized cultures." According to the 2011–2015 U.S. census estimates about the racial makeup of zip code 11203, which is in Brooklyn, 89.9 percent of the population there is black or African American.[8]

FIGURE 14.2

Alice Backer, above, helps a participant in a Wikipedia skill-share. Backer, of AfroCROWD, has partnered with Brooklyn Public Library for Wikipedia skill-building events that serve Brooklyn's community of people of African descent.

Credit: Jim.Henderson (own work), CC BY-SA 4.0

As skill-building events, educational programming that focuses on increasing the online representation of people of African descent on Wikipedia serves the goals of the library. "We want people to learn how to create and share their work so that they are able to become a part of the cultural fabric," said Marrone. This fabric is a hybrid space; "publics" are online and offline. Skill-shares at the library bridge these publics in the library's Info Commons, an open classroom that has library laptops, Wi-Fi, and flexible seating. AfroCROWD at the library is an example of an outreach campaign that champions local communities and encourages ongoing education for all.

Dallas, Texas

Skill-building, community outreach, and feminism caught the attention of library staff at the Dallas Public Library. In 2016, the noticeable gaps in Wikipedia's coverage of women and the arts were the reason why Tiffany Bailey, manager of the Fine Arts Division at the library, got involved. She was approached by Consuelo Gutierrez of the Cedars Union, an incubator for the arts, and was joined by Kate Aoki of the Dallas Architecture Forum, to organize an editing event at the library that focused on women and the arts. Bailey, Guiterrez, and Aoki, who were all new to editing, used and adapted a toolkit prepared by the organizers of Wikipedia's Art+Feminism movement to teach themselves to edit Wikipedia and to teach their patrons. In other words, they got their start editing through collaboration and conversation about Wikipedia among themselves and their patrons. Their Art+Feminism event was held all day in March 2017 and included editing workshops, refreshments, and children's activities hosted by the children's library staff. "In this political climate, we felt Wikipedia editing on this topic was timely and important," said Bailey. "Art+Feminism was a great fit: we endeavor to teach new skills and promote [information] literacy—to empower people to do things with technology."

During her event, Bailey got to know patrons by their first names and they had conversations about how to research and bring online visibility to the history of Texan women in the arts. The event was successful in spurring curiosity and conversation about the Dallas Public Library's collection of resources about local art history, women in the arts, and representation of women online. "People came up to me and said, 'We're thrilled this is happening at a public library,'" said Bailey. Moreover, Wikipedia now joins the menu of digital media that the library has been incorporating into its programming and outreach. The Dallas Public Library also uses social media platforms such as YouTube, Facebook Live, Facebook, Instagram, and Twitter to reach out to patrons, raise the visibility of library holdings with stories and events, and bridge online and offline publics. While Bailey and her staff are still learning how to edit Wikipedia themselves, organizing an Art+Feminism event was a catalyst for their involvement.

San Francisco, California

The need to improve the representation of diverse local communities online was not lost on two public librarians in San Francisco. Christina Moretta and Andrea Davis collaborated to organize The Queerest Wikipedia Edit-a-Thon at the San Francisco Public Library in 2016. As in Brooklyn, their event bridged the Wikipedia editing community with community members and patrons who had an interest in learning Wikipedia. The event also had a subject-matter focus: to understand and improve the quality of content on Wikipedia related to San Francisco's queer history and culture.

Davis and Moretta recognized that Wikipedia's editor demographics—more than 80 percent of its editors are white males—does not reflect the diversity of San Francisco. The lack of diversity has also shaped Wikipedia's content. As mentioned, there are fewer articles about women, and research suggests there are also linguistic biases that devalue nonwhite male perspectives. However, Davis, a teen librarian, considered these asymmetries and gaps as opportunities to build bridges between the communities—particularly in a large city such as San Francisco. To organize and promote The Queerest Wikipedia Edit-a-Thon, Davis and Moretta sought out local Wikipedians to join the event. Davis and Moretta posted a "geo-notice" on the user pages of Wikipedia editors who had identified as living in the Bay area. The outreach paid off—at The Queerest Wikipedia Edit-a-Thon, an experienced Wikipedian, Britta Gustafson, gave a short, helpful overview of Wikipedia for participants. Of the twenty attendees, about a third were Wikipedia editors, setting the stage for thoughtful conversations about their diverse community as well as the way that information gets included in Wikipedia.

For Davis, these conversations made the event successful. People got to know each other. Davis was also pleased that the library staff did "a song and dance about library materials" and some Wikipedia editors who participated got library cards for the first time. After the editing event, the local WikiSalon invited Davis and Moretta to make a presentation about what a library can do for Wikipedia. While the organizers initiated the event to highlight and improve Wikipedia's coverage of San Francisco's queer history and culture, unexpected outcomes included bridge-building work between the library and local Wikipedia editors who had not yet discovered what their city's public library offers.

The events in these three cities demonstrate the way that Wikipedia's biases—which are partially the outcome of a minority of the population contributing to the encyclopedia and partially the result of gaps and prejudices in secondary reference materials—are catalysts for library involvement in Wikipedia. Partnership-building and serving diverse local communities and histories equally play a role in inspiring new library staff members to embrace Wikipedia as a project and a community to get to know better. The events that these libraries host require staff time to program, but they also synchronize with the service goals of the libraries. Moreover, the events are useful, community-focused activities that give library staff an incentive to work as Wikipedia editors who are fluent in editing best practices. As editors themselves, public library staff can take a lead in supporting newcomers and have the expertise to adapt and apply Wikipedia's guidelines to incorporate their library's community service goals. "As librarians, it is our job to connect library users with the information that they seek." As a new editor, Moretta, found Wikipedia more user-friendly than she anticipated. Davis echoed this and observed that today's Wikipedia is not the Wikipedia of ten years ago.

Copyright-Free Images

In 2016 Moretta uploaded a historic photo of an avenue in Laurel Heights to her Instagram account, using social media to give visibility to a #longgone #lostplace. The photograph was taken in the middle of Divisadero Street, looking straight up Ellis Street to the Calvary Cemetery, an embankment crowded with white gravestones, seemingly waiting for a cable car to rumble up the hill on the rails sunk in the cobbled stones; a horse, with the carriage behind, appears stopped on the south side of the street, near a wide sidewalk with quintessential row houses. Electricity posts and lines flank the top and sides of the photograph.

Today an apartment complex crowns the embankment and the cemetery is figuratively buried, since it was relocated in the 1930s. The historical image doesn't have to be similarly hidden, however. Wikipedia offers public libraries an opportunity to bring offline, copyright-free references and resources such as this photograph to a wider audience. Like many U.S. public libraries, the San Francisco Public Library is a custodian to millions of historic photographs and works on paper featuring San Francisco and California. Many of the images are in the public domain (which in 2017 were works created before 1922). In a brainstorming conversation after their editing event, Moretta described a plan to use Wikipedia editing to expand public access to these works—and to use the works as starting points and illustrations for articles to point Wikipedia readers to the evocative visual archive that she manages at the San Francisco Public Library. Moretta described uploading a set of copyright-free photographs to Wikimedia Commons in preparation for a future event. That tack, she said, would provide a list of resources specific to San Francisco's history and culture. Moretta would also prepare, and work from herself beforehand, a list of articles that participants use as starting points for the images.

Bringing Offline References Online

In San Francisco, Davis and Moretta are making plans for more Wikipedia events to serve their library and make more offline resources accessible online. In this next section of the chapter, we will gain insight into how they, and other public library staff, have used Wikipedia to teach information literacy and guide more patrons to free resources online—including library catalogs. These examples of bringing offline references online are attentive to the way that references can ameliorate the online underrepresentation of their diverse communities with Wikipedia. Finally, these examples showcase how other libraries have gotten started with editing more generally by bringing offline references online during a citation campaign.

Citations That Link to Library Collections

Bringing offline resources online does not need to be limited to digitizing and uploading copyright-free photographs. Books are the go-to offline reference source that public libraries are familiar with managing. As a tertiary reference, Wikipedia depends on verifiable secondary sources as references for articles; in other words, URLs are neither the preferred nor the only allowable reference source: books, articles, and other materials are warmly welcomed as verifiable references to build the tertiary source. Moreover, as of March 2017, offline book references on Wikipedia can now hyperlink to public holdings in libraries' collections. This is possible thanks to a partnership between the Wikimedia Foundation and OCLC. ISBNs can now be used to generate Wikipedia citations that link to WorldCat—the largest database of books in the world, spanning the collections of more than 72,000 libraries. The citation tool previously only worked with URLs, DOIs, and PubMed IDs. When the tool is used to generate a reference, then the reader who clicks on that reference will be guided to the WorldCat entry for the material, as well as the closest library where the reader can check it out.

Wikipedia's role as a popular platform that can guide readers to more free, offline references was attractive to Allison Frick, a youth services librarian in Philadelphia at the Glenside Free Library, a branch of the Cheltenham Township Library System (Glenside, PA). In May 2017, Frick partnered with a university librarian to organize a one-hour information literacy event with Wikipedia as the starting tool to discuss information literacy skills for Internet research. For Frick, engaging with Wikipedia helps computer users at all levels to evaluate and improve their online experiences; at her event, some of the participants were new to using computers and she started with the very basics—discussing how to turn on the computer and double-click on a browser. Wikipedia is a way she can help patrons go online and access more free reference materials. With a smile, Frick summarized: "Now, an Internet search that goes to Wikipedia can guide you to library resources. ISBN citations take you to WorldCat, to a library catalog—then you can check out books for free!" Her enthusiasm epitomizes how a one-hour information literacy with Wikipedia is a model others can easily adopt.

"When someone says you shouldn't use Wikipedia because it's unreliable or because their teacher said not to, I respond: well, yes you can," said Frick. Wikipedia is accessible and a jumping-off point for information seekers. "Wikipedia gets your brain ready to do more research." She's unabashed about promoting Wikipedia as valuable for its work-in-progress imperfections. "Even in good articles, there are going to be biases—based on what kinds of topics have or haven't gotten coverage or how something is organized," she said. "But these kinds of gaps are not a good reason not to use Wikipedia! If you see a gap, use that as an opportunity to figure out how to do it better. You can edit Wikipedia. Don't accept that other people are not writing about things that matter to you; you have permission to do something, too."

Wikipedia can start a conversation about Internet information literacy and being a knowledge producer online as well as a consumer. By engaging with Wikipedia, public librarians can discover and then discuss with patrons how referencing takes place on Wikipedia. Librarians can also point patrons to the editorial back channels of Wikipedia, such as talk pages and notice boards, to show how consensus is built about claims made on Wikipedia, and the importance of online "civility." Unlike posts made in social media, or decisions driven by search engine algorithms (which are unavailable to the public), the Wikipedia community has made their policies, guidelines, and editing histories transparent. These guidelines—which cover addressing the authority of credible material—are useful guideposts that public librarians can use to discuss best practices in both online and offline source evaluation.

Staff Events: #1lib1ref and Beyond

Adding citations is one of the easiest ways for library staff to begin their engagement with Wikipedia. A few public librarians interviewed for this project were at libraries that joined the Wikipedia Library's #1lib1ref campaign in 2017. The campaign called upon library staff to add one citation—#1lib1ref is an acronym for "one librarian, one reference"—to a Wikipedia article with a "[citation needed]" tag. The International Federation of Library Associations and Institutions (IFLA), a campaign partner, supported the effort to add citations to Wikipedia by publishing a complementary infographic (see figure 14.3) guiding the public on how to spot "fake news."

IFLA also urged library staff, as authoritative standard-bearers of information verification, to edit Wikipedia. And analysis of the edit summaries after the campaign that was initiated suggests that approximately 1,000 references were added to Wikipedia by about 1,000 librarians.[9] Participation was made easy by the combination of a practical call for one simple action and the use of the "Citation Hunt" randomizer tool to give users the chance to easily browse unsourced snippets on Wikipedia (which are flagged with the template [Citation needed]). This tool provides anyone who is interested in contributing with a starting point to contribute, thereby lowering the barriers to participation.

According to library staff, the simple call to action framed Wikipedia editing as sensible and doable. Librarians reported that when their libraries established editing stations with coffee for staff to contribute, fueling editing with caffeine and team collaboration, many staff members participated and had conversations

FIGURE 14.3

How to Spot Fake News

Courtesy of International Federation of Library Associations and Institutions.

about Wikipedia and their collections. Scheduling in staff time and making space for editing ensure that public librarians, who are indeed well-positioned to add authoritative references to Wikipedia, have the necessary time and support to contribute. Moreover, this is also an opportunity to incorporate their libraries' collections online. Although Wikipedia references can be links to websites, best practices encourage the use of more credible sources such as books and peer-reviewed articles. By adding a citation or including recommended reading, public libraries can use Wikipedia to point patrons to sources that they have access to using databases.

This section of the chapter has described three ways that libraries have gotten involved, mostly on their own, in Wikipedia editing. Wikipedia can inspire creative forms of outreach: organizing an event around copyright-free images is an example of this kind of outreach, community engagement, and collection visibility. Second, library staff can incorporate Wikipedia editing into information literacy events. And staff can also make edits using Wikipedia's ISBN tool, which connects Wikipedia readers to books in libraries via WorldCat. Understanding this tool, and referencing guidelines more generally will help patrons more confidently navigate the Internet and access the free reference materials that are available to them at the library. Finally, staff events at the library that encourage librarians to edit through a simple call to action are often successful in introducing library staff to the Wikipedia editing community, and they improve the encyclopedia.

Let's now discuss how to measure the impact of different forms of engagement. On one hand, as described in general terms, editing and outreach can raise the profile of libraries online. But what should be emphasized is that this is a way to meet patrons where they are, online. Approximately 50 percent of Wikipedia's incoming web traffic comes from search engines, according to a June 2017 report from Alexa.com. Incorporating library resources on Wikipedia could sound like self-promotion, but it's actually a form of community engagement with users who may not otherwise know how to access library materials from the commercial Internet. "It's critical to do programs that connect the public to reliable sources of information that are free. As library staff, we sometimes forget [that databases] cost a lot. This is a form of gatekeeping," said Andrea Davis. Editing Wikipedia can help to offset this gatekeeping. The issue of barriers to access is important for librarians to remember, emphasized Paul Flagg, who recently finished his MLIS degree at the University of Southern Florida and is a staff member at the John F. Germany Public Library in Tampa. The home page is a central portal to library resources, such as paywalled digital databases and local information, and these important channels can be difficult for patrons to navigate and often do not show up in indirect information inquiries with search engines. As a result: "Most people will go online to search and use Wikipedia," said Flagg.

Wikipedia has free tools and software that can help libraries understand their impact. This could be important to a staff member like Jared Mills, manager of reader services at the Seattle Public Library, who explained that his large urban library system has sought to update and improve the user experience of his library's website on the open web. But such updates are time- and resource-intensive. Moreover, it can be technically difficult to search engine optimize a library's collections, databases, and so on. "We know we could do more," said Mills. "We're trying to do a better job so people can still get that help even if they cannot make it to a branch." Editing Wikipedia does not require local server maintenance. The Wikimedia Foundation also has freely accessible and adaptable tools to use to measure page views and editing histories; these are ways to assess impact in terms of numbers of page views and edits.

Beyond meeting patrons online, library staff learning to edit and to work with the Wikipedia community build the profession in new ways. Davis recalls the invigorating staff discussions she had with colleagues about citations and the life of information online when they ran their Wikipedia event, and their desire to receive more training. She reflected that information professionals are often accustomed to critically analyzing among themselves. "Editing Wikipedia takes criticism to the next level: you have agency," she said. "Editing makes much more sense to me as an information professional than critique alone." By learning together how the online encyclopedia's articles have been co-created and becoming familiar with the suite of tools that contributors have developed to ensure that contributions are robust and verifiable, librarians can work within the Wikipedia system to counter the persuasive narrative that "everything is already online." And once they're involved, library staff are in a powerful position to take on different roles in the Wikipedia community in order to govern and grow the project.

CONCLUSION

Why Wikipedia? From the boroughs of New York to the borderlands of Texas, the perspectives of public librarians in this chapter suggest that Wikipedia has been—and can be—an opportunity to expand the boundaries of their librarianship. There are many platforms that public librarians can and do engage with on the open web, and Wikipedia's community, strengths, and weaknesses can be understood as calls to action for library staff to get involved in order to redress inequalities and engage with their communities, and other communities online, in new ways. The stories here have been gathered to benchmark what public library staff have already been doing, and to demonstrate opportunities to do more to serve communities, expand services, and meet patrons online.

These stories also demonstrate that when librarians slowly learn to incorporate editing Wikipedia into their work, they can thoughtfully focus on those aspects of the encyclopedia that are most important to them and their work. From adding citations to organizing articles, connecting with other editors on WikiProjects, and copyediting, there are many ways to participate. It takes time to become accustomed to the quirks of a new organizational culture—and while it is the only nonprofit in the top 100 Internet properties, Wikipedia is no different from any other organizational system or online collaborative community in this respect. When library staff, as cultural custodians of information, learn best practices for successful engagement, they can decide what forms of editing they are most suited for and bring their knowledge and suite of Wikipedia skills to their communities.

The outcomes can be extremely rewarding. Public librarians explain their successes in editing and doing outreach to their communities with Wikipedia with pride, knowing that they've guided the online public to reliable information by editing. They are pleased to help patrons understand how the online encyclopedia is created by reaching a civil consensus among editors and achieving agreement on ways that it can be improved. Wikipedia is a powerful ally for public libraries, and Wikipedia needs libraries. Major search engines in the United States usually list Wikipedia articles among their top results; Wikipedia's data is also used to populate knowledge bases such as Google's Knowledge Graph. "We had good conversations about citations on Wikipedia," said Davis about the editing event she held in 2016. Out of those conversations, Davis said she was encouraged because the participants were asking questions about reliability and looking hard at links as well as talk pages. They saw the Internet in a new way: "That's where our success was," she said.

For library staff, Wikipedia is an opportunity for them to do librarianship in a new way. Mary Phillips, a reference librarian at the Carnegie Library of Pittsburgh, explained how she focuses on copyediting articles and adding citations. She decides what to edit by letting herself fall into a "Wikipedia rabbit hole." She urges other librarians not to be afraid of Wikipedia, but to join her in improving the encyclopedia: "[Librarians are] experts in recognizing authority. We are experts in how people interact with information that is mediated. We are uniquely positioned to help this resource become the best it can be. I add citations. I match my skillset to improve the quality of this resource. I'm a librarian on Wikipedia."

NOTES

1. Wikipedia + Libraries: Better Together home page: www.webjunction.org/explore-topics/wikipedia-libraries.html.

2. For updated statistics, see the "Featured Article" page on Wikipedia: https://en.wikipedia.org/wiki/Wikipedia:Featured_articles.

3. David Peterson, February 19, 2017, "Twin Cities Libraries Hesitate to Lend Internet Hot Spots," *Star Tribune*, www.startribune.com/twin-cities-libraries-hesitate-to-lend-internet-hot-spots/414169893/.

4. "Fact Sheet: Mobile Phone Ownership in the United States," Pew Research Center, January 12, 2017, www.pewinternet.org/fact-sheet/mobile/; Horrigan, "Libraries 2016."

5. Sara Sanchez, "Segundo Barrio, Chihuahuita on Endangered List," *El Paso Times*, October 5, 2016, www.elpasotimes.com/story/news/local/el-paso/2016/10/05/segundo-barrio-chihuahuita-endangered-list/91548474/.

6. Sanchez, "Segundo Barrio."

7. https://en.wikipedia.org/wiki/Wikipedia:WikiProject_Women_in_Red#librarian_in_residence.

8. Source: U.S. Census Bureau, "2011–2015 American Community Survey 5-Year Estimates," https://factfinder.census.gov/faces/tableservices/jsf/pages/productview.xhtml?src=CF.

9. See analysis of the downloadable metadata at www.webjunction.org/news/webjunction/1lib1ref-highlights.html.

15

Becoming a Wikipedian

MERRILEE PROFFITT

made my first edits to the English-language Wikipedia on March 22, 2005. I know this because everything on Wikipedia is completely transparent, so my edits are preserved for all to see. On that day, I did almost everything wrong. My edits violated policies and "pillars" I knew nothing about—conflict of interest, neutral tone, unsourced materials. And yet, some kind souls came along and made my contributions better. I learned and improved. But I didn't feel like I belonged. And I didn't edit very often.

I remained intensely curious about Wikipedia, and about the role that libraries might play in it. From what I had observed, Wikipedia was committed to making knowledge free and open, which is very similar to the ethos of libraries. I am fortunate to work as a program officer in OCLC Research, and in my position, I am encouraged to think broadly about the future of libraries and to undertake small-scale experiments on behalf of the library community. What would a collaboration between Wikipedia and libraries look like? For example, if a library/Wikipedia collaboration could be fostered, could the citations that are the core of every Wikipedia article lead back to libraries? These citations can include everything from links to news sites to peer-reviewed articles and books. Although many of the items cited are available online, many more books and journals are locked up in copyright or under licensing terms. But libraries make these pay-walled materials freely available to the communities they serve. The problem is the relative invisibility of libraries on the open web. If a Wikipedia reader found a citation to a book and wanted to learn more, she could search for the title of that book and would probably be led to Amazon or another source where she could buy the book. Her local library would not appear as one of the top links offered by a search engine, and would probably not even be in the top 100 links.

The notion of "collaborating" with Wikipedia proved to be challenging, and part of what inhibited me from making progress was the difficulty of making sense of the Wikipedia ecosystem, which can be confusing and off-putting from an outsider's perspective. Wikipedia is fostered by the Wikimedia Foundation (alongside a number of "sister" projects, such as Wikidata, Wikimedia Commons, and Wikisource). But the Wikimedia Foundation doesn't manage Wikipedia— that is done by the volunteer Wikipedia community. But the community is, as I discovered, very broad and diverse, and made up of individuals with a variety of motivations. Some enjoy creating articles and then taking them through Wikipedia's version of a peer review process. Some like administrative tasks and volunteer in spaces like Article for Creation (AFC), Articles for Deletion (AFD), or ArbCom (the Arbitration Committee). (As a side note, Wikipedians seem to love acronyms as much as librarians do, and at times I have had the experience of swimming in an unfamiliar acronym soup.)

I could see that there were many possibilities for libraries and archives to harness the power and gravitational pull of Wikipedia to bring attention to their collections and services—but I could also see that there were a number of tensions inherent in doing so. A 2009 case study shared by the University of Washington revealed tensions between archivists, who were editing articles in an attempt to add links to relevant finding aids, and Wikipedians, who were trying to prevent "link spam" from polluting the project.[1] Here were two allied communities that were at loggerheads with one another, and both were "right" in their own way. But there was no clear dialogue between the two communities. What, I wondered, would Wikipedians want from librarians?

In 2009 I was fortunate to be introduced to Adrianne Wadewitz, who was then working on her PhD in British literature at Indiana University. Wadewitz was a digital humanist and an active "Wikipedian." This was the first time I had heard that term. In a phone call, Wadewitz was generous with her time and ideas (something I would later come to value in my many contacts with Wikipedians). What would Wikipedians want from librarians? "Access to the collections you license," she said. As someone affiliated with an academic institution, she had access to a wealth of licensed resources, but the majority of Wikipedians do not. This wasn't something I could see happening (en masse, at least). We talked about some other ideas and at the end of the call she encouraged me to keep going: librarians should be part of Wikipedia. We agreed to keep in touch and I continued to ponder about what contributions libraries could make to Wikipedia. What could OCLC as an organization contribute?

I continued to edit Wikipedia very sporadically—I didn't know anyone else who edited Wikipedia and I never gained full facility with wikitext markup (which is sort of HTML-like). In 2010 I read about Liam Wyatt, an Australian Wikipedian who served as Wikipedian in Residence (WIR) at the British Museum in London. This, I decided was what we needed, and what I in particular needed to help make sense of the still-confusing Wikipedia world. As time went on, more institutions announced that they had brought onboard a WIR: the National Archives, the Smithsonian, the British Library . . . Why not OCLC?

While I was looking for more information about Wikipedians in Residence, I found a corner of Wikipedia that looked friendly and welcoming—GLAM (Galleries, Libraries, Archives, and Museums). Through a link I was able, finally, to contact a group of people who were able to help answer some of my questions. Phoebe Ayers (then a science librarian working at UC Davis) was the first person I met who was both a Wikipedian and a librarian. Ayers encouraged me to talk to some WIRs and thought that OCLC sponsoring a WIR was a great idea. I wound up connecting with the WIRs at the National Archives and at the Smithsonian Institution, who were able to provide me with background about what they had been able to do as well as draft job descriptions. Armed with this information, I asked for and received strategic funding for a short-term position that would enable us to figure out what contributions OCLC and libraries more generally could make to Wikipedia.

OCLC was fortunate to hire the Wikipedian Maximillian Klein as our WIR, and together we worked on a number of different projects, most having to do with integrating library authority controls into Wikipedia and (later) Wikidata.[2] But more importantly (for my own story), I had broken the logjam and had now established contacts within the Wikipedia community.

The year 2012 was a big one for me. I attended several edit-a-thons (and helped with the organization of a few of those). I found that the edit-a-thon setting provided some key ingredients that were important for me to learn and grow as an editor. First, I had time that I was able to purposefully dedicate to editing Wikipedia. Like many women who work full-time, I have little leisure time.[3] Second, if I had not come to the event with a specific purpose in mind (to improve a particular article, for example), I could usually draw from a list of suggested articles, or work pairwise with another editor to focus on an article in tandem. Finally, I could use the time to ask questions and advice of other more experienced editors. These seasoned veterans were both helpful and thoughtful in giving coaching and encouragement. Frequently they would share small but useful tools that made their own editing easier. Without exception, I have come away from edit-a-thons feeling not only smarter and more confident, but also knowing that I had made the encyclopedia a little better.

I also attended my first Wikimania in 2012. Wikimania is a sort of gathering of the tribes for all Wikimedia projects. It is a very well-attended and international conference, reflecting the nature of the larger Wikimedia movement. That year, there were more than 1,400 attendees from 87 countries. The event is organized and run by volunteers, and many of the people attending are taking vacation time and paying their way with personal funds. It is the norm for people to attend conference sessions all day and then spend time in the evenings and around the edges of the meeting editing or hacking (many of the tools and gadgets that are used in Wikimedia projects have been developed by volunteers rather than by Wikimedia Foundation software engineers). At that Wikimania I also learned about Wikidata, then a new project. I was fascinated by this project, and I believe it will be key to library interests and to Wikipedia's intersections with library data.

It is very inspiring to be in a group of people who are committed to a common purpose and who have given themselves not only permission but a mandate to change the world. I have spent my career in a world with a lot of rules and protocols. Wikipedia, to be sure, has plenty of rules and protocols. But among its "pillars" and policies there are principles that guide one to bend the rules when necessary and to change and evolve structures that aren't working. (See figure 15.1 for one interpretation.) One of the things I love best about Wiki culture are admonitions like "Be bold!" or "Just fix it" or (my favorite) "Ignore all rules: If a rule prevents you from improving or maintaining Wikipedia, ignore it."

Back in 2005 when I started editing Wikipedia, I admit to feeling like a bit of a fraud. I was slow and everything seemed unnatural. There was documentation, but there was almost too much of it. I was probably suffering from impostor syndrome. But with time and a bit of practice, with support from others who

Five Pillars of Wikipedia

By Giulia Forsythe, CC BY 2.0

want me to succeed, and with the advent of the Visual Editor, I have gained a lot of confidence.

Over time I've embraced that I too am a Wikipedian. I have come to understand that the things that made me excellent in my work life make me a natural Wikipedian. I understand and appreciate what makes for a quality source (sources are the backbone of a good article). I love doing research and I know how to find those sources. If I can't find or physically locate them, I can make use of services provided by libraries to help me (reference librarians and interlibrary loan are your friends). I have a curiosity about the "truth" and an instinct to double-check things. These are qualities that make me a good Wikipedian—and a good "Wikibrarian," a blend of librarian and Wikipedian. I also have come to recognize that there are different ways to be a Wikipedian. Thankfully, some people have the time and inclination to do the deep research that is required to bring an article to feature article status. Others spend their time on administrative tasks. My strength is in organizing events and speaking and writing about Wikipedia; and in continuing my own passion, which is to bring librarians into closer contact with the encyclopedia.

Over time I've come to believe that every librarian is already a Wikipedian; they just don't know it yet. Your path to editing Wikipedia may be different than mine. You may more naturally grasp the basics or not need as much personal support as I did. You may struggle in different ways and need different types of help. Things I did not know when I started—how to read a talk page, how to interpret the edit history of an article, how to find project pages—are skills that are easy for anyone to pick up. Even if you never edit Wikipedia, I urge you to take a small amount of time to learn about the anatomy of the encyclopedia. Becoming Wikipedia-literate will give you greater insight into what you are seeing on any given article, including known strengths and weaknesses.

After I spoke with my first Wikipedian, Adrianne Wadewitz, I continued to follow her work as she began to address issues related to the gender gap and representation of women in Wikipedia. She was, like so many Wikipedians I've met, passionate and clear-eyed about her ability to make small changes that can add up in the aggregate. I always assumed that at some point our paths would cross and I would have the opportunity to meet her in person. I regret that this didn't happen before her untimely death in 2014. When I think of her I think of the work that she did, that I do, and that we all do to make the information world better for all. It is important work, and work that is well worth doing. I hope you will "be bold" and join me and so many others on a path of blending our library work with the Wikipedia world and take your own first steps as a Wikibrarian.

NOTES

1. Ann Lally, "Using Wikipedia to Highlight Digital Collections at the University of Washington," *The Interactive Archivist*, May 18, 2009, http://interactivearchivist.archivists.org/case-studies/wikipedia-at-uw/.

2. You can read about the work that Klein and I did in greater details in the OCLC Research blog, *HangingTogether*.

3. In 2011 the former executive director of the Wikimedia Foundation, Sue Gardner, shared some of the many reasons why women don't choose to edit Wikipedia. Among the reasons listed are spare time and lack of confidence, two things that have prohibited me from editing in the past. See Sue Gardner, "Nine Reasons Women Don't Edit Wikipedia (in Their Own Words)," https://suegardner.org/2011/02/19/nine-reasons-why-women-dont-edit-wikipedia-in-their-own-words/.

ABOUT THE CONTRIBUTORS

KENNING ARLITSCH is dean of the library at Montana State University, where he leads a research library actively engaged in student success, statewide collaboration, and the university's research enterprise. In his 24-year career as a professional librarian, he has held positions in library instruction, digital library development, and IT services. His funded research has focused on search engine optimization, as well as measuring the impact and use of digital repositories. He writes a regular column in the *Journal of Library Administration* and serves on the editorial board of *Library Hi Tech*. Arlitsch holds an MLIS degree from the University of Wisconsin-Milwaukee and a PhD in library and information science from Humboldt University in Berlin, Germany. His dissertation on Semantic Web Identity examined how well research libraries and other academic organizations are understood by search engines.

LIANNA DAVIS is the director of programs and deputy director for Wiki education at Wikipedia. With more than seven years' experience in running programs connecting Wikipedia and academia, Davis is one of the world's leading experts on teaching with Wikipedia. She has played a pivotal role in creating Wikipedia education programs in eight countries worldwide and has supported the work of volunteers in more than fifty additional countries. She has a master's degree in communication, culture, and technology from Georgetown University and a bachelor's degree in communication studies from the University of Puget Sound.

KELLY DOYLE is the Wikipedian in Residence for Gender Equity at West Virginia University Libraries. She earned her BA degree in English literature from the University of Delaware and her MA in English literature from the College of Charleston. Prior to her present position, she worked at the Avery Research Center for African American History and Culture in Charleston, South Carolina. Doyle has spoken about her work at the Department of State's Office of Global Women's Issues, the Library of Congress, the Women's Media Center, and the National Democratic Institute.

THERESA EMBREY is the chief librarian at the Pritzker Military Museum & Library. She has written articles and given conference presentations on history, genealogy, and library technology topics.

JASON EVANS was appointed as a full time Wikimedian at the National Library of Wales following a two-year residency there. Evans works to advocate for open access within the culture sector by openly sharing library data and demonstrating the benefits to the organization and the public. He has hosted dozens of Wikipedia "edit-a-thon" events and has managed a number of volunteer projects to enrich and reuse open-access content. Evans is a regular contributor to digital heritage conferences, and has a particular interest in language and linked open data.

BOB KOSOVSKY is the curator of rare books and manuscripts for the Music Division of the New York Public Library. He also taught classes in the Extension Division of Mannes College, now a division of The New School. He has been a Wikipedia editor since 2006 and serves on the board of Wikimedia New York.

MAIRELYS LEMUS-ROJAS works as the metadata librarian at Indiana University–Purdue University Indianapolis University Library, where she is responsible for the strategic coordination and management of metadata for all digital collections. She holds an MS degree in library and information studies from Florida State University with a concentration in web design/technology and networking, and she also holds graduate certificates in museum studies and information architecture. Since her previous appointment at the University of Miami Libraries, she has been working on exposing curated library data to open knowledge projects like Wikipedia and, more recently, Wikidata.

ANDREW LIH is the author of *The Wikipedia Revolution: How a bunch of nobodies created the world's greatest encyclopedia* and is a noted expert in online collaboration and digital news innovation. He was the recipient of the 2016 US National Archives Citizen Archivist of the Year award for his work with Wikipedia and heritage institutions and a 2015 Knight Foundation grant. He has been associate professor of journalism at the University of Southern California and American University and he started the new media program at the Columbia University Graduate School of Journalism in 1995. He has been a speaker at South by Southwest (SXSW), the Online News Association, TEDx, and Wikimania.

JAKE ORLOWITZ is the founder of The Wikipedia Library. A longtime editor of Wikipedia since 2007 and an English Wikipedia administrator, he has created and contributed to tools for teaching new editors how to use Wikipedia and helping experienced contributors do better research. He works for the Wikimedia Foundation running the Wikipedia Library Program full-time and lives in Santa Cruz with his wife and stepdaughter.

LYDIA PINTSCHER has been contributing to free software projects for more than ten years. She studied computer science at the Karlsruhe Institute of Technology in Germany. Today she is the product manager of Wikidata, Wikimedia's knowledge base, as well as the president of KDE e.V, a registered non-profit organization that represents the KDE Community.

MONIKA SENGUL-JONES is the OCLC Wikipedian in Residence for 2017–2018 for the Wikipedia + Libraries: Better Together project, funded by the Knight Foundation and the Wikimedia Foundation. She is a communication and media studies scholar completing her doctorate in the Department of Communication and the Science Studies Program at UC San Diego, and she is experienced in qualitative research methods. She earned a master's degree in gender studies at Central European University. Sengul-Jones has edited Wikipedia since 2012.

JUSTIN SHANKS is the digital scholarship librarian at Montana State University. In this capacity, he is responsible for fostering innovative forms of digital scholarship and access while also providing guidance for engaged digital teaching and research. Shanks's research involves Semantic Web Identity and associated implications for institutional visibility, research dissemination, and open data. As the interim department head of Library Informatics and Computing, he guides a service-oriented department that is responsible for web design, hardware maintenance, data management, and user experience. Shanks is also codirector of Montana State University's Data Infrastructure and Scholarly Communication (DISC) group. He is a PhD candidate in science and technology studies at Virginia Tech; his dissertation investigates the dynamics of technology and pedagogy in contemporary higher education.

SARA SNYDER heads the Media and Technology Office of the Smithsonian American Art Museum. From 2007 to 2014 she served as webmaster at the Smithsonian's Archives of American Art. She holds an MLS degree in information studies and an MA in American history from the University of Maryland, College Park. She has been contributing to Wikipedia since 2007, and has presented on Wikipedia as well as other digital projects at the meetings of professional organizations such as SAA, ARLIS, CNI, MCN, and AAM, as well as at the Smithsonian, the National Archives, and the Library of Congress.

ALEX STINSON is the GLAM-Wiki strategist at the Wikimedia Foundation, where he develops infrastructure, capacity, and best practices for Wikimedia's global volunteer community to partner with galleries, libraries, archives and museums (GLAMs). While at Wikimedia, he developed the #1lib1ref campaign, which engages librarians in improving Wikipedia's references, and he supported the IFLA's Opportunity Papers on Wikipedia and Libraries. Stinson has a master's degree in English literature and previously worked in digital humanities, where he supported digital-inflected pedagogy and digital research projects which shared humanities knowledge with the public. He has been contributing to Wikipedia since 2005.

TIM THOMPSON is the discovery metadata librarian at Yale University. Previously, he was the metadata librarian for Spanish and Portuguese at Princeton University. He is involved with projects to advance linked data for libraries and archives and help implement new approaches to resource description.

LILY TODORINOVA has been the undergraduate experience librarian at Rutgers University since 2014. Her work centers around student engagement, information literacy, and emerging technologies. Todorinova is interested in understanding how novice researchers find their scholarly voice and how the library can leverage the open web environment, including Wikipedia, in promoting critical thinking and information literacy. She is also the vice chair/chair elect of the ALA Reference and User Services Association's Emerging Technologies Section.

YU-HUNG LIN is an innovative librarian who has worked in several different types of libraries. Throughout his career, Yu-Hung has explored and adapted emerging technologies to enhance the efficiency of library services. He tends to be an optimist who likes to come up with new and creative ways to do things effectively.

INDEX

10/31/18